Local Public, Fiscal and Financial Governance

Brian Dollery • Harry Kitchen
Melville McMillan • Anwar Shah

Local Public, Fiscal and Financial Governance

An International Perspective

palgrave
macmillan

Brian Dollery
School of Business
University of New England
Armidale, NSW, Australia

Harry Kitchen
Department of Economics
Trent University
Peterborough, ON, Canada

Melville McMillan
University of Alberta
Edmonton, AB, Canada

Anwar Shah
Governance Studies
Brookings Institution
Washington, DC, USA

ISBN 978-3-030-36724-4 ISBN 978-3-030-36725-1 (eBook)
https://doi.org/10.1007/978-3-030-36725-1

This Palgrave Macmillan imprint is published by the registered company Springer Nature Switzerland AG.
The registered company address is: Gewerbestrasse 11, 6330 Cham, Switzerland

Preface

This book is a part of a two volume series on local governance: *Local Public Finance and Economics: An International Perspective* as volume 1 and *Local Public, Fiscal and Financial Governance: An International Perspective* as volume 2. This series is intended to serve as a comprehensive guide/reference for policymakers, practitioners, policy analysts and interested researchers, scholars and students in local public governance and local public finance and economics worldwide. The series would also be of interest to government officials, policymakers and public policy students internationally as it provides a comprehensive coverage of issues and presents a synthesis of lessons from worldwide experiences in local economic and fiscal governance. The series would also serve as useful reference books for undergraduate and graduate courses in public economics. The existing literature on local public finance and economics has typically a country-specific focus, mostly of an industrial country, for example, *State and Local Public Finance* by Ronald Fisher, published by Routledge in 2016, has a US focus. Also, the literature does not give special attention to local public governance issues. This series attempts to fill this void by providing a state-of-the-art synthesis of the academic literature and supplementing it with lessons of experience from both industrial and developing countries. The series further presents one of the most comprehensive treatments of local economic and fiscal governance issues. Some of the newer topics covered include neo-institutional perspectives on the role of local government, tax instruments for environmental protection, output-based intergovernmental transfers, fiscal rules and fiscal discipline, combating corruption, measuring, monitoring and evaluating local government performance, municipal mergers, intermunicipal cooperation and political economy of local government reform. In view of this, we hope that this series would be of interest to a wider range of audience in both industrial and developing countries.

Armidale, NSW, Australia	Brian Dollery
Peterborough, ON, Canada	Harry Kitchen
Edmonton, AB, Canada	Melville McMillan
Washington, DC, USA	Anwar Shah

Acknowledgments

This book represents the knowledge gained from several decades of research and teaching local public economics to graduate and undergraduate students in Australia, China, Japan and North America. In addition, it captures the practical experiences of policy-makers and practitioners from industrial and developing countries gained through policy advice, senior policymakers and high-level executives' retreats, conferences, workshops, seminars and short courses. The authors are grateful to students, practitioners and policymakers around the globe for enriching their knowledge with the insights gained from these interactions.

The authors are also grateful to their families and the editors of Palgrave Macmillan for their support and encouragement for completion of this volume.

Brian Dollery, Armidale, New South Wales, Australia
Harry Kitchen, Peterborough, Ontario, Canada
Melville McMillan, Edmonton, Alberta, Canada
Anwar Shah, Washington, DC, USA

Contents

About the Authors

Brian Dollery is Professor of Economics in the UNE School of Business and Director of the UNE Centre for Local Government at the University of New England, Armidale, NSW, Australia. He has previously worked at Yokohama National University, Rhodes University and the University of South Africa. Recent books include *Perspectives on Australian Local Government Reform* (2015), *Funding the Future: Financial Sustainability and Infrastructure Finance in Australian Local Government* (2013), *Councils in Cooperation: Shared Services and Australian Local Government* (2012), *Local Government Reform: A Comparative Analysis of Advanced Anglo-American Countries* (2008), *The Theory and Practice of Local Government Reform* (2008), *Reform and Leadership in the Public Sector* (2007) and *Australian Local Government Economics* (2006). Over the past two decades, Brian has closely worked with local government across all Australian states, largely in the area of municipal mergers, shared services, financial sustainability and urban water.

Harry Kitchen is a professor emeritus in the Economics Department at Trent University, Canada. Over the past 20 years, he has completed more than 100 articles, reports, studies, and books on issues relating to local government expenditures, finance, structure and governance in Canada. In addition, he has served as a consultant or advisor for a number of municipal and provincial governments in Canada and the federal government, and has worked on projects in Russia and China. In 2013, he was awarded The Queen's Diamond Jubilee Medal for policy analysis and research contributions to municipal finance, structure and governance in

Canada. In 2017, he was appointed visiting scholar at the Institute of Municipal Finance and Governance, Munk School of Global Affairs, University of Toronto.

Melville McMillan is a professor emeritus in the Department of Economics and a fellow of the Institute of Public Economics at the University of Alberta, Canada. McMillan's research and teaching interests are in public economics, particularly urban and local economics, fiscal federalism, and the demand/supply of public goods and services. He has published in these areas and has advised governments and organizations nationally and internationally (e.g., the World Bank). Although "retired", McMillan remains actively involved in academic and policy matters.

Anwar Shah is a senior fellow (non-resident) at Brookings Institution, Washington, DC, USA; advisor/consultant to the World Bank; and Distinguished Visiting Professor of Economics, Southwestern University of Finance and Economics, Chengdu/Wenjiang, China. He has previously served the Government of Canada (Ministry of Finance) and the Government of Alberta, and served on the UN Intergovernmental Panel on Climate Change. He has published more than two dozen books in English, Spanish, Chinese, Vietnamese and Russian and numerous articles in leading economic journals on governance, public management reforms, budget reform, federalism, local governance, fiscal reforms and global climate change issues.

With special contribution by:

Ernesto Crivelli is Senior Economist in the European Department at the IMF, Germany. Previously he worked in the IMF's Fiscal Affairs Department, where he provided technical assistance on a wide range of tax policy issues. Before joining the IMF, he was a senior fellow of the Max Planck Institute. He has published on tax policy, tax administration, aid, and fiscal decentralization issues. He received his PhD from the University of Bonn, Germany.

List of Figures

List of Tables

PART I

Introduction and Overview

CHAPTER 1

Introduction

1.1 Introduction

The role of local government has expanded in a large and increasing number of countries. This shifting of responsibilities is a product of a quiet, even silent, revolution over several decades during which countries have been re-examining and revising the roles of their governments. Shifting responsibilities and authority to local government—that is, decentralization—is a widely observed outcome and notably so in developing and transition countries where political decision-making is commonly highly centralized.

Much effort and many resources have gone into promoting economic growth and reducing poverty, the results and effectiveness of which are often questioned. Where citizens have little voice in determining local public services, expanding the role of local government through decentralization is recognized as offering potential for enhancing economic well-being and expanding faith in government. Realizing that potential, however, is challenging. There are many examples of successful decentralized countries, but decentralizing countries successfully is difficult. Part of the difficulty is that there is no one best model. Patterns of decentralization among successful countries are diverse and they have evolved in the context of history and culture. Efforts to decentralize must recognize the country context, but even in designing a basic structure, although the principles are straightforward, there are many possible pitfalls and diversions as well as, often significant, opposing interests. Hence,

B. Dollery et al., *Local Public, Fiscal and Financial Governance*,
https://doi.org/10.1007/978-3-030-36725-1_1

decentralization programs have had mixed results. The objective of the exercise is to enable people to be more engaged in their government and for local governments to do more for their people. Furthermore, success requires that governments represent local preferences; that is, they be responsive, transparent, accountable, equitable and honest. In effect, empowering local governments and empowering their citizens. Achieving these ends, however, is demanding.

This book is part of a two-volume set aimed at assisting those pursuing decentralization and specifically seeking expansion of the role of local governments and the empowerment of their citizens. The initial volume, *Local Public Finance and Economics: An International Perspective*, focused on principles and best practices for local government. The main topics there covered organization and responsibility assignment, service delivery, sources of own revenues, intergovernmental transfers and borrowing. This volume, *Local Public, Fiscal and Financial Governance: An International Perspective*, extends the previous analysis. The major topics are fiscal and financial management, pursuit of government integrity and accountability, and reform imperatives. Volume I was primarily concerned with local government design to achieve a quantity and quality of local public services matching local preferences and enhancing local well-being. Volume II encompasses a broader perspective as reflected by the term governance. Local governance is a more comprehensive concept defined as the formulation and execution of collective action at the local level to serve the public interest. It encompasses the direct and indirect roles of public and private institutions and organizations and the networks within and among them that structure local collective decision-making. As such, this approach draws additionally upon fields including public choice, new public management and the new institutional economics. In part due to the emphasis on governance, public administration and administrative issues receive considerable attention in this volume. The governance perspective is believed to provide a stronger foundation for analyzing the pressures that globalization and the information revolution place upon citizen-state relations at the local level and to enable better policies for local government to address both market and government failures.

1.2 Overview

This section provides both an overview and a summary of the topics in the book and summaries of the chapters. The chapter reviews are organized by book parts and in numerical order.

1.2.1 Part II: Local Public, Fiscal and Financial Management

Part II is an examination of a number of the more conventional topics of local public finance, but it extends the analysis by delving further into options and alternatives. The chapters in Part II cover tax and particularly property tax administration, budget and accounting methods, and fiscal discipline.

1.2.1.1 Chapter 2: "Local Tax Administration"

The success of any local tax system depends critically upon its administration. A successful administration must treat taxpayers (and potential taxpayers) fairly, be efficient and keep corruption and evasion to a minimum. Issues to be addressed in striving for a successful local tax administration are examined in Chap. 2. A central question is who should be responsible for the administration of local taxes. Should it be central governments, the independent local governments, some blend of the two or, perhaps, an autonomous agency? Central administration affords advantages in scale and scope and separation from local taxpayers while local administration, for example, offers familiarity with local conditions, association with local government (use and need for funds), and diligence in collecting local taxes. Autonomous agencies can provide potentially advantageous independence from politicians and from the civil service. The typical arrangement is a mix of central and local administration with the senior government determining the local tax base (primarily a revenue assignment matter) and being responsible for establishing standards for local tax administrative staff and (perhaps with local government associations) staff training. Local governments should be responsible for setting local tax rates. Assignment of the administration of the collection, enforcement and auditing of the taxes depends upon the capacity of local government and the degree of autonomy that central government is prepared to grant. Improving local tax administration has many facets. Among those are identifying taxpayers, minimizing ambiguities and loopholes, coping with the informal economy, controlling corruption, improving compliance, enforcing collection, handling appeals and undertaking performance reviews. Local tax administration can be complex, but establishing an effective and fair system is critical.

1.2.1.2 Chapter 3: "The Practice of Real Property Taxation in the World"

Property taxes are widely used and are an important and growing source of own revenue for local governments. As such, Chap. 3 serves as a primer on property tax practices worldwide. Some of the major features are noted here. Across OECD (Organisation for Economic Co-operation and Development) countries, property taxes amount to 1.6% of GDP (gross domestic product) on average. In a sample of developing and transition countries, the average is only 0.005% of GDP but that amounts to 40% of local government taxes. Taxes on real property—that is, land and improvements—dominate property taxes and the immobility of such property makes it suitable for local taxation. Since expenditures in improvements are sensitive to taxation, property tax rates applied on improvements may be lower than those on land. Assessments for property taxes are typically on market value, especially in developed countries. But even there, although more so in developing and transition countries, an alternative tax is sometimes used, one that relies on readily identified characteristics such as area and/or use. Market values are most readily estimated where there is an active property market and property characteristics are well known, but where market transactions are unusual, value might be approximated from depreciated cost or discounted income. While assessments of capital value are most common, rental value is used in some places. It is customary that senior levels of government regulate assessment methods to ensure uniform practices, but it is ideal if the local authorities set their own tax rates so as to better match local taxes with local preferences. Different types of property (e.g., residential, commercial, industrial, agricultural) may be taxed at different rates. For example, residential rates are frequently lower than those on commercial and industrial properties. For political reasons, taxes from non-residential property usually subsidize residential services—a feature that can distort the property tax as a benefit tax within municipalities. Certain types of properties (e.g., religious and government buildings) are subject to special consideration. In addition, special arrangements may be made to promote economic development or renewal and/or to reduce property tax burdens on particular groups (especially low-income households). In addition to local general-purpose governments, property taxes often support a variety of services provided by special districts (e.g., school authorities with independent taxing powers). Because boundaries typically do not coincide, to ensure the same tax rates apply across overlapping jurisdictions and to provide proper information in the case of determining senior government aid to local authorities, senior governments may need to ensure that valuations relative to the assessment bases (e.g., market value) are uniform across local governments. As with other forms of taxation, a property tax system will be accepted only if it is considered fair which includes having a trusted complaint and appeal mechanism. Real property taxation is a valuable and important source of revenue for local government but one that seems underutilized especially in many developing and transition countries.

1.2.1.3 Chapter 4: "Municipal Budgeting and Accounting"

Budgets are an essential tool of municipal government. They are vital for financial planning and management, for contributing to accountability and transparency, and for avoiding corruption and misappropriation. The roles and methods of budgeting and accounting in municipal government are reviewed in Chap. 4. Two types of budgets are necessary, operating budgets (which focus on resources used up during the, typically annual, budget period) and capital budgets (which address infrastructure financing and outlays). Regardless of the type, budgets have historically been oriented toward financial control—that is, monitoring the inflow and scrutinizing the outflow of funds. More recently, budgets have come to embrace also an output focus and contribute increasingly to expenditure effectiveness through expanded use for management and planning. Because senior governments are (actually or implied) financially responsible for municipal governments, municipal budgets are commonly subject to senior government requirements. Typically, operating budgets must be balanced while borrowing is possible (within limits) for financing capital investments. Senior governments can assist municipal governments (as well as other local authorities and its own agencies) by pooling borrowing requirements, borrowing on their behalf and then on-lending to the individual units. This reduces transaction costs and often interest costs—especially for smaller municipalities. In part, the recommendations of accounting organizations have led to a movement from accounting on a cash basis to accrual (or modified accrual) accounting. Fund accounting—that is, accounting in separate funds for the finances associated with different municipal activities for compliance and/or management reasons—is a common feature of municipal accounting. Regular and timely reporting is important for effective budgeting and accounting. Reporting includes annual independent audits. Reliable municipal budgets and accounts serve a range of services and interests. Notably, they are valuable internally for the use of policymakers and management, for external interests (e.g., citizens, lenders) and for senior government monitoring.

1.2.1.4 Chapter 5: "Local Fiscal Discipline"

Fiscal discipline is most evident where there is a tradition of fiscal conservatism and well-developed and strong fiscal institutions. Even in such cases, avoiding fiscal indiscipline is likely to require clear and enforced fiscal rules—especially at the subnational level. Subnational, and particularly local government, is susceptible to fiscal lassitude due to weak citizen accountability, interest group capture and heavy reliance upon intergovernmental transfers from governments only weakly adverse to bailouts. Where the incentives for self-imposed discipline are weak, fiscal rules (if backed by senior-level political will) can help. In Chap. 5 the reasons for fiscal indiscipline and approaches to establishing fiscal discipline are explored. Among the effective measures are restricting borrowing to financing only capital expenditures and debt limits. Measures to enhance budget transparency and accountability to local citizens can assist but that still demands citizen attention and concern. Successful fiscal discipline is more probable with a combination of rules, empowering budgetary institutions and, of course, enforcement and responsibility for outcomes. Essential, overall, is political will and that normally depends upon citizens and their representatives together having to bear the consequences of disciplinary failures.

1.2.2 Part III: Local Government Integrity and Performance Accountability

Concerns about increased corruption are cited frequently as a criticism of decentralization. The prospects of more or less corruption are explored in Chap. 6 in the context of local infrastructure investment. Controlling corruption improves government performance, but measuring and monitoring local government performance is a more recent initiative and is examined in Chap. 7. When undertaken voluntarily by local governments, the prospects of performance assessment being utilized effectively and generating rewards are improved.

1.2.2.1 Chapter 6: "Local Public Infrastructure and Corruption"

Criticisms of decentralization include the concern that decentralization promotes corruption—that is, the abuse of public office for private gain or exercise of public powers against public interest. The material in Chap. 6 reviews the fundamentals of corruption in general before examining and contributing to the understanding of corruption as it might arise through the decentralization of infrastructure investment to local government. Although largely unexplored, this perspective is important because local infrastructure represents a large (and normally disproportionate) part of national infrastructure, contributes substantially to citizen well-being and represents amounts of funds that appeal to those inclined toward abuse of power. In addition, it is a topic that provides scope for assessment of whether corruption might be greater or less with decentralization. Corruption is a product of poor governance: that is, the failure of the norms, traditions and institutions by which government authority is exercised. Corruption is an old problem, basically the principal-agent problem, and can be studied in the context of that literature and through the new public management and new institutional economics lenses. Besides being a continuing issue, corruption has many forms, is universal and found in widely varying degrees across countries. Does decentralization—and decentralization of infrastructure investment in particular—aggravate the corruption problem? The evaluation indicates that there are factors (e.g., closer personal relations and potential for interest group capture of local government) that may make decentralization a breeding ground for corruption. On the other hand, there are characteristics (e.g., greater awareness, greater competition and lower transactions costs) that may reduce the potential for corruption. The conceptual models are inconclusive, and empirical analyses, confounded by flawed data, are challenging to interpret. Yet, the few studies specific to infrastructure suggest that decentralization leads to improvement. Clearly, there are opportunities for further research. Nonetheless, there are insights into enhancing integrity in decentralized infrastructure investment. In many cases, making the environment for infrastructure services operate more competitive will generate improvement. Where poor governance is the primary culprit, institutional reform (with all its challenges) will be essential. Regardless, the nature of corruption is very case specific and reforms need to be tailored to the situations in each country and locality.

1.2.2.2 *Chapter 7: "Measuring and Monitoring Local Government Performance"*

Political decentralization and democratization have spread rapidly in developing and transition countries since 1990. Realizing the benefits of those movements, however, has proven elusive largely due to lack of adequate citizen empowerment—often despite notable efforts by local governments. Chapter 7 provides insights into the approaches used in efforts to ensure and enhance local government performance, conceptual foundations, and positive and negative experiences. Performance monitoring measures may be mandatory (as imposed by senior government) or voluntarily undertaken by local government. Examples of common mandatory measures include requiring audited financial statements and restrictions on debt. Examples of voluntary measures include benchmarking programs and sharing information with the public (extending transparency). A FAIR governance framework is recommended—that is, one that is fair, accountable, incorruptible and responsive—and mechanisms for implementation are outlined. An overview of practice indicates that higher-order governments' involvements are typically requirements to ensure fiscal discipline and fiscal sustainability. While some senior governments impose service delivery reporting requirements on local authorities, such disclosures may function better when they are local initiatives. Examples of failed monitoring efforts can often be characterized as being intrusive and overreaching while generating little or no local benefit. Overall, local governments perform best when their activities are transparent and they are accountable to their constituents.

1.2.3 *Part IV: Local Government Reform Imperatives*

Growth, technological change and certainly decentralization are major forces motivating local government reform. Municipal mergers have been a common policy instrument although the evidence of such consolidations generating net benefits is mixed. Intermunicipal (or, more broadly, intergovernmental) cooperation is an alternative mechanism by which it may be possible to realize the benefits of scale or internalization while minimizing the loss of independence. Essentially all local government reforms are controversial. Exploring the political economy of local government reform can be insightful. These three topics are examined in separate chapters in this section of the book.

1.2.3.1 Chapter 8: "Structural Reform: Municipal Mergers"

Municipal mergers are a frequently advocated and practiced reform of local government systems. The pursuit of cost savings through scale and scope economies and technical/administrative efficiencies (and perhaps other benefits realized via accompanying reforms) are the prime motivation. The trade-offs usually noted are diminished choice and competition and a more constrained democracy. Mergers are controversial and have thus been subject to considerable investigation. The conceptual and empirical perspectives on mergers are examined in Chap. 8, including—in addition to scale and scope and administrative capacities—possible impacts from internalizing spillovers and effects on municipal growth. None of the literature leads to definitive conclusions. To illustrate, Chap. 8 concludes that despite the grounds for anticipating economic benefits from mergers, especially in terms of cost savings through scale and scope economies, these expectations have not been confirmed by the weight of empirical evidence. In addition, it appears that local democracy thrives best, at least in terms of political participation, in smaller jurisdictions. The mixed evidence on the benefits of size perhaps explains the wide variation in the average size of local governments across countries. Mergers, it seems, require evaluation on a case-by-case basis.

1.2.3.2 Chapter 9: "Intermunicipal Cooperation"

Intermunicipal cooperation is an option for municipalities facing the (often disappointing) prospects of mergers and an option for consideration by local authorities considering alternative delivery systems. Intermunicipal cooperation is primarily motivated by the search for lower costs, improved service quality and/or other benefits from expanded production and delivery systems for particular services that seem not to be available from contracting with private providers or providing individually. Intermunicipal cooperation takes a wide variety of forms, for example, from informal mutual service agreements to autonomous organizations (e.g., corporations) owned by municipalities. Chapter 9 begins with an overview of the various kinds of arrangements and a survey of numerous taxonomies and features seen to characterize those arrangements. Of particular note is that intergovernmental cooperation—while typically horizontal, can also be vertical—adds flexibility at the task or function level, to the standard central, intermediate and local governmental structure. Turning to conceptual considerations, intermunicipal cooperation facilitates creating service units of more optimal size—a feature consistent with the objective of subsidiarity—while retaining local democratic oversight if not actual decision-making. Those units may involve coordination, joint supply and/or intergovernmental contracts. The primary objective of intermunicipal cooperation is typically to realize cost savings (and/or improved services for the expenditures made) by achieving what may be classified broadly as scale and/or scope economies. Other potential benefits may be improvements achieved through the internalization of externalities and/or advantages that materialize from improvements in or improved utilization of administrative and technical capacities. Transaction costs are a major barrier to successful intermunicipal agreements. Transaction costs involve particularly the costs of bringing the potentially cooperating municipalities together and then keeping them together. This aspect depends very much upon the nature of social networks, the extent or establishment of interpersonal trust and the development of shared understanding. The potential cost of those responsible for not meeting the expectations of municipal governments or living with the consequences—that is, agency costs—is another obstacle. A final potential, and only recently recognized, problem is one that might be called unexpected residual costs. In essence, following an intermunicipal agreement, all or some of the cooperating municipalities may find themselves bearing greater costs than previously in meeting responsibilities not covered by the agreement (e.g., due to loss of economies of scope and funding unanticipated transactions costs). A survey of recent empirical studies seeking evidence demonstrating the benefits of intermunicipal cooperative agreements found the numbers scant and the results contradictory. The problem, in part, is that service quality and change are frequently difficult to measure. Nonetheless, intermunicipal cooperative agreements are many and persistent.

1.2.3.3 Chapter 10: "Political Economy of Local Government Reform"

The reform of local government, even when seen as improving, is controversial. In addition, reform proceeds unevenly, it is discontinuous and typically particular to the specific environment. The consequence is that, beyond the well-recognized "progressive public administration" and "new public management" eras, local government reform has been challenging for scholars seeking to account for its genesis, nature and implementation. The complexity of the subject stems partly from it ranging from being comprehensive to it being quite narrow and specific to a particular aspect of the local public sector; for example, structural, financial, functional, jurisdictional (as with the scope of authority and competence), and organizational and managerial. The investigation in Chap. 10 distills and guides the reader through the substantial and varied literature, both theoretical and empirical. The theoretical thread encompasses the conceptual contributions on the motivations and shaping of reform and the analytic systems focus on diagnosing and guiding reform—sources of government failure, the influence of the new institutional economics (especially transactions costs and agency costs) and the role of policy leadership. The diversities of reform and institutional differences complicate empirical analysis and commonly constrain it to comparisons among similar countries and/or specific types of reforms. Demonstrated here is a study of reforms in 6 Anglo-American countries and another of 28 European countries. A major conclusion from the first was that despite substantial reforms and changes implemented, the operation of local government was not fundamentally transformed. The European countries clustered into six different types. A relatively common feature was central/state governments downloading more responsibilities than resources and that, in turn, prompted various reforms individually or collectively by the local governments themselves. Overall, it appears that universal general policy measures are few.

1.3 Conclusion

Local governance, in looking broadly at collective action at the local level, encompasses a wide perspective of the local public sector. It opens for further consideration alternative tax and tax administration systems, a broad range of budgeting and accounting tools, and expands substantially the examination of local public management and public administration. Curtailing corruption requires the engagement of citizens and civil society. The structure of local government, inter-local and local-state relations are important to local residents. Citizens can be very sensitive to changes in those arrangements (perhaps especially so for mergers) and hence engage in and expect participation. This volume has been directed to discussions of these topics. It is hoped that the book will inform and assist those who are pursuing greater empowerment and improved performance of local government.

PART II

Local Public, Fiscal and Financial Management

CHAPTER 2

Local Tax Administration

2.1 Introduction

The ultimate success of a local revenue system depends on the way in which local revenues are administered; after all, the best system in the world is of little use if it cannot be administered in a way that minimizes corruption and evasion and is fair, efficient and effective in its impact on taxpayers.

Revenue systems collectively include local taxes, user fees and charges, fines and penalties along with other miscellaneous revenues. Their administration and use in developing and transitional countries often differ from those in developed and industrial countries (Bahl and Bird 2018; Mikesell 2013). This difference is often attributed to a relatively larger agricultural sector that is not easily taxed in the former and because a high proportion of the economic activity in these countries occurs in the informal (shadow) economy and, therefore, not taxed (Bird 2003, p. 3). This informal economy which erodes the local tax base, it has been suggested, is largely driven by corruption (Schneider 2006; Schneider and Enste 2000). Exemptions that are perceived to be the result of a bribe also undermine the trust in government and the compliance with revenue laws (Dreher and Herzfeld 2005). A recent empirical study found that corruption is negatively associated with overall tax revenue (Baum et al. 2017).

These factors have combined to produce tax systems in transition and developing economies that have been capricious and potentially confiscatory, often resulting in negotiated tax liabilities (Berkowitz and Li 2002).

B. Dollery et al., *Local Public, Fiscal and Financial Governance*,
https://doi.org/10.1007/978-3-030-36725-1_2

This has created an environment in which bribery is prevalent and it has produced a business climate that is often hostile to new investment and the growth of small business (McCarten 2005, p. 5). More directly, there is evidence to suggest that the relative burden of bribes paid (to avoid high taxes) is higher for small enterprises in the formal sector (Clarke and Xu 2002) in these countries. In addition, it has been suggested that the high tax and regulatory environment in post-communist countries were directly responsible for driving much of the economic activity into the informal sector (Johnson et al. 1997).

The combination of inappropriate tax policies and weaknesses in the administration of local taxes has contributed to problems for developing and transitional countries. Less than comprehensive and uniform local tax systems have led to inadequate, unfair and inefficient tax collection systems, resulting in higher taxes on those who pay and less revenue from the local tax base leaving local governments with fewer public services than would otherwise be desired. The lack of accountable and transparent structures has a negative impact on tax compliance, leading to the possibility of more corruption and more tax evasion (Aghion et al. 2016). This can have a distorting effect on locational decisions of firms/businesses and the subsequent public sector investment that municipalities need to provide a reasonable quality of life for their citizens. To overcome this, it has been argued that specialized taxpayer offices should be established with anti-corruption agencies a part of a solid tax administrative system (IMF 2015; Stiglitz 2004).

Unfortunately, there is no easy or comprehensive solution for addressing the kinds of problems noted above. There are, however, a few administrative initiatives that could be taken to improve the administrative structure and to avoid many of the pitfalls or problems that often surface in local tax administration.

The remainder of this chapter is organized in the following way. Section 2.2 briefly outlines administrative structures frequently used for local taxes. In a general way, Sect. 2.3 highlights some of the major issues with local tax administration. Section 2.4 summarizes the chapter.

2.2 Local Administration Responsibility

Even though the property tax is the most prevalent local tax, local governments around the world rely on a variety of taxes. In the Nordic countries, for example, local governments rely on income taxes—property and sales taxes are non-existent as a local tax. In countries that were, at one time, part of the British Commonwealth or influenced by it, local governments generally rely on property taxes. In most countries, local governments have access to only one tax; however, in a few countries or states within the country, local governments have access to more than one local tax (Kitchen et al. 2019, chapters 8, 9 and 10).

Finally, there is considerable variation in the fiscal discretion that local governments have in determining their tax base and setting their tax rates. Some have no discretion at all, while a few have discretion over both the base and the rate. The most common option is for local government to have control over rates, although often restricted by limits, but not over the base.

In practice, international experience suggests that local autonomy and local control of the tax system are enhanced if the administration of the tax is also local (Mikesell 2013). Tax administration takes a variety of forms. Of the possibilities, complete centralization of all local tax administration or complete autonomy for local authorities seldom exists. A mix of the two is more common. As well, some developing countries have introduced an independent revenue authority to collect and administer taxes. Each of these options is now described briefly.

2.2.1 Central Administration

In countries where the central government has sole and exclusive control over all taxes, central administration is the only option. Here, taxes are levied in a uniform and consistent manner across all local jurisdictions with the actual administration performed centrally or through a number of dependent regional authorities operating under the administrative umbrella of the central government. Elements of a centrally administered system frequently include the following: collection of taxes that include both central taxes and any subnational taxes that may exist; a regulatory environment that is the same across the entire country; a taxpayer registration system that is uniform across the country; taxpayer identification numbers that are used by all levels of government; compatible and combined revenue and taxpayer accounting information systems; and uniform delinquency control and audit programs (Mikesell 2013, pp. 91–92).

2.2.2 *Independent Administration*

Independent local administrations involve responsibility for both enacting tax legislation (including the choice of taxes, defining the tax base, setting rates) and administering all taxes. This structure has much more fiscal autonomy than local governments operating in a centralized administrative system or a system with a mix of central and local administration. Independent local administration is also more likely to exist where senior levels of government do not share in the taxes employed by local governments.

2.2.3 *Mix of Central and Local Administration*

In most countries, local tax administration is shared by the local government as well as by a senior level of government (the central government in unified countries and the state/provincial/regional government in federal countries). Sharing responsibilities varies from country to country, but the most common practice is for the senior level of government to assume responsibility for administrative issues around the tax base including creating a taxpayer registration system, assigning taxpayer identification numbers, designing accounting and audit programs, training tax collectors, and sometimes collecting and enforcing tax collection, while local governments are responsible for setting local tax rates.

A few examples of this are listed here.

- In Sweden, Norway, Finland and Denmark, local governments piggyback onto central government's personal income tax by setting their own personal income tax rates (Lotz 2012).
- In some states in the United States, local governments set their own income and/or sales tax rates and piggyback onto the state income and sales tax base. In a few states, however, local governments collect their own income and sales tax revenues (Mikesell 2010, 2011).
- Municipal governments in Switzerland levy supplements to the cantonal personal income tax by levying a local income tax rate that is a percentage of or multiple of the cantonal tax rate (Mikesell 2013, p. 94). This is akin to "piggybacking".
- In Canada, municipalities are responsible for setting local property tax rates, collecting local taxes and enforcing collection, but determination of the property tax base (assessment), reassessment of the

property tax base and training of assessors are the responsibilities of the province or an independent assessment authority (Dahlby and McMillan 2019; Kitchen and Tassonyi 2012).

2.2.4 Semi-autonomous Independent Agency

A number of countries, including Malaysia, New Zealand, Singapore, Ghana, Kenya, Malawi, Rwanda, South Africa, Tanzania, Uganda, Zambia, Bolivia, Ecuador, Guatemala, Columbia, Guyana, Mexico, Peru and Venezuela, have adopted semi-independent revenue authorities for the administration and collection of national (Taliercio 2004, p. 2) and, on occasion, subnational taxes. These agencies are not generally designed for administering and collecting local taxes, but they could be used for this purpose.

Organizationally, these agencies have been set up outside the civil service and granted the legal status of semi-autonomous authorities. Depending on the country, they generally report to the Ministry of Finance or similar ministry or department. The authority is contracted to deliver agreed results and its management is contracted on fixed-term contracts and has significant independence in financial, personnel and operational matters. Furthermore, these authorities are designed with a number of autonomy-enhancing features, including self-financing mechanisms, boards of directors with high-ranking public and private sector representatives, and separate personnel systems (Taliercio 2004, p. 2).

2.3 Issues in Local Tax Administration

A number of issues frequently surface in any discussion of local tax administration. At the outset, there is the issue of whether or not local taxes should be administered and collected locally; or by a centralized level of government; or by an independent or semi-independent tax authority.

In addition, there are a variety of other functions that local tax systems and tax administrators have tried to upgrade over the past few years. For example, local tax administrators have improved their organizational and management skills. Second, they have strengthened the legal and regulatory framework in which they work. Third, they have broadened the tax base by identifying and registering taxpayers and potential taxpayers. Fourth, they have initiated programs/practices to improve taxpayer compliance. Fifth, they have improved their capacity to process the information flows resulting from additional information collected from taxpayers and a variety of government departments/ministries. Sixth, they have developed their risk-analysis capacity to focus on cases involving potential tax violators. Seventh, they have strengthened their investigation, audit and enforcement capacity. Eighth, they have initiated improved appeals procedures. Ninth, they have improved their analytical capacity and ability for carrying out studies on tax burdens, collection trends, compliance gaps and impacts of policy changes. Tenth, they have implemented procedures to reduce corruption. Each of these is discussed below.

2.3.1 Level of Administration

2.3.1.1 Central Administration

Centralized administration of the local tax system, either through assigning all responsibilities to the central government or from smaller municipalities contracting with larger cities to perform all administrative functions, has a number of advantages. First, because administrative costs are mainly fixed in nature, centralizing administration will reduce compliance and collection costs. The opportunity to spread fixed costs over a larger tax base leads to lower per unit costs. One study on property assessment in the state of Georgia (United States) concluded that a 10% increase in the volume of assessment led to an increase in total administration costs of 3% (Sjoquist and Walker 1999).

Second, a centralized administrative structure increases the probability that local taxpayers will be treated uniformly and in an unbiased and consistent manner throughout the region or jurisdictional area. A centralized system improves the extent to which tax authorities deal at "arm's-length" with local taxpayers. It minimizes the possibility that local administrators will play favorites by giving special treatment to certain taxpayers. As well, it is better able to cope with tax avoidance and evasion and to resolve problems created by cross-border transactions, especially for any tax with a mobile base (Bahl and Bird 2018, p. 212).

Third, the introduction of modern technology and the growth in professional staff in local tax administration have meant that economies of scope and scale are more likely to be achieved in centralized systems where coordination of specialists and related activities are more easily handled (Bird and Zolt 2008). This has led to a worldwide reduction in the number of local tax offices (OECD 2015).

Fourth, a centralized administration system increases the possibility that the same procedures and processes will be followed everywhere. A single taxpayer identification number permits tax administrators to collect all relevant information on all taxpayers and enhances their ability to administer the tax system, collect taxes and complete tax audits.

Fifth, larger administrative structures are better positioned than smaller administrative units to make use of specialized technology and equipment (computers for record keeping and tracking of taxpayers, etc.), to offer specialized training programs for staff, to employ specialized personnel that can deal with complex assignments that could prevent tax evasion or avoidance, to deal with taxable activities that cross regional or local jurisdictional boundaries and to pay higher salaries and thus reduce the attractiveness of corruption (Mikesell 2013).

Sixth, centralized tax administration may improve the transparency of the overall tax system because taxpayers will not be confused over who does what, who is responsible for answering what questions and who enforces tax collection and undertakes tax audits. There is only one tax authority.

2.3.1.2 Local Administration

For those who subscribe to the subsidiarity principle (government services should be provided by the level of government closest to the taxpayers), there may be a basis for defending local tax administration because it may offer the following advantages.

First, local units are likely to be more familiar with local conditions and better able to register taxpayers, collect taxes and enforce the collection and auditing function. If local governments control the choice of a tax and its administration, they are in a better position to determine their tax base, set their tax rate, enforce tax collection and pursue tax audits. All of this reflects local preferences; for example, local authorities may wish to pursue different enforcement policies than a central authority might desire in order to better balance tax payer equity (local choice) with revenue generation (Alm 1999).

Second, supporters of a local administrative structure argue that transparency and accountability are improved when local governments collect and administer the taxes they levy. As long as taxpayers know which level of government is responsible for each tax, they are better able to hold governments accountable for their actions (Bird and Slack 2014). This is often lost when one level of government collects a tax that is levied by another level of government such as where local governments piggyback a local tax rate onto a tax employed by a senior level of government.

Third, the existence of many local administrative units permits experimentation in new and innovative techniques, including the application of information technology, barcoding and imagining to tax administration (Bahl and Bird 2018, p. 212). These may be tried in specific jurisdictions, and if they succeed, the techniques can be used elsewhere. If they fail, the impact and confusion are restricted to a small area and the fallout from the failed experiment is minimized.

Fourth, local administration means that local governments have access to their revenues immediately and that they do not have to wait for funds to be remitted by the central authority. Slow and inaccurate payment has been a common complaint by local governments in the United States whose sales or income tax is administered by the state government. As well, when state governments in the United States experience budget problems, it has not been uncommon for them to delay scheduled payments (in the form of transfers of centrally collected local taxes) to their local governments (Mikesell 2013). Local administration also eliminates disputes that can occur over the division of centrally collected revenues across local governments and between local governments and the central government where taxes are shared.

Fifth, local administration would better protect regional or local interests in disputes over the allocation of business and personal tax revenues collected from businesses or individuals who work in multiple jurisdictions. These interjurisdictional allocation disputes can be highly contentious and it is alleged that central authorities have less interest than local authorities in resolving them because the central authority has nothing to gain or lose. Their revenue will not be impacted and the only decision is over the division of revenue between competing local jurisdictions (Mikesell 2013).

Sixth, in some developing countries, local tax administration is a way of generating employment. This has been noted in Tanzania, for example, where small local taxes and charges have been implemented to create employment for people in the administration and enforcement of these taxes and charges (Fjeldstad 2001, p. 4).

Seventh, local authorities may be more diligent than central authorities in enforcing local tax collection because the latter have an incentive to concentrate on their own taxes rather than on those collected for local governments (Bahl and Bird 2018, p. 212). This, however, may not be a problem if local governments permit the collecting authority to retain a portion of all local taxes collected. This is the practice in the United States, where the state collects sales taxes for local governments (Mikesell 2011). On the other hand, if the fee is substantial, local authorities may prefer to collect their own taxes.

Eighth, local authorities may be preferred over a centralized authority in many developing countries where there has been no tradition of paying taxes. To put it simply, local authorities may have a better chance of implementing new taxes and bringing potential taxpayers into the tax system. Taxpayer compliance, here, is alleged to be higher than it would be under a centralized system that may be seen as distant and considerably removed from the local community (Burgess and Stern 1993, p. 799).

Ninth, since tax authorities (politicians and civil servants) are viewed by many taxpayers as rapacious, the existence of a number of independent local tax authorities can inject an element of competition across taxing authorities (McLure and Martinez 2000). This intermunicipal competition may assist in protecting taxpayers from unfair and potentially corrupt tax collection systems because taxpayers who are aware of what is happening in neighboring jurisdictions will be better informed and better positioned to challenge what is happening in their own jurisdiction.

2.3.1.3 Central or Local Administration: Which Should It Be?

A number of arguments have been presented in support of each of these structures. In the end, a choice must be made—central or local? This choice might be based on a number of factors, but it will likely revolve around the capacity of local governments to administer their own taxes and the willingness of more senior levels of government to permit them to run their own system.

Where local governments have the capacity to administer their own taxes as they do in developed countries, the choice may depend on the tradeoff between benefits from economies of scale in tax administration and a willingness on the part of a senior level of government to give municipalities more local autonomy, at least in setting tax rates, if not in determining the tax base.

Where local authorities do not have the capacity to administer local taxes either because they have never administered one or because they have insufficient resources (poorly trained personnel, lack of computerized tax records, etc.) to administer it properly, arguments generally support central administration.

When all arguments are weighed, certain aspects of tax administration could benefit from centralization while others could benefit from local decisions. For example, the local tax base within each country should be standardized so that location decisions are not distorted. Educating, training and setting standards for tax administrators could benefit from centralization. Tax collection, enforcement and auditing could be done centrally although this may create problems if the central authority is not given an incentive to carry out this function thoroughly, effectively and efficiently. Perhaps the best incentive would come from paying the central authority to collect taxes, as is currently done in a few countries. Local governments, however, should be given responsibility for setting local tax rates. International experience tells us that municipalities that raise the money they spend are more accountable, transparent and efficient in the services for which they are responsible.

2.3.2 *Reforming Local Tax Administration*

Local government revenue reform is a topic that has generated considerable interest in a number of countries in recent years. It ranges from arguments in support of giving cities in Canada, for example, access to additional tax sources (Kitchen and Slack 2016) to arguments in support of reforming existing administrative revenue structures to help them become more transparent, accountable and efficient in developing and transitional countries (Bahl and Bird 2018). Of these two areas of concern, the latter are the center of discussion here.

Many developing and transition governments have embarked on ambitious tax and revenue reform agendas. This includes modernizing taxpayer registration, strengthening payment systems, improving collection enforcement, developing effective audit programs, developing better taxpayer services, introducing automation and computerization, implementing unique taxpayer identification numbers, monitoring taxpayers (McCarten 2005, p. 11) and initiating programs to improve tax compliance. In a few countries, this has also included the creation of semi-autonomous tax and revenue administration agencies. These issues are amplified below.

2.3.2.1 Semi-autonomous Independent Agency

These authorities have been adopted in developing countries to overcome problems created by inadequate and restrictive government civil service systems and public management systems. Their autonomy is considered to be an antidote to the failure of political systems to build effective accountability mechanisms to prevent politicians from intervening to grant favors such as lowering taxes on specific taxpayers, exempting specific taxpayers/properties from taxes or harassing political opponents through unnecessary tax audits.

A separate body operating independently from the civil service, it has been suggested, is better able to pay higher salaries to attract more competent and specialized professional staff (experts in tax and auditing). It has also been suggested that it is less likely to be subjected to patronage appointments when compared with the civil service. Indeed, it was this problem that led some to view the introduction of a semi-independent revenue authority as necessary to bypass the inadequacies of the civil service in Bolivia following the change of government in 1997 (Taliercio 2004, pp. 5–7).

Common to most agencies are special financing mechanisms. There are two basic variations—one where the agency receives a fixed percentage of revenue collected and the other where the agency receives a variable percentage of all revenues collected. In either case, these structures provide tax collection agencies with an incentive to increase revenues collected. The downside of this, however, is the possibility that these agencies will become overly and unfairly aggressive in their tax collecting role, potentially violating taxpayers rights to fair and reasonable treatment under tax law and practices.

Increased reliance on semi-independent tax authorities in developing countries, it has been suggested, has been driven by politicians who want to create a credible commitment to taxpayers that their tax administration is competent, effective and fair. Furthermore, it is the autonomous nature of these authorities that is important and permits politicians to make this claim. Increased autonomy, the hypothesis goes, leads to higher tax compliance and increased tax collections. One econometric study that tested this hypothesis concluded that autonomy matters. Perceptions of greater levels of autonomy are associated with perceptions of better performance with the autonomy variable being consistently significant (statistically) across a variety of models. As well, separate case studies supported the hypothesis that performance indicators improved most when autonomy was high and least when autonomy was low (Taliercio 2004).

2.3.2.2 Strengthening Management

Introducing changes that strengthen the management of the tax system may not be easy, yet it is extremely important. Improving management almost always requires fundamental changes in the behavior of managers and staff. In most developing and transitional economies, bad management policies and practices have existed for so long that it is very difficult to change them. As well, in many countries, the administration of the revenue system is often constrained by laws and regulations that severely reduce the flexibility of the managers to move resources around to achieve a more efficient and optimal use of them.

The first task in tax administration and functions is identifying and registering taxpayers. This is best achieved when all taxpayers and potential taxpayers are assigned taxpayer identification numbers (TINs). Here, each taxpayer is identified by a number that may be used for all taxes—income tax, value-added tax and property tax. Such a system is preferred over a system where a different taxpayer number is assigned for each tax. To avoid problems and to increase the effectiveness of the registration system, the TIN should not include taxpayer characteristics that may change over time (such as economic activity, type of taxpayer or address). Strict controls should be placed on TINs so they cannot be duplicated; cannot be assigned to more than one taxpayer, and each taxpayer can only be assigned one number; only one TIN for each company; and a TIN should not have too many digits (World Bank 2002a). Reliance on effective identification numbers is a key requirement for the proper implementation of a tax system. This should minimize the non-filer problem and help to improve the overall equity and effectiveness of a local tax system.

Improving the management of tax administration systems is one of the most challenging tasks, especially in developing and transitional economies. Projects in Latvia, Russia and Columbia have focused on strengthening "the capacity of managers for setting strategic goals; formulating operational policy; managing financial, human, information and physical resources effectively; supervising, monitoring and evaluating performance; improving coordination; anticipating and resolving operational problems; enforcing internal control systems; preventing corruption; improving mechanisms to redress taxpayer grievances; and interacting with stakeholders" (Gill 2003, p. 12).

Tax officials must be adequately compensated, so that they do not steal to live. They should be professionally trained, promoted by merit and judged by their adherence to the strictest standards of legality and morality. To remove temptation, tax collections should be kept out of tax administration and channeled through banks. Officials should have relatively little contact with taxpayers and even less discretion in deciding how to treat them (Bird 2003, p. 16). Reliance on updated and effective information technology including the use of computers and the automation of as much of the tax function as possible is equally important because this will improve the administrator's capacity to manage effectively the local tax system (Bahl and Bird 2018, pp. 211–14).

2.3.2.3 Controlling Corruption

Corruption has been defined "as the abuse of public office for private gain" (World Bank 1999, p. 1). Corrupt actions include theft of public property and acceptance of bribes for special favors or tax considerations. Corruption diminishes the effectiveness of the tax system, treats taxpayers unequally and leads to a general distrust and dislike of local governments. Policies and practices that eliminate or reduce the depth and range of corruption are important, especially in developing countries where tax administrative structures tend to be weaker and more susceptible to corruption.

To counter corruption, some countries have delinked the salaries of tax administrators from the salaries of other civil servants, thus giving management the freedom to pay market salaries. It is not clear, however, what the size of the salary differential would need to be to effectively reduce corruption. Moreover, such increases may impose a considerable burden on local budgets in developing countries (World Bank 1999).

Columbia dealt with corruption by preparing *Corruption Risk Maps* that are designed to provide procedural changes to reduce opportunities for corruption (McCarten 2005, p. 31). Latvia and Jamaica have strengthened internal control systems (including computerized management information systems, automated financial management and human resource management systems) that have reduced the discretion that revenue officials have in tax administration and they simplified procedures to be followed (Gill 2003, p. 13).

Creating a centralized data processing center has a number of advantages. It permits tax authorities to take advantage of economies of scale in tax administration by serving as a center for registering taxpayers, processing returns, accepting payment, remitting refunds, maintaining taxpayer accounts, detecting non-filers and maintaining correspondence with taxpayers. The United States has these centers and other countries have also created them (Gill 2003, pp. 11–13). They reduce the contact between taxpayers and officials, thus reducing the opportunity for corruption (McCarten 2005, p. 18). Any remaining interaction between tax officials and taxpayers should be through standardized processes that are easy for internal audit and transparent to all parties (McCarten 2005, p. 21).

Automating as many of the tax administrative tasks as possible reduces the possibility of bribery (Mikesell 2013). This has included restricting access of employees to scanned copies of original records to prevent tampering, and creating auditing trails of administrative decisions and changes made to taxpayer current accounts (McCarten 2005, p. 31).

When combined with higher salaries for tax administrators and stiff penalties for malfeasance, the creation of semi-autonomous collection agencies in some African countries (e.g., Kenya, Uganda and South Africa) reduced the amount of corruption (Taliercio 2004, p. 26). In addition, reliance on independent taxpayer surveys can help identify elements of the tax administrative structure or individual tax offices that harbor severe corruption (World Bank 1999).

At the local level, taxes should be designed so that they are broad based, with relatively few exemptions if any at all, low tax rates, and structured so that local administrative officials have little discretion over the base and none over the tax rates. Both of these should be determined by politically elected councils, not determined or altered by local tax administrators (Fjeldstad 2002).

2.3.2.4 *Strengthening the Legal and Regulatory Framework*

Many countries have introduced changes to remove ambiguities or loopholes that permitted tax evasion and unintended tax avoidance. This has involved strengthening taxpayer registration requirements by introducing compulsory taxpayer identification numbers for all existing and potential taxpayers. Revenue authorities have been given more power to collect and enforce tax collection as well as stronger penalties for non-payment and non-compliance. Rules and regulations, in many countries, have been simplified to permit the exchange of information between different departments and different government agencies, thus facilitating more effective implementation of tax laws and enforcement. Rules and regulations that reduce the discretion of local revenue authorities have been enacted as have grievance and appeal procedures to improve the fairness, effectiveness, transparency and accountability of the local tax system.

2.3.2.5 Improving Compliance

Voluntary tax compliance does not have a long history in many developing and transitional countries. To correct this, tax administrators have or should concentrate on facilitating compliance, monitoring compliance and dealing with non-compliance (Bird 2003, p. 7). Facilitating compliance consists of providing taxpayers with information including clear instructions on why there is a local tax, how it works and how it should be paid. Fortunately, in many countries efforts are being made to improve tax compliance by simplifying tax forms, reducing the number of steps to be followed, automating most of the tax administrative function, introducing electronic tax filing and payment of taxes (Gill 2003, pp. 14–15; McCarten 2005, p. 15). As well, administrative staff are frequently available in offices or on telephone lines or through the internet to answer questions and provide assistance. Of a more specific nature, some countries have introduced creative and innovative strategies to make potential taxpayers aware of the concept of taxes and why taxes should be paid. This has included awareness-raising campaigns through the media, advertisements on public transit, inclusion of material in school curricula, school plays on tax issues and fairy tales concentrating on tax compliance (McCarten 2005).

Accountability mechanisms should be improved between taxpayers and governments if transparency, answerability and controllability are to be improved (Moore 2004). Mechanisms to do this, it has been suggested, have three components: first, transparency or the ability of taxpayers to see that government decisions or processes are implemented in accordance with known rules and mandates; second, answerability or the obligation to provide legitimate reasons for government decisions; and third, controllability or institutional checks and controls to prevent mismanagement and abuse of power and to ensure that corrective measures are adopted when the rules are violated (Gloppen and Rakner 2002). It is also important that tax systems be neutral in their impact on private sector decision-making.

Taxpayer compliance is also higher in countries that provide easy accessibility to service and information so that taxpayers can fulfill their tax obligations. This service includes personal services at tax offices or other convenient and accessible places, telephonic information service and information through pamphlets, folders, forms, internet service, advertisements in papers and commercials on radio and television. A second important aspect is the prompt processing of taxpayer applications (e.g., tax payer refunds) or complaints (World Bank 2001).

Effective taxpayer service systems improve the integrity and effectiveness of local tax administration and produce fewer errors in tax reporting and more reliable tax returns, thus permitting the tax authorities to spend their time focusing on detecting intentional errors and tax evasion.

2.3.2.6 Enforcing Tax Collection

Tax enforcement is perhaps the weakest area in tax administration in most developing countries. Effective enforcement procedures are necessary if tax collection and tax compliance are to be improved. One tool for improving compliance is to use a computer system that identifies non-filers and those who have not paid their full tax liability immediately after the due date. Quick notification heightens the perception that the administrative authority knows the delinquents and is about to pursue them.

Enforcement can also be improved if tax authorities develop and use a system for risk analysis that selects specific taxpayers/properties for detailed investigation, audit and physical inspection, if necessary. Reliance on risk analysis is better than random selection because it permits the tax authority to identify taxpayers/tax cases that are most likely to avoid or evade taxes.

Strengthening audit capacity is another way in which enforcement can be improved. The purpose of an effective tax audit is to achieve a preventative effect because the risk of detection, when combined with strong enforcement procedures and high penalties/fines, provides an incentive for taxpayers to comply voluntarily with the tax system. Reducing tax evasion is also linked to the perceived fairness of any tax system and, as such, is a useful mechanism for increasing taxpayer compliance. In fact, in many countries, tax audits produce less than 1% of total tax revenue; yet they are critical, for it is their preventative effect that is more important than the additional revenue they generate (World Bank 2002b). Maximum preventative effects of effective tax audits are achieved by targeting high-risk or potentially high-risk groups of taxpayers; thus appropriate selection of audit targets is a key element of an audit strategy.

Finally, permitting tax authorities to impose fines on delinquent taxpayers has proven to be an effective instrument for increasing tax compliance. The trick is to determine the appropriate penalty. Fines that are too high provide an incentive for taxpayers to bribe tax officials; hence, it has been suggested that fines/penalties be lower but highly visible (Ott 1998).

2.3.2.7 *Handling Appeals*

Appeals procedures should be designed so that they are not long and expensive. This should consist of an appeals body that is neutral and transparent and independent of the administrative tax agency. In some countries, this is handled by a tax court. A good appeals process assists in improving voluntary compliance because it increases the taxpayer's trust in the fairness of the tax system.

2.3.2.8 *Introducing Performance Measures*

Establishing performance measures for tax administration and collection is one way in which local tax authorities could measure the effectiveness of their system. These measures could be benchmarked against similar measures in other taxing jurisdictions. This would provide an indication of the extent to which a local tax authority was operating in an efficient, effective and fair manner. Furthermore, if performance measures for a particular tax authority are out of line, in a negative way, with other comparable authorities, there is a basis for reviewing the administrative structure and reforming it to improve the local system. If the measures are out of line in a positive way, the system may be a model to be emulated by other comparable authorities. It is unlikely that every local tax authority has the resources to construct and adopt every possible performance measure; nevertheless, the following lists some of the measures that could be used. The final choice in a country or locality will depend on the availability of data and the capacity of the tax authority to collect the requisite information and carry out the task.

- The ratio of taxes levied to gross domestic product (GDP): lower ratios vis-à-vis similar tax collection systems elsewhere may indicate a less effective tax collection system and provide an incentive to review the current tax structure with the intent of improving its performance.
- Ratio of taxpayers and potential taxpayers (number of registrants) to total population: the higher this ratio, the more effective the tax collection system because it is likely that a higher percentage of taxpayers have been identified and, therefore, brought into the tax system. Evasion and avoidance is likely to be lower and compliance higher.
- Tax revenue as a percent of tax base: the higher the ratio, the more effective the tax collection system.
- Actual tax revenue collected as a percent of budgeted tax revenue: the higher the ratio, the more effective the tax system.

- Tax arrears as a percent of total taxes collected: the higher the ratio, the less effective the tax system.
- Tax administration costs as a percent of tax revenue collected: the higher the ratio, the lower the efficiency of the tax system.
- Number of taxpayer appeals as a percent of total taxpayers: the lower the percent, it is more likely that the tax system will have a higher rate of compliance and be more effective and fair in its operation.

2.3.2.9 Dealing with the Informal Economy

The informal economy is one in which cash or barter transactions dominate the regular or formal economy. This is especially prevalent in developing countries. Because the informal economy is based on cash or bartering, local income taxes are ineffective. Value-added taxes tend to work better, but these are almost never used by local governments. Local sales and selective excise taxes are not uncommon but they are also difficult to enforce. Local property taxes tend to be most effective because they can be based on property values or area/size of property and not likely to be a component of the informal economy since they are immobile and visible and, therefore, capable of being taxed.

One problem that exists with property taxation in developing and transitional economies is that the tax is often based on a relatively narrow base with a comparatively high tax rate. This has led to a considerable amount of bribery where local taxpayers pay local tax officials to ignore them when it comes to taxation or to treat them leniently for tax purposes. If the bribe is less than the tax liability, taxpayers have an incentive to opt for the informal sector. Reducing bribery opportunities through tax administrative reforms appears to improve the attractiveness for small enterprises to join the formal sector (McCarten 2005, p. 11). In fact, there is some evidence to suggest that the effective burden of bribes is higher on smaller enterprises when compared with larger enterprises (Clarke and Xu 2002). If bribes can be eliminated, enterprises in the informal sector have an incentive to join the formal sector where they substitute payment of taxes for payment of bribes.

2.4 Summary

The ultimate success of any local tax system depends on the way in which the local tax is administered. In practice, local tax administration takes a variety of forms. These range from complete centralization of local tax administration to complete autonomy for local authorities, although the latter seldom exists. The most likely option is a mix of the two with the central authority being responsible for such things as determining and valuing the local tax base; educating, training and setting standards for tax administrators; tax collection, enforcement and auditing as long as the central authority has an incentive to carry out this function thoroughly, effectively and efficiently. Local governments, however, should be given responsibility for setting local tax rates at the very least and possibly for collection and enforcement.

A number of issues frequently surface in discussions of local tax administration. At the outset, there is the issue of whether or not local taxes should be administered and collected locally; or by a centralized level of government; or by an independent or semi-independent tax authority.

In addition, there are a variety of other functions that local tax systems and tax administrators have tried to improve on over the past few years. Local tax administrators have tried to improve the organization and management of their agency. Second, they have tried to strengthen the legal and regulatory framework in which they work. Third, they have broadened the tax base by identifying and registering taxpayers and potential taxpayers. Fourth, they have initiated programs/practices to improve taxpayer compliance. Fifth, they have improved their capacity to process the information flows resulting from additional information collected from taxpayers and a variety of government departments/ministries. Sixth, they have tried to develop their risk-analysis capacity to focus on cases involving potential tax violators. Seventh, they have strengthened their investigation, audit and enforcement capacity. Eighth, they have initiated improved appeals procedures. Ninth, they have improved their analytical capacity and ability for carrying out studies on tax burdens, collection trends, compliance gaps and impacts of policy changes. Tenth, they have implemented procedures to reduce corruption.

References

Aghion, P., Akcigit, U., Cagé, J., and Kerr, W. 2016. Taxation, Corruption, and Growth. NBER Working Paper 21928. Cambridge, MA: National Bureau of Economic Research.

Alm, James. 1999. Tax Compliance and Administration. In *Handbook on Taxation*, ed. Bartley Hildreth and James A. Richardson. New York: Marcel Dekker.

Bahl, Roy, and Richard M. Bird. 2018. *Fiscal Decentralization and Local Finance in Developing Countries, Studies in Fiscal Federalism and State-Local Finance.* Northampton: Edward Elgar Publishing.

Baum, Anja, Sanjeev Gupta, Elijah Kimani, and Sampawende Jules Tapsoba. 2017. Corruption, Taxes and Compliance. IMF Working Paper. WP/17/255. Accessed 28 Jan 2019.

Berkowitz, Daniel, and Wei Li. 2002. Tax Rights in Transition Economies: A Tragedy of the Commons? *Journal of Public Economics* 76 (3): 369–398.

Bird, Richard M. 2003. Administrative Dimensions of Tax Reform. International Tax Program Paper 0302. Toronto: Joseph L. Rotman School of Management, University of Toronto.

Bird, Richard M., and Enid Slack, eds. 2014. Local Taxes and Local Expenditures in Developing Countries: Strengthening the Wicksellian Connection. *Public Administration and Development* 34 (4): 359–369.

Bird, Richard M., and Eric Zolt. 2008. Technology and Taxation in Developing Countries: From Hand to Mouse. *National Tax Journal* 61 (4): 791–821.

Burgess, Robin, and Nicholas Stern. 1993. Taxation and Development. *Journal of Economic Literature* 31 (2): 762–830.

Clarke, G.R.G., and L.C. Xu. 2002. Ownership, Competition, and Corruption: Bribe Takers Versus Bribe Payers. World Bank Working Papers WP2783, February.

Dahlby, Bev, and Melville McMillan. 2019. What Is the Role of Property and Property-Related Taxes? An Assessment of Municipal Property Taxes, Land Transfer Taxes, and Tax Increment Financing. In *Funding the Canadian City*, ed. Enid Slack, Lisa Philipps, Lindsay M. Tedds, and Heather L. Evans, 45–73. Toronto: Canadian Tax Foundation and Institute on Municipal Finance and Governance.

Dreher, A. and Herzfeld, T. 2005. The Economic Costs of Corruption: A Survey and New Evidence. *SSRN Electronic Journal*, https://doi.org/10.2139/ssrn.734184, June.

Fjeldstad, Odd-Helge. 2001. Fiscal Decentralization in Tanzania: For Better or for Worse? 10. CMI Working Paper 2001. Bergen: Chr. Michelsen Institute.

———. 2002. Fighting Fiscal Corruption: The Case of the Tanzania Revenue Authority, 3. CMI Working Paper 2002. Available at www.ids.ac.uk/gdr/cfs/activities/Fjeldstad%20Wp.pdf

Gill, Jit B.S. 2003. *The Nuts and Bolts of Revenue Administration Reform.* Washington, DC: World Bank.

Gloppen, Siri, and Lise Rakner. 2002. Accountability Through Tax Reform in Developing Countries: Illustrations from Sub-Saharan Africa. *IDS Bulletin* 33 (3): 1–17.

International Monetary Fund (IMF). 2015. Current Challenges in Revenue Mobilization: Improving Tax Compliance. IMF Policy Paper, Washington, DC.

Johnson, Simon, Daniel Kaufman, and Andrei Shleifer. 1997. The Unofficial Economy in Transition. *Brookings Papers on Economic Activity* 28: 159–239.

Kitchen, Harry and Enid Slack. 2016. More Tax Sources for Canada's Largest Cities: Why, What, and How? IMFG Papers on Municipal Finance and Governance Series No. 27. University of Toronto. Available at http://munkschool.utoronto.ca/imfg/resources/

Kitchen, Harry, and Almos Tassonyi. 2012. Municipal Taxes and User Fees. In *Tax Policy in Canada*, ed. Heather Kerr, Ken McKenzie, and Jack Mintz. Toronto: Canadian Tax Foundation, ch. 9.

Kitchen, Harry, Melville McMillan, and Anwar Shah. 2019. *Local Public Economics and Finance: An International Perspective*. Cham: Palgrave Macmillan.

Lotz, Jorgen. 2012. You Get What You Pay For: How Nordic Cities Are Financed. IMFG Papers on Municipal Finance and Governance Series, University of Toronto No. 7. Available at http://munkschool.utoronto.ca/imfg/resources/

McCarten, William. 2005. *"The Role of Organizational Design in the Revenue Strategies of Developing Countries: Benchmarking with VAT Performance," Mimeograph*. Washington, DC: The World Bank Institute.

McLure, Charles, and Jorge Martinez-Vazquez. 2000. *"The Assignment of Revenues and Expenditures in Intergovernmental Fiscal Relations", a Paper Prepared for the Core Course on Intergovernmental Relations and Local Financial Management*. Washington, DC: World Bank Institute.

Mikesell, John L. 2010. The Contribution of Local Sales and Income Taxes to Fiscal Autonomy. In *Municipal Revenues and Land Policies*, ch. 6, ed. G.K. Ingram and Y.-H. Yang. Cambridge: Lincoln Institute of Land Policy.

———. 2011. Consumption and Income Taxes. In *Greenbook*, chapter 10 International City Managers Association.

———. 2013. Administration of Local Taxes: An International Review of Practices and Issues for Enhancing Fiscal Autonomy. In *A Primer on Property Tax Administration and Policy*, ch. 4, ed. William J. McCluskey, Gary C. Cornia, and Lawrence C. Walters, First ed. Chichester, West Sussex, UK: Wiley-Blackwell.

Moore, M. 2004. Revenues, State Formation, and the Quality of Governance in Developing Countries. *International Political Science Review* 25 (3): 297–319.

Organization for Economic Cooperation and Development (OECD). 2015. *Tax Administration 2015*. Paris.

Ott, Katarina. 1998. Tax Administration Reform in Transition: The Case of Croatia. Occasional Paper No. 5, Institute of Public Finance. Available at www.ijf.hr/eng/ops/ijf-ocp5.pdf

Schneider, F. 2006. Shadow Economies and Corruption All Over the World: What Do We Really Know? IZA Discussion Paper No. 2315. Bonn: Institute for the Study of Labor (IZA).

Schneider, F., and D. Enste. 2000. Shadow Economies: Size, Causes, and Consequences. *Journal of Economic Literature* 38 (1): 77–114.

Sjoquist, David L., and Mary Beth Walker. 1999. Economies of Scale in Property Tax Assessment. *National Tax Journal* 52 (2): 207–220.
Stiglitz, Joseph E. 2004. *Development Oriented Tax Policy.* Initiative for Policy Dialogue, Tax Task Force (Mimeograph), Columbia University.
Taliercio, Jr., Robert. 2004. Designing Performance: The Semi-Autonomous Revenue Authority Model in Africa and Latin America. World Bank Policy Research Working Paper 3423. Washington, DC: The World Bank.
World Bank. 1999. *PREM Notes.* Available from www1.worldbank.org/prem/PREMNotes/premnote33.pdf
———. 2001. *Taxpayer Services.* Available from www1.worldbank.org/publicsector/tax/taxpayers.html
———. 2002a. *Registration.* Available from www1.worldbank.org/publicsector/tax/registration.html
———. 2002b. *Tax Audit.* Available from www1.worldbank.org/publicsector/tax/valuation.html

CHAPTER 3

The Practice of Real Property Taxation in the World

It is simply and solely the abundance of money within a state (which) makes the difference in its grandeur and power.
The art of taxation consists in so plucking the goose as to obtain largest amount of feathers with the least possible amount of hissing.
—Jean-Baptiste Colbert, Minister of Finance, France, 1666–1685.

3.1 Introduction

Local property taxes are important sources of own revenues for local governments around the world. However, their potential as a source of own revenues are not fully exploited especially in the developing countries due to inefficiencies in tax administration. Even in industrial countries, use of this tax instrument in dealing with urban sprawl remains to be seen. Regardless of the special design of property taxes to deal with urban sprawl advocated later in this chapter, McMillan (2016, 2017) shows that having simply greater reliance on property taxes as a source of local revenue reduces urban sprawl. This chapter presents a synthesis of global practices in real property tax to make this knowledge readily accessible to practitioners and students.[1] It is intended to serve as a primer on worldwide practices on real property taxes. It highlights the importance of the tax in local finances, discusses various variants used around the world (*see* Almy 2013;

[1] This chapter is based upon Shah (2016). It also draws heavily upon an excellent and comprehensive survey on this subject by Almy (2013).

B. Dollery et al., *Local Public, Fiscal and Financial Governance*,
https://doi.org/10.1007/978-3-030-36725-1_3

Mikesell 2013). It also reflects on what is taxed, what is taxed preferentially and what is not taxed. It details the process of property tax rate determination. It details valuation methods and data requirements; assessment cycles and review and appeal mechanisms. The failure to establish a credible valuation system will erode taxpayers' confidence, compliance, and revenue performance. It describes principles and practices on property tax relief mechanisms. It also provides perspectives on institutional arrangements for property tax administration including assessment of property value, tax compliance, penalties, enforcement mechanisms and dispute resolution mechanisms. It clarifies the perspective roles of various orders of government in property tax policy, legislation, regulation, rate and base determination, valuation, collection and compliance.

3.1.1 Importance of Real Property Tax as a Source of Local Finance in an International Context

Local property taxes as a percentage of GDP in 2013 ranged from a low of 0.3% of GDP in Estonia to a high of 3.8% of GDP in France with 2.7% of GDP in the USA; 2.8% of GDP in Canada and 2.9% of GDP in Luxembourg (*see* Table 3.1). Typically, in former British heritage countries local property taxes as a percentage of GDP exceed 1% of GDP. Among OECD countries, local government reliance on property taxes as source of local financing varies from a low of 3% in Sweden to a high of 96% in Ireland. On average, OECD local government finance 26% of total expenditures from local property taxes. For developing countries such data is scant and available for only a handful of countries (*see* Tables 3.2 and 3.3). These data suggest that Latin American countries typically rely on property taxes for one-third of local government financing. Central and Eastern Europe, East Asia and Pacific and Africa regions have lower reliance on property taxes. The PRC raises only 4.7% of local revenues from recurrent taxes on real estate. However, in the Republic of South Africa, real property tax revenues account for 97% of local own source revenues. Overall in developing countries real property taxes account for 39.5% of local own revenues. Figure 3.1 presents data on the real property taxes as a percentage of GDP from IMF's Government Finance Statistics 2012 for the world sample. Figure 3.2 presents data for the same sample on real property taxes as a percentage of local tax revenues. Both figures show a wide range across the World Sample.

Table 3.1 Relative importance of property taxes in the OECD countries

	PT % GDP	*Local share*	*L PT% GDP*	*LGR %GDP*	*LPT/LGR*
Location	*2013*		*2013*	*2013*	*2013*
Australia	2.37	0.626	1.48362	2.4	0.618
Austria	0.724	0.893	0.646532	3.22	0.200
Belgium	1.5	0.96	1.44	3.48	0.413
Canada	3	0.922	2.766	4.17	0.663
Czech Republic	0.47	0.999	0.46953	7.51	0.062
Denmark	1.842	1	1.842	15.22	0.121
Estonia	0.305	1	0.305	5.97	0.051
Finland	1.293	1	1.293	16.13	0.080
France	3.807	0.999	3.803193	8.22	0.462
Germany	0.923	1	0.923	4.95	0.186
Greece	2.176	1	2.176	2.3	0.946
Hungary	1.324	1	1.324	4.65	0.284
Ireland	2.181	1	2.181	2.26	0.965
Israel	2.706	0.997	2.697882	3.59	0.751
Italy	2.692	1	2.692	8.98	0.299
Japan	2.661	1	2.661	9	0.295
Korea	2.51	0.867	2.17617	5.94	0.366
Luxembourg	2.878	1	2.878	4	0.719
Mexico	0.29	0.669	0.19401	1.07	0.181
New Zealand	1.962	1	1.962	3	0.654
Norway	1.233	0.839	1.034487	7.97	0.129
Poland	1.3	1	1.3	6.58	0.197
Portugal	1.114	1	1.114	4.98	0.223
Slovak Republic	0.445	1	0.445	2.22	0.200
Slovenia	0.689	1	0.689	5.91	0.116
Spain	2.148	1	2.148	4.14	0.518
Sweden	1.066	0.534	0.569244	17.99	0.031
Switzerland	1.784	0.705	1.25772	6.24	0.201
United Kingdom	2.05	0.52	1.066	4	0.266
United States	2.834	0.967	2.740478	6.5	0.421
OECD	1.74	0.916	1.59384	6.09	0.261

Source: Author's calculations based on data from OECD (2015)

Note: *PT* property taxes by all levels, *LPT* local property taxes (includes school taxes), *LGR* local government revenues

Table 3.2 Developing and transition economies: Relative importance of local property taxes as a percentage of GDP and of local taxes (LT)

Country	*Year*	*%GDP*	*%LT*
Bolivia	2007	0.005	0.103
Bulgaria	2009	0.009	0.624
Cape Verde	2009	0.005	0.713
Colombia	2009	0.006	0.289
Cyprus	2009	0.001	0.169
Georgia	2009	0.009	0.706
Honduras	2009	0.007	1
Hungary	2009	0.003	0.127
Jamaica	2007	0.002	0.606
Kazakhstan	2009	0.006	0.138
Kenya	2009	0.001	0.421
Korea, Republic	2009	0.006	0.15
Kyrgyzstan	2009	0.007	0.237
Latvia	2009	0.006	0.107
Lesotho	2008	0.001	0.975
Lithuania	2009	0.003	0.1
Mauritius	2009	0.001	0.515
Moldova	2009	0.001	0.029
Mongolia	2009	0.002	0.063
Morocco	2009	0.004	0.364
Paraguay	2009	0.003	0.545
Peru	2009	0.002	0.648
Russia	2009	0.003	0.166
South Africa	2009	0.011	0.979
Thailand	2009	0.003	0.256
Tunisia	2009	0.001	0.181
Ukraine	2009	0.031	0.052
AVERAGE	2009	0.005	0.395

Source: Almy (2013), OECD (2015)

Overall while the relative importance of property taxes in local government revenues is roughly comparable in industrial and developing countries, developing countries raise less revenues from property taxes as a percentage of GDP (*see* Table 3.4). In terms of trends, relative importance of local property tax revenues have been increasing in a majority of industrial countries since the 1990s (McMillan 2008), whereas in the 2000s they have been constant in United States and Canada and decreased in Spain and United Kingdom.

Table 3.3 Relative importance of local property taxes as a source of local revenues in non-OECD countries, 2000/2001

Region/country	*Property taxes as a % of local own source revenues*
Central and Eastern Europe	
Russia	7.0
Ukraine	9.3
Latin America	
Argentina	35.0
Chile	35.1
Colombia	35.0
Mexico	58.7
Nicaragua	6.4
Asia	
China	4.9
India	7.0–41.0 (various states)
Pakistan (1996)	35.5
Indonesia	10.7
Philippines	13.4
Thailand (2008)	4.9
Africa	
Guinea	32.0
Kenya	15.0
South Africa	21.0
Tanzania	4.0
Tunisia	32.4

Source: Bird and Slack (2004)

3.1.2 Property Transactions Taxes as a Source of Local Finance in an International Context

Property transaction taxes are practiced worldwide and imposed as documentary stamp duties (originated in Holland in 1624), property and/or real estate transfer taxes, real estate excise tax, deed recordation or registration or transfer taxes, mortgage transfer tax and conveyance taxes (*see* Sexton 2010; Bahl 2004).

These taxes in the United States are usually imposed by states on the gross sales price of a property (Youngman 2016). In addition, mortgage taxes may be imposed on the total amount of mortgage financing for the purchase of the property. Tax rates in the United States vary from a low of 0.01% in Colorado to a high of 4% in parts of Pennsylvania. Even within a state, there may be large variations in city/county component across

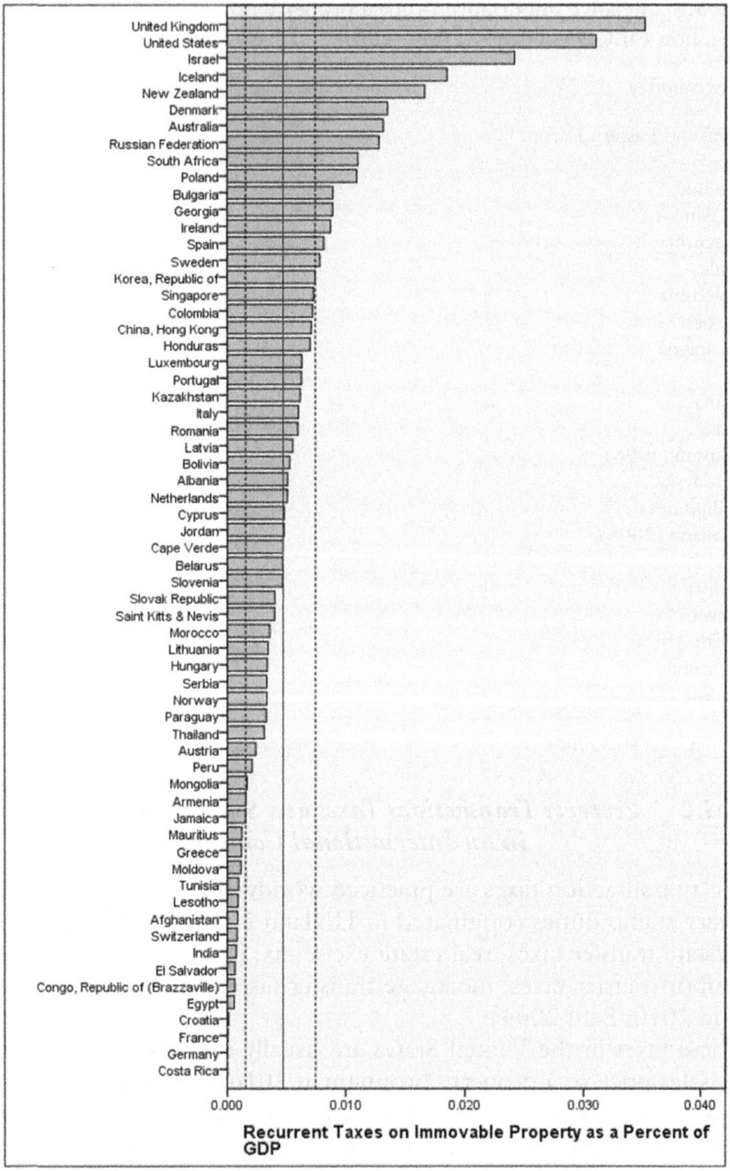

Fig. 3.1 Property tax effort in relation to GDP. (Source: Almy 2013)

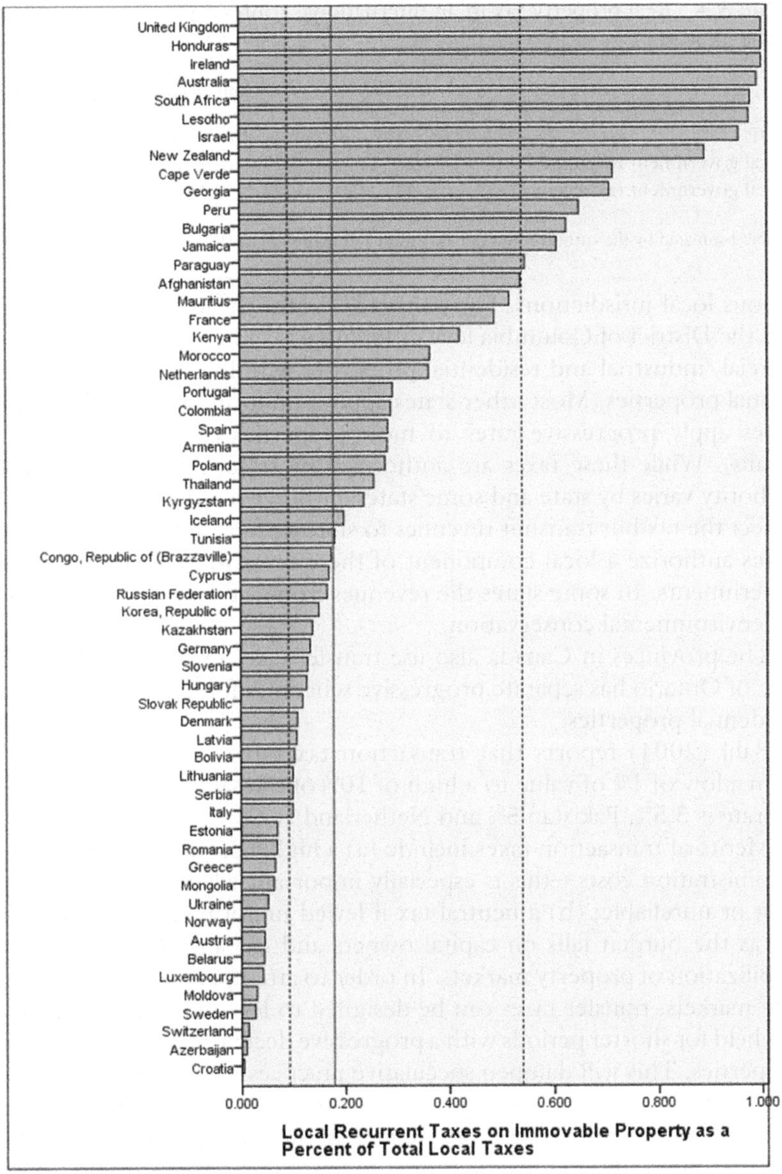

Fig. 3.2 Relative importance of local property tax in local taxation. (Source: Almy 2013)

Table 3.4 Real property tax in an international context (percentage in relation to the indicator)

	OECD	*Developing countries*	*PRC*
GDP	1.6	0.5	1.1
Local government revenues	26	16	4.7
Local government tax revenue	44	40	NA

Source: Estimated by the author from OECD (2015) and IMF-GFS (2013)

various local jurisdictions. For example, California, four additional states and the District of Columbia levy differential tax rates on residential, commercial/industrial and residential properties with lower tax rates for residential properties. Most other states apply a uniform single rate and a few states apply progressive rates to most properties (*see* Sexton 2010 for details). While these taxes are authorized by state legislation, collection authority varies by state and some states authorize county governments to collect the tax but transmit revenues to state general fund revenues. Some states authorize a local component of these taxes to be retained by local governments. In some states the revenues from these taxes are earmarked for environmental conservation.

The provinces in Canada also use transfer taxes extensively. The province of Ontario has separate progressive schedules for residential and non-residential properties.

Bahl (2004) reports that transaction tax rates vary across countries from a low of 1% of value to a high of 10% of the same. Germany transfer tax rate is 3.5%, Pakistan 5% and Netherland at 6%.

Merits of transaction taxes include (a) a highly productive tax with low administration costs—this is especially important where cadasters do not exist or unreliable; (b) a neutral tax if levied uniformly; (c) a progressive tax as the burden falls on capital owners and (d) an important tool for stabilization of property markets. In order to attempt cooling of hot property markets, transfer taxes can be designed to levy high rates on properties held for shorter periods with a progressive decline in rates for long-held properties. This will dampen speculative practices.

Demerits of the transaction taxes include (a) greater volatility in revenues than with annual property taxes; (b) higher rates required to generate property tax equivalent revenues dues to fewer transactions; and (c) higher rates discourage factor mobility and impose high excess burdens on businesses (*see* Sexton 2010 for the US evidence).

3.1.3 What Is a Real Property Tax and Its Potential Tax Base?

Real property tax is a tax that is imposed on real property. A comprehensive base for the tax would include all types of real property. Real property encompasses real estate, realty, land, improvements (structures and fixtures) attached to land. Real property taxes vary by type of real property. Real property is usually classified as:

Residential: Single family or multifamily housing units
Commercial: business property including office space, shopping centers, stores, theatres and entertainment facilities, hotels and parking facilities;
Industrial: warehouses, factories, land in industrial districts, power plants, communications towers, machinery and equipment
Linear properties: power lines, telephone lines, gas lines, cable lines;
Agricultural/rural: farms, timberland, ranches and orchards; or
Special purpose: Religious and charitable institutions, think tanks and research institutions, schools, hospitals, sports complexes, parks and playgrounds, cemeteries and crown properties (government-owned land and buildings).

A comprehensive tax base for the real property tax would include all of the above except land and improvements owned by special purpose institutions. However, most countries levy real property taxes on residential, commercial, and industrial properties. A small number of countries impose a tax on agricultural land. Only a handful of countries, for example Canada, impose such taxes on linear properties. However, in Canada, this varies from province to province and by property type (see Kitchen et al. 2019a, chapter 9).

In transition countries with public ownership of land, leasehold rights could be treated as private property and taxed (Asian Development Bank 2013). Alternately there could be a supplemental tax on land use in addition to the tax on improvements which are privately owned (Hong 2013).

There are two types of real property taxes: general real estate taxes (also called ad valorem taxes) and special assessment and improvement taxes—sometimes called frontages taxes or charges imposed per linear front foot of the property. Both are levied against specific types/parcels of property and automatically become liens on those properties. The general real property tax comprises taxes by various governments and agencies or special taxing jurisdictions. Special taxing jurisdictions may levy supplementary rates on municipal/government-determined tax base. These jurisdictions include: school boards, hospital boards, drainage districts, water and sanitation districts and parks, forest preserves and recreation districts.

3.1.4 *Property Tax Variants Around the World*

Real property taxes commonly include annual/recurrent taxes on land and/or structures (Bird and Slack 2005; UN-Habitat 2013). For providing water sewer and other utilities to newly developed areas sometimes additional frontage taxes (per liner front foot of the property) are also imposed for a defined period to recover capital costs of utilities. In some countries real property taxes include taxes on power lines, pipelines, and cable lines. Less frequent are recurrent taxes on net worth (assets minus liabilities). Estate/inheritance taxes, taxes on fixed assets such as machinery and equipment and taxes on financial transactions and capital transfers are often included in the broader classification of property taxes as done by the IMF's Government Finance Statistics and the OECD's Revenue Statistics. Table 3.5 presents a worldwide view of imposition of recurrent taxes on immovable real property only.

Table 3.5 shows that a large majority of countries impose taxes both on land and structures. Some countries, for example Brazil, have in addition a separate tax on rural lands. Only six countries levy a land tax only and

Table 3.5 Immovable property tax variants—a world view (number of countries)

Region	*Land tax only*	*Building tax only*	*Land and building tax*	*Total imposing real property tax*	*Number of countries with no real property taxes*
Africa	0	3	44	47	5
Asia	1	0	39	40	6
Australia and Oceania	4	0	9	13	9
Europe	0	0	44	44	3
North America and the Caribbean	1	1	30	32	4
South America	0	0	13	13	0
World	6	4	179	189	27

Source: Author's calculations based upon basic data from Almy (2013)

Table 3.6 Real property tax collection and administration—a world view

Region	*C*	*CRL*	*CR*	*CL*	*R*	*RL*	*L*	*ALL*
Africa	12	0	0	6	0	1	28	47
Asia	9	0	0	9	1	4	15	38
Australia & Oceania	1	1	0	1	0	4	6	13
Europe	1	1	0	8	1	4	17	32
North America & Caribbean	10	0	0	3	0	2	15	30
South America	0	2	0	0	1	0	8	11
World	33	4	0	27	3	15	89	171

Source: Author's calculations based upon basic data from Almy (2013)

Notes: *C* center, *CRL* central/regional (provincial)/local, *CR* central/regional, *CL* central/local, *R* regional, *RL* regional/local, *L* local

four countries levy a building tax only. Twenty-seven countries do not levy any recurrent tax on real property.

World practices also vary in terms of the level of government having administrative responsibility for the tax. Table 3.6 shows that in a large majority of countries, responsibility for collection of taxes and retention of revenues lies with the local governments. Nevertheless, in 33 countries real property tax is a central levy and in 27 countries it is a joint central-provincial levy and in 15 countries, it is a provincial-local levy. In most countries with local government collection either central or provincial government retain roles in base determination while local governments are given autonomy in rate setting and collection.

3.2 Property Tax Valuations

3.2.1 How Property Values Are Assessed Under Non-market or Hybrid Approaches?

Market-based property valuations pose significant difficulties if the property markets are not well developed, have fewer market-based transactions, cadastral value record system is not well developed or simply the cost of administering market value-based system is seen too prohibitive or the complexity of such system and challenges associated with reliable data and information systems, makes introduction of such a system politically and administratively infeasible. In view of these impediments, many countries around the world—a few OECD countries but mostly developing and transition economies—have developed non-market or hybrid assessment approaches to raise revenues from property taxes (*see* McCluskey and Franzsen 2013, for a worldwide survey of these approaches). The following paragraphs provide a brief overview of these approaches.

3.2.1.1 Non-market Valuation Approaches

These approaches typically take the form of area in square meters of land, finished area/floor space, location, type and age of the property and its use as discussed below.

Physical Characteristics of the Property as the Basis of Taxation

This is usually done by using land area or building square meters or both and applying a tax rate differentiated by location. Other adjustment coefficient such as quality of construction and access to various public services and utilities and soil quality and productivity for rural/agricultural land, could also be used. Such assessments are less demanding in terms of data, are objective and easier to do and represent a less costly alternative especially for jurisdictions not having a system of cadasters for property valuation. The system also does not require frequent updating and minimizes complaints and disputes and costs of dispute resolution.

Local jurisdictions in some cases are divided into different zones with a differential unit value per square meter assigned to land area and finished area (floor space) for each zone to determine property values. The zonal unit values are sometimes adjusted by type of property, occupancy, age, structure and use factors. Various types of residential and non-residential properties, owner-occupied and rental properties, quality and type of construction, age of the building, and type of use of non-residential properties such as hospital, educational institutions, industrial commercial and hotels are assigned different factors. These factors are then used to adjust unit values for individual properties. In the Czech Republic, differential adjustment factors on a progressive scale by municipal population size grouping, varying from a coefficient of 1.0 for towns with municipal population less than 1000 to a coefficient of 4.5 for metropolitan Prague are also applied (*see* McCluskey and Franzsen 2013). Countries adopting the area-based valuations differ regarding the adjustment factors and methods used to adjust zonal or individual property values. Israel does not value properties but instead differential property tax rates per square meter are imposed based upon actual use, location, type and age of property. Area-based evaluations are practiced in various countries in Asia, Africa and Central Europe. Area-based approaches offer a pragmatic approach to property taxation in data scarce or imperfect property markets. Adjustment factors represent an attempt to make these approaches somewhat fairer in application. A simple physical characteristics–based system is, however, commonly perceived as unfair unless appropriate adjustments are made to reflect quality and access. These adjustments, however, represent a tradeoff in terms of simplicity and objectivity and fairness objectives. Nevertheless, it is possible to design physical characteristics–based systems that offer a superior and less costly alternative to value-based systems.

3.2.1.2 Hybrid Valuation Approaches

Hybrid valuation approaches practiced in various countries include using the purchase price of the property as the basis of evaluation and leaving it unchanged till the property is resold or adjusting it annually by a price index. This practice of valuation was adopted in California following the passage of Proposition 13 which fixed assessed value at 1975–76 levels unless a property is resold and limited the annual increases in assessed values to a maximum of 2%. Under this approach, property tax burden of identical properties would vary depending upon how frequently they were transacted in the market place leading to unfair heavier tax burden on some property owners.

Another approach to property valuations is so-called property value banding system is used in the United Kingdom for its Council Tax. Under this system, each property is assigned to fall within a particular band or range of property values. Tax liability is then determined by applying an adjustment factor to the property tax payment to be made in reference to a property in the median value range, with below median value properties paying a lower tax and higher than median value ranges paying a higher tax. For example, United Kingdom uses an eight-band classification of properties with the lowest band paying about 0.66% of median value tax and the highest band paying twice the median value tax. The advantages of this approach are the simplicity of administration in property tax determination as it obviates the need for individual property valuation more precisely. There is also less need for annual updating of values due to the large bandwidth of each band. This explains why the United Kingdom reevaluates properties only once in 20 years as opposed to annual revaluations under the market-based property valuation systems. The simplicity is also appealing to citizens as attested by the popularity of the Council tax in United Kingdom. The demerits of this approach is the substantial difference in tax burdens across bands associated with assignment of properties closer to the bottom or the top ends of the bandwidth to a higher or lower band involves a very contentious subjective judgment. Since the approach aims to achieve only a rough justice such assignments are highly contested leading to highly costly and time-consuming appeals.

3.2.1.3 Flat Lump Sum Taxes and Charges

Under this approach every property either on an area wide basis or in a specific classification zone pays an equal lump sum tax. This tax is easiest to administer as it requires minimal information. However, it is not a fair tax as properties of varying valuations would pay the same charge. Ireland levies a uniform flat charge on all residential properties that are not owner occupied. In Australia, several local governments levy a flat charge differentiated by residential densities or by size and location of apartment. In New Zealand some rural settlements levy a uniform flat annual charge per property. In Tanzania flat rate charges vary by property location, use and size.

Non-market or hybrid approaches to property taxation represents pragmatic approaches to local finance in scarce data environments.

3.2.2 How Property Values Are Assessed Under Market-Based Approaches?

Property assessments are carried out to arrive at a measure of monetary worth of the property. To have a monetary worth, a property must be desirable, have a market demand, be in relatively scarce supply and legal ownership and use rights must be transferable with relative ease.

3.2.2.1 Reference Point for Market-Based Valuation

There are several options to serve as reference point for such valuation:

Market value: an estimation of the most probable price, the property is expected to fetch in an open and competitive market. This is usually the probable price with the best alternative use of the property;
Restricted market value: an estimation of most probable value with the current use of the property;
Market price: The price at which the property is actually sold; and

Notional or normative value: rough approximation of value based upon a normative view.

Beyond a reference point, valuation requires a determination of the bases to be used—would it be current annual rental value or the capital value of the property. These options are discussed below:

Annual rental value–based system: Annual rental value serves as the basis for taxation. Under such a system, a tax can be levied either on the owner or the occupier of the property (as done in United Kingdom). Such a system is useful in jurisdictions where rental properties dominate the housing market and there are fewer sales transactions. If levied on occupiers, this system widens the tax net to a larger number of taxpayers with potential benefits in terms of citizen participation in government affairs. Determination of annual rental value is relatively easier but poses significant difficulties in such determination for non-occupied properties. A tax on occupier, however, raises significantly the costs of tax collection, administration and compliance due to large number of mobile taxpayers. Annual rental value also poses a psychological hurdle for policy makers as the tax rates would have to be higher to yield equivalent revenues compared to capital value basis as discussed below.

Capital value–based system: Capital value of the property is based on the present value of costs and benefits of ownership of the property over its lifetime. Valuation of the property on capital basis is therefore a daunting task as it requires a very data-intensive analysis. Annual rental value conceptually is simply the fraction obtained by dividing the capital value by the life of the asset if costs and benefits are fully capitalized. That is why some countries using annual rental value define such value as a percentage of capital value in their laws (*see* Almy 2014). Most countries use capital value as the basis for property taxation. This preference is based on the fact that capital value taxation is imposed on owners of the property and therefore number of taxpayers are substantially reduced. Further, there is a greater certainty in tax compliance as tax liabilities are placed as lien on the property. Political economy considerations also favor capital value as the basis as tax base is large requiring a lower rate of property tax to yield given amount of revenues. Taxing capital owners also has a degree of political appeal due to its positive impact in reducing income inequalities.

3.2.2.2 *Principal Approaches to Market-Based Property Valuation*

There are three commonly used approaches to valuation of properties for property tax purposes.

The Sales Comparison Approach: This approach assumes that market value of a property is directly related to the recent sales prices of similar/comparable properties. The approach requires detailed information on hedonic (site, structure and public amenities) characteristics of comparable properties sold in a recent period. Similarities and dissimilarities of various properties with the subject property are then analyzed to approximate market value of the property. The principal factors for which adjustment must be made include property rights, deed restrictions and easements, financing concessions, conditions of sale, date of sale and location. This approach is most useful when there are a large number of sale transactions available with detailed data on each property. This is typically the case for single family residences, condominiums and small commercial properties which are frequently traded (*see* Table 3.7).

The Cost Approach: The cost approach is used when the property being valued is new or nearly new; or in situations where few comparable sales figures are available or when the improvements are unique or specialized. The cost approach is based on the assumption that a purchaser

Table 3.7 Market-based approaches to property valuation

Approach	*Determination of current market value*	*Property type*
Sales comparisons	Comparison of sales prices of comparable properties	Single residences Condominium Small commercial
Cost approach	Current market value of land plus cost of improvements minus depreciation	Manufacturing plant Unique Special use (limited market data)
Income approach	Income potential (capitalization of income minus expenses)	Income producing (rental) properties such as Hotel apartments Office buildings

Source: Galaty et al. (2000), Almy (2013), Saskatchewan (2012)

would not pay any more to purchase a property than it would cost to buy the land and then rebuild the same improvements. Value for properties that are assessed using the cost approach are determined by using the following formula:

$$\begin{aligned} &\textit{Total prooperty value} = \textit{current value of land} \\ &+\textit{cost of improvements} - \textit{accrued depreciation} \end{aligned}$$

where accrued depreciation includes normal wear and tear (physical depreciation), a change in needs (functional obsolescence) and style (style obsolescence) of a building, or even in loss in value because of its location (external obsolescence). The cost of improvements can be assessed either by using reproduction cost or the replacement cost method. Reproduction cost is the construction cost at current market prices of an exact duplicate of the subject improvements. Replacement cost is the cost to construct an improvement similar to the subject property using current construction methods and materials. Replacement cost is frequently used in appraising old structures because it eliminates obsolete features and takes advantage of current construction materials and costs. Both the cost approaches can be approximated by one of the following methods (Galaty et al. 2000):

Cost per square meter method: Cost per square meter of a recently built structure is used to estimate the cost of the subject property. This is the most widely used method.

Unit in place method: It estimates the cost per unit of major building components including material, labor and overhead costs and applies these to quantity need for each component to derive total cost per component. The sum of individual components represents the cost of new structure.

Quantity survey method: The quantity and quality of all materials and labor are estimated on a unit cost basis. Indirect costs are added to derive total costs.

Index method: Under this approach original cost is updated using a construction price index.

The cost approach is useful in assessing manufacturing/industrial properties.

The Income Approach: This approach assumes that income-producing properties are bought and sold based on their income-earning potential. The value of the property is determined by dividing the estimated net operating annual income by the required rate of return (also called the capitalization rate). This approach is used to assess the value of rental properties such as apartment buildings and rental office buildings.

The Special Case of Government Properties and Foreign Embassies: Higher government (crown), foreign embassies, international organization properties are typically exempt from local property taxation. These properties nevertheless benefit from local services. For this reason, these organizations exercise corporate social responsibility by paying annual grant-in-lieu of taxes. The municipality evaluates these properties as office properties and assesses their values accordingly and then applies the relevant mill rate to determine the amount of grant it will request from relevant entities.

3.2.2.3 Assessment of Special Properties

A number of properties typically are not subject to market value assessment techniques (Alberta 2004, 2010). These include the following:

Farmland: Farmland is assessed on the basis of its productive potential; that is, the ability to produce income from the growing of crops and/or the raising of livestock. The productive potential of farmland is determined using a process that sets the value for most productive soil and then makes adjustments for less than optimum conditions. Assessing farmland on the basis of productive value, however, raises some issues. For example in Alberta, Canada, productive value assessments are very low relative to market value for farming (e.g., 1/8). There is the issue of land for agriculture versus farm/rural residences (assessed and taxed separately from land in Alberta) and low taxes (land only) for intensive farming operations such as feedlots, confined swine and poultry (with the capital structures not taxed). It is useful to assess farm land at productive value when near urban developments and having much high speculative values anticipating urban development.

Linear Property: These properties have distribution lines or other facilities and may cross municipal boundaries. Linear property includes: oil and gas wells; pipelines to transport petroleum products; electric power generation, transmission and distribution facilities; telecom systems, including cellular telephone systems; and cable television systems. These properties are typically assessed at the provincial/state levels.

Machinery and Equipment: The assessment of such assets takes into account purchase price, depreciation and obsolescence factors.

Railways property: The assessed value of railways property is a fixed dollar amount based upon the annual tonnage transported on the railways right of way. Railways companies are required to provide such information on an annual basis.

Assessment of Public Leasehold Land: Assessing public leasehold land represents a formidable challenge for tax purpose. Hong (2013) notes two important challenges. First, relationship between land lease contract (term and provisions) and property value requires examination but research on this topic is not available due to inadequate sales and other information that is needed to conduct such research. The remainder duration of the lease matters for such valuation. A long-term lease adds value if the current location is consistent with the intended economic activity. On the other hand, if the use of the current land is of short-term interest only, with a relocation in mind in future the long-term lease would adversely affect a purchaser's bid price and capital value determination would represent a difficult task. A second challenge arises from determining rental value of leasehold land based upon its highest and best use. This is because there may be significant divergence of contract rent from fair market rent (rent based from highest and best use in arm's length transactions) especially for leasehold estates with long-term leases with no provisions for frequent updating of rents. This would also be a problem for leasehold properties which were leased at low charges to accommodate social, economic policy and industrial development objectives Benchetrit and Czamanski (2004).

3.2.2.4 Assessment of Individual Properties Versus Mass Appraisal Methods

So far our analysis has focused on determination individual property values for tax purposes. Such an approach, however, is costly, time consuming and has significant elements of subjectivity inviting taxpayers' criticisms. In response to these concerns local governments in OECD countries are increasingly adopting the so-called mass appraisal techniques. Mass appraisal is the process of valuing a group/class of properties as of a given date using econometric models. The econometric models used for this purpose typically use hedonic regression techniques which specify that house value is a function of its physical attributes (land and structure attributes), site characteristics (its location, its access to public service amenities), property taxes and nuisance factors (e.g., air craft and traffic noise, air and water pollution, local incidence of crime). Various factors either affect property values positively or negatively. The models allow estimation of these effects per unit of individual attribute. Predictive accuracy of such models can also be tested. Mass appraisal techniques allow more objective assessment and frequent updating of a large number of properties at substantially lower cost than individual property assessment and limit individual assessor biases in assessing properties. Such mass appraisal techniques are also helpful in an analysis of assessment errors associated with individual property assessment methods. For example, predicted market values can be compared to assessed values to determine a relationship of assessment to market values. Mass appraisal methods can also assess data from various sources such as fiscal cadasters (physical characteristics and assessed values), multiple listing service (property characteristics), land titles and records (ownership, area), tax records (assessed value and tax liabilities), geographical information systems (location and public amenities data) to test the consistency, reliability and accuracy of data.

3.2.2.5 *Assessment Dates and Cycles*

Each jurisdiction announces a valuation date to complete the valuation process. Under mass appraisal methods all property valuations are updated by the valuation date. Jurisdictions following individual property valuations typically use a three- to five-year cycle to update all properties with fraction of properties being reassessed each year through rolling evaluations as has been the practice in Canada and the USA. In the interim years the reassessed property values are updated using a macro index. Some US jurisdictions provide a phase in period for the new assessment to take effect. The IAAO recommends that property must be re-evaluated at least every six years. Austria, Estonia and United Kingdom are the exceptions where no re-evaluations have been done during the past two decades (Almy 2014).

3.2.2.6 *Property Valuation Record*

Property information has been traditionally collected by field inspections and recorded in a fiscal cadaster which contains detailed attributes of a property as well as its appraised value. In the private sector, realtor's associations developed the so-called Multiple Listing Service which provides detailed data on properties offered for sale and their sale prices. In addition, an assessor's task has been made simpler by the emergence of private real estate websites like Zillow, Trulia, Realtor, Redfin and many other websites in the United States that may have geographical mapping, data and areal imagery and 3-D tours of properties. Sweden has implemented taxpayer declarations that limit the needs for field inspections to collect data needed for property valuations. More recently, there is a trend toward geographical information systems that provide a more comprehensive view of all relevant attributes needed for property valuation in one data base as currently practiced in Iceland, Northern Ireland and New Zealand (Almy 2014).

3.2.2.7 Assessment Complaints and Appeal Mechanisms

Almost all countries provide a process for filing complaints and formal review mechanisms. While the institutions would vary by jurisdiction, there are a few common steps involved in all such processes. If an owner of an assessed property feels that the assessment is either inaccurate or unfair, a call to the local assessment office is the first step in raising one's concerns. The assessor may request to inspect the property to determine if an error was made. If the assessor agrees that the original notice is in error, a corrected notice may be issued. If the assessor and the property owner cannot come to an agreement, the property owner may begin the formal complaint process with the officially designated agency responsible for such review—usually a semi-autonomous quasi-judicial agency/board constituted by local or provincial legislation. If the property owner is not satisfied with the review agency decision, then he/she may resort to the court system for redress. Figure 3.3 highlights this process in a Canadian jurisdiction.

3.2.2.8 Ensuring Uniformity of Assessment Across Local Jurisdictions: Equalized Assessments

Equalization of assessment in a provincial or state jurisdiction may be necessary because: (a) there is often no fixed percentage in relation to market value at which a property must be assessed; (b) local governments enjoy significant discretion in tax administration and as a result assessed values as a percentage of market values may vary significantly across local jurisdictions; (c) special taxing jurisdictions such as school boards may not have the same taxing boundaries as municipal governments that are responsible for assessing properties; and (d) the province would need data on

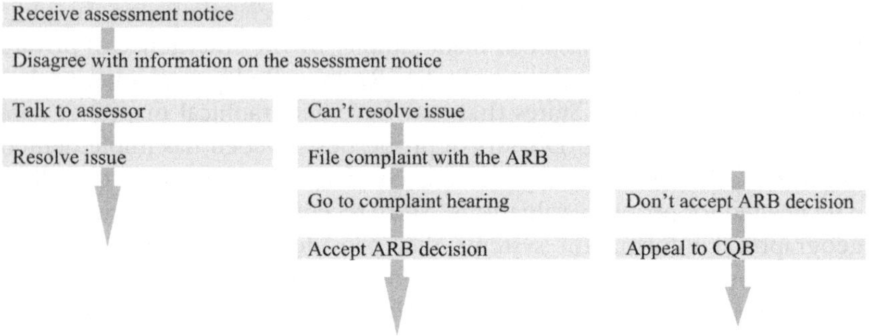

Fig. 3.3 The complaint system in the province of Alberta, Canada. (Notes: *ARB* Assessment Review Board, *CQB* the Court of Queen's Bench of Alberta. Source: Alberta 2015)

assessments that are comparable to serve as the basis of general purpose and specific purpose transfers.

To deal with above concerns, provincial/state officials may either ask the local officials to certify each year the relationship of assessed value to market value in aggregate in their jurisdiction or estimate market value themselves to arrive at the equalization rate. The equalization rate is the ratio of total assessed value to total market value. This is used as an adjustment factor to ensure all jurisdictions have a fixed and equal relationship to market values. The resulting assessments (total assessed value/equalization rate = equalized assessment) are called equalized assessments. Of course, the equalized assessment would equal total actual assessments if all municipalities assessed their properties at 100% of market value.

In order for a school district, that overlaps more than one municipality, to fairly distribute the property tax levy (total amount of school taxes to be collected) the levy needs to be divided in proportion to the total market value of each municipal segment. This allows for an equitable distribution of taxes based upon the market value of each municipality or segment. For example, School District AB need to raise $1 million through property taxes. The district contains Town A and Town B. Each town has a total assessed value of $10 million. If the $1 million tax levy simply were allocated on the basis of the assessed values, the taxpayers in both towns would evenly split the levy, with each town paying $500,000. However, through equalized assessments, the state/province determines that the two towns have different levels of assessment. Town A has an equalization

Table 3.8 The use of equalized assessments in fairer interjurisdictional distribution of tax burden

	Town A	*Town B*
Assessed value (AV) of each town	$10 million	$10 million
Equalization rate of each town	33.33	50.00
Market value of each town	$30 million	$20 million
Market value of school district AB=$50 million		
Percent of market value (and, therefore, percent of levy) for each town	60%	40%
Tax levy to be raised from each town	$600,000	$400,000
Tax rate for each town (Tax levy ÷ Assessed value) × 1000	$60 per $1000 AV	$40 per $ 1000 AV

Source: New York, State of (2011)

rate of 33.33 and Town B has an equalization rate of 50.00. Table 3.8 illustrates how a fairer allocation of levy is achieved among these two towns.

Apart from the apportionment of taxes among municipal jurisdictions and distribution of provincial/state grants, equalization rates are used in a variety of situations (*see* New York 2011):

fiscal rules: establishment of tax and debt limits;

allocation of costs among jointly operated services among participating municipalities;

determination of state/provincial assessments or state approval of local assessments (state-owned lands);

determination of ceilings (railroad and agricultural values) and exemptions;

apportionment of sales tax revenues and joint indebtedness; and

as evidence in court proceedings on the issue of assessment inequity.

3.3 How Property Tax Rates Are Determined?

In OECD countries, determination of municipal mill rate is the responsibility of municipal councils. Each year, municipal councils determine the amount of money they need to operate the municipality. From this amount, the council then subtracts projected revenues from other sources such as other taxes, user charges, licenses and permits and higher order grants. The remainder is the amount of money the municipality would need to raise through property taxes to meet balanced operating budget requirements. This revenue requirement is then used to calculate the tax rate. The tax rate is determined as follows:

$$\frac{\textit{Municipal residual revenue requirement}}{\textit{Aggregate assessment base of the municipality}} = \textit{Tax rate}$$

The tax rate is typically expressed in tax revenue per thousand dollar of assessed value and termed as the municipal mill rate. For example, a mill rate of one means that tax liability is one dollar per thousand dollars of assessed value. The tax rate is applied to assessed value of individual properties to determine individual liability. Some municipal jurisdictions may practice a split-mill rate taxation where there is a separate tax rate for land and for improvements and also there could be separate tax rates for commercial and industrial properties as compared to residential properties. In that event, the municipal council decides on the proportion of revenues to be raised from various types of assessments. In such determination, it may be guided by the cost of provision of municipal services to residences versus businesses. There also may be requirements for raising revenues for financing school education for school boards or for the province or state. In that event, a school board or the province/state determines how much revenue it needs to raise from property taxes and determines the school/education mill rate by dividing revenue requirements by property assessments and then requests the municipal jurisdictions to levy and collect supplementary school taxes by the specified education mill rate. Municipalities include the education property tax on their property tax bills to property owners. Municipalities collect education tax dollars from their tax payers and remit these to the school board or the province as the case may be. Some jurisdictions, for example the province of Alberta, Canada, gives individual property owners a discretion in deciding the allocation of their education tax bills either to public (government schools) or to non-government schools. In this case, the municipality will be obligated to split the collected money among public school boards and non-public school board and remit accordingly.

Property tax rates may also differ by the type of property; for example, farmland may be taxed at lower rate than urban land and commercial/industrial properties may be taxed at differential rates due to local tax policy objectives.

3.4 Differential Taxation of Various Types of Property

Property tax regimes in some countries impose differential tax rates on land and structures and also based on land use of the properties. The following paragraphs reflect upon the conceptual rationale and legal practices in various countries practicing such differential taxation.

3.4.1 *Differential Taxation of Land and Improvements*

The conceptual case for differential taxation of land and improvements rests on the ground that land is a fixed asset with fixed finite supply, and therefore, a tax on land would be negatively capitalized in land prices reducing the price of land just as public services would be positively capitalized into land prices leading to an increase in land prices. If the property tax serves as a benefit charge for public services, the net effect on land prices may be zero thereby limiting the distortionary effects of such taxation. A positive tax on land consistent with service benefits, therefore, is advocated. The supply of structures and improvements, on the other hand, is considered sensitive to any changes in tax burdens and taxes discourage such investments. In the interest of advancing local economic development agenda, while a positive tax on land is desirable, a similar tax on improvements is not desirable. This provides a justification for a positive tax on land and zero tax on improvements. Economic theory further suggest that land taxation should have a rising tax gradient as one moves from city core to the periphery to encourage compact urban development and discourage urban sprawl.

The design of property tax, however, usually does not follow this guidance. Not a single country in the world has a rising tax gradient. In fact, opposite may be true. For example, Ukraine imposes a positive tax on land and zero tax on improvements but positive tax on land has a declining tax gradient as one moves from city core to the periphery (*see* UN 2011, p. 74). This is because both the tax rate and property valuations are higher at the core than the periphery. Jamaica uses a fixed tax rate to tax unimproved land only. A number of countries tax both land and improvements at differential rates. For example, the city of Pittsburgh, United States, taxed land at a higher rate (4%) than improvements (1%). UN (2011) lists the names of countries with such differential taxation but does not provide details (*see* Table 3.9).

Table 3.9 Countries having land value taxes or split rate taxes on land and improvements

Region	*Countries*
Africa	Kenya, Namibia, Swaziland, Zimbabwe
Asia	Japan, South Korea, Taiwan, South Korea
East Asia and Pacific	Australia, Fiji, New Zealand, Papua New Guinea, Solomon Islands, Vanuatu
Latin America and the Caribbean	Bahamas, Barbados, Belize, Grenada, Jamaica, Mexico
Europe	Denmark, Estonia, France, Ukraine
North America	Canada, USA

Source: UN (2011), Table 7.5, p. 67

3.4.2 *Differential Tax Treatment of Residential, Commercial/Industrial and Agricultural Properties*

A theoretical case for differential property tax treatment of residential, commercial, industrial and agricultural properties rests on the service benefit principle. The service benefit principle states that residences should be taxed for services to residents and businesses for services to business and to promote local economic development there should be no cross-subsidization among residential and non-residential properties. The costs of local public service provision benefit vary for these classes of properties; therefore, local effective tax rates for each class of property should be set in such a way as to recover annual operating cost of service provision plus annualized capital costs and congestion cost charges. This principle, however, is universally neglected by policy makers in both OECD and developing countries as politicians find it politically expedient to levy higher burden on non-residential properties to cross-subsidize services to residences. To place a limit on such cross-subsidization, the province of Alberta has legislated that non-residential mill rate (property tax rate per thousand dollar of assessed value) must not exceed five times the same for residential mill rate. New Brunswick legislation requires that the non-residential tax rate must be 1.5 times the residential rate. This is the only province with a fixed relationship. Ontario set up 'ranges of fairness' in property taxation. Over time, this is designed to lower the non-residential tax rate vis-à-vis the residential rate.

A 2015 US study (COST 2015, p. 18) finds that on average tax/benefit ratio (assuming 25% of educational spending benefits businesses) for state-local business taxes is 1.80 for the nation as a whole. Local property taxes contribute significantly to this lop-sided incidence as they constitute 74% of total business taxes at the local level. A 50-state comparative study by the Lincoln Institute of Land Policy (2015) shows that most US local jurisdictions impose a heavier burden of taxation on commercial properties relative to residential properties (*see* Fig. 3.4). Average effective tax rate ratio (aggregate actual tax collections divided by aggregate market values) on the two types of property shows a high ratio of 4.3 in the New York State to a low of 0.86 for the state of Maryland. Only in five states this ratio is lower than 1.00.

Among residential properties, apartment building have on average higher effective tax rate relative to other residential properties. The relative effective tax ratio varies from a high of 5.2 in New York City, New York, to a low of 0.86 in Baltimore City, Maryland. Figure 3.5 traces these ratios for major US cities from 1998 to 2014.

3.4.2.1 *Rural Properties*

On conceptual grounds, rural properties due to relatively limited access to local services are expected to pay a lower burden of property taxes. This is indeed the practice in OECD countries. Table 3.10 reports differential

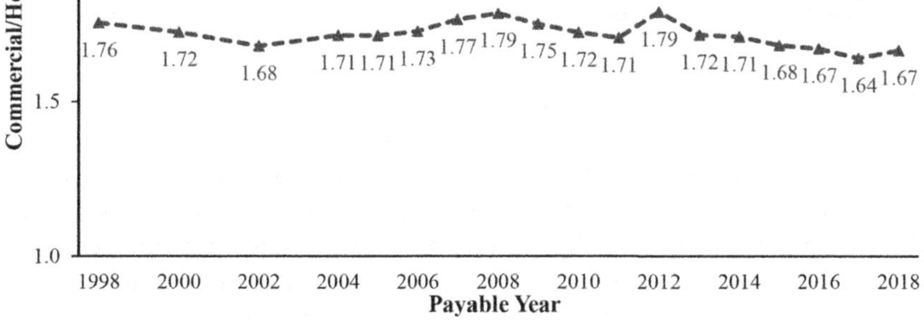

Fig. 3.4 Commercial-residential effective tax rate ratio—US averages, 1998–2014. (Source: Lincoln Institute of Land Policy (2015), p. 11)

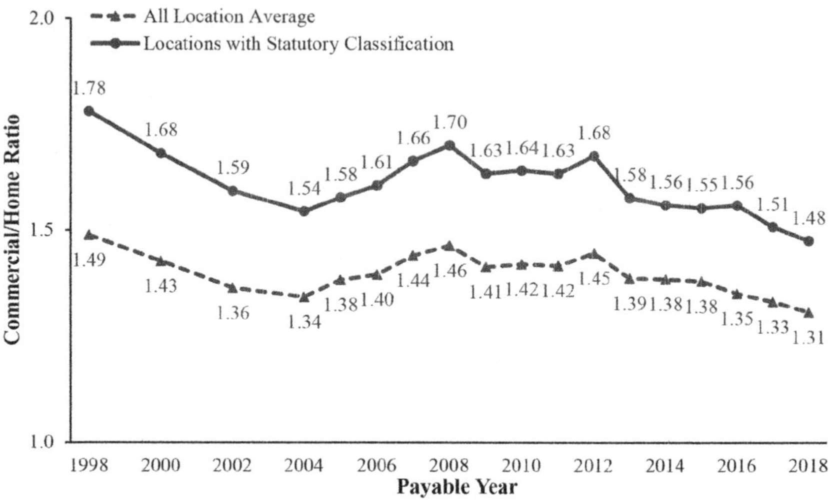

Fig. 3.5 Ratio of apartment effective property tax rate to other residential properties effective property tax rates: US large urban areas, 1998–2014. (Source: Lincoln Institute of Land Policy (2015), p. 13)

Table 3.10 Comparative urban versus rural average effective property tax rates in the United States

Property class	*Sample property value (in $000)*	*Urban average effective tax rate (%)*	*Rural average effective tax rate (%)*
Homestead	150	1.49	1.39
Apartment building	600	1.94	NA
Commercial	100	2.10	1.70
Industrial	100	1.50	1.22

Source: Lincoln Institute of Land Policy (2015), various pages

taxation of urban and rural property in the United States. The table shows that while rural properties are taxed more lightly than urban properties, the differences in average effective property tax rates are not very dramatic. The reason for this surprising result may be that rural municipalities are more resource constrained and, therefore, may rely more heavily on land and property taxes compared to their urban counterparts. Perhaps also that due to a lack of local public services in rural areas capitalization of net benefits results into lower market values for similar structures—especially residential property in rural areas.

3.4.3 *Differential Tax Treatment of Government Properties: Grants-in-Lieu-of-Taxes*

As discussed earlier, in most countries, local government does not have the authority to levy taxes on higher order government properties. However, higher order governments, at least in OECD countries are open to compensating local governments for local public services received through so-called grants-in-lieu-of-taxes (GILOT) and these payments can be equivalent to local property taxes and other charges or a fraction thereof at the option of the higher order government. In Canada, the federal government has traditionally made payments on its otherwise legally tax exempt property located in various local jurisdictions. Since 2000 such payments are made by the Public Works and Government Services Canada as authorized by the Payments in Lieu of Taxes Act, 2000. These payments by eligible provincial properties are either authorized by legislation (in a majority of provinces) or by executive orders or policies of different provinces and the federal government. Typically, federal and provincially owned properties with a few exceptions (that vary by province) make such payments. In Ontario, Quebec, Newfoundland, the Northwest Territories, and Nunavut, healthcare and educational facilities are included in GILOT programs. Ontario is an anomaly when it comes to payments in lieu for provincial hospitals, universities, colleges, and penal institutions. Instead of a payment or grant based on assessed value, these institutions pay a fixed amount, often referred to as the "heads and beds" tax. The current rate is $75 per bed for hospitals, $75 per resident place for penal institutions, and $75 per full-time student equivalent for qualifying post-secondary institutions. To illustrate the revenue shortfall, the city of Toronto in the early 2000s received payments in lieu of taxes (PILOTs) of $10.2 million for universities, colleges, hospitals, and correctional facilities. If these properties had paid property taxes similar to other properties, it was estimated that the yield would have been between $29 million (based on the residential rate) and $100 million (based on the commercial rate). All provinces and territories with the exception of Newfoundland and Prince Edward Island pay the full amount of taxes that would otherwise be levied. Both these provinces pay partial amounts only. These payments are either made on application by municipality to the provincial and federal governments as is the case in Alberta, Saskatchewan, Quebec, Nova Scotia, Prince Edward Island, the Northwest Territories and Nunavut or by the provincial governments on their own accord as in rest of the provinces. Only in four provincial/territorial jurisdictions, local governments are offered appeal opportunities against provincial assessment of own properties (*see* Muniscope 2010 for policy/legislative details on individual jurisdictions).

In the United States, under federal law, local governments receive compensation for a reduction in their revenues due to the presence of federally owned lands. This "Payments in Lieu of Taxes" (PILOT) program is administered by the Department of the Interior (DOI) and does not cover military or Indian lands. The DOI uses a complex formula to calculate these payments. However, these payments must be authorized through annual budget appropriations bill by the US Congress (*see* Cornia 2013). Incidentally, federal government does not pay PILOT for iconic landmarks or other federal buildings in the District of Columbia presumably because the district receives a large federal grant.

In United Kingdom, prior to April 1, 2000, crown properties made only voluntary contributions for local services—the so-called ex gratia contributions in lieu of rates (CILORs). The Local Government and Rating Act of 1997 came into force effective April 1, 2000, and made all crown property liable to be assessed for local rates just like any other type of property. As a result, all iconic buildings including the Palace of the Westminster and the Tower of London are now being assessed for property tax liability using normal valuation methods (*see* McCluskey et al. 2013b). The Buckingham Palace is assessed for two components—commercial (the part that is open to visitors) and residential (living quarters of the Royal family).

In Malaysia, the Federal Constitution Article 156 authorizes payments for local services by the federal government. These payments are negotiated bilaterally annually. In 2010, the federal government paid an effective tax rate of 8.75% to local government. This compares favorably to commercial properties which were taxed at 12% rate (*see* McCluskey et al. 2013a, b, op.cit., p. 18).

Recent reforms toward valuing government properties based upon current use and charging these for local services received is a welcome trend. The valuation of iconic buildings for such purpose represents a major challenge and typically "replacement cost" method for assessing buildings with appropriate allowances for depreciation and assessing land values based upon best alternative use represent approximate methods to meet this challenge.

3.4.4 *Property Tax Treatment of Non-profits: Payments-in-Lieu-of-Taxes*

PILOTs represent the voluntary payments as a substitute for property taxes made by tax exempt non-profit organizations. A large majority of these organizations offer education (university, college, schools), health (hospitals, clinics) religious, arts and culture (private museums), housing and social services. Voluntary PILOTs have been justified as these non-profits expand the access of social services and, therefore, lessen the need for public intervention. Kenyon and Langley (2019) provide an additional justification for PILOTs. They provide a vehicle for charging for public services to non-profits and recover at least partially costs of local services. However, there are ramifications for such a tax treatment.

First, property tax exemption is not targeted to local benefits but instead higher-valued properties receive more benefits. Second, some non-profits who operate on state, national or international basis, may not provide any service to local area but benefit from local services. This contributes to a higher burden of taxation on local residents while benefits of such taxation is exported to outside jurisdictions who do not pay for such services.

In the United States nearly 60% of localities receive these payments through long-term contracts with non-profits (*see* Langley et al. 2012). Overall, these organizations contribute roughly 1% to local revenues and pay only a small fraction of taxes that would be due if they were liable for taxation. As these organizations do not contribute a fair share of the costs of services they receive, concentration of these in a small locality can have detrimental effect on local finances. In recent years, a small Texas town with concentration of religious organizations took the unusual step of preventing entry of new religious groups. An oversupply of these institutions erodes local tax base while increasing the demand and costs of associated municipal services. Voluntary basis of such payments lead to inequity in charging for public services. Also, refusal to make such payments by a non-profit would entail costly and unproductive litigation by local government. To overcome this problem, it may be better to replace voluntary basis of these payments for non-voluntary municipally assessed "contributions" that take due account of demand and supply considerations for local area of specific non-profits. This will give local councils some leverage over the supply of non-profits as well as ensure stability in local revenues. Kenyon and Langley (2019) argue that "PILOTs are most suitable for non-profits that own a large amount of tax exempt property and provide modest benefits to local residents relative to their tax savings" (p. 3). They commend the city of Boston for creating systematic PILOT program that promotes horizontal equity while raising more revenues than bilaterally negotiated agreements. They further suggest that charging higher user fees to non-profits may be a good alternative to PILOTs.

3.4.5 *Property Tax Treatment of Religious and Charitable/ Non-profit Properties*

Religious and charitable organizations typically provide social welfare services thereby reducing the need for such services to be provided by the local public sector. In recognition of this role, such organizations often receive tax exemption from local property taxes. Concentration of such organization in a single municipal jurisdiction can, however, be curse as it can dramatically shrink municipal tax base to provide local services as happened recently in several local jurisdictions in the state of Texas, United States. To ward off against such a possibility, local government would be well advised to have objectively determined limits (e.g., property tax base that can be exempt on religious or charitable grounds cannot exceed 10% of aggregate property tax base for the municipality) imposed to limit the number of such organizations that can receive such tax exempt status given the size of tax base for the local jurisdiction.

3.4.6 *Property Tax Treatment of Informal and/or Illegal Properties*

In developing countries, especially in urban areas, large tracts of public lands are informally or illegally occupied and various structures are erected that are not formally sanctioned and may not conform to local building codes. Slums and shanty towns represent examples of such properties but there are many other examples where public lands are illegally occupied or the private construction do not conform to local land use zoning codes.

Some private lands may also have slum housing as the owners may consider this as a tax avoidance strategy on vacant land and hold land for speculative purposes. These properties, especially slums, represent a major challenge for property tax administration because these properties do not receive any public services and are not taxed. Typically, the income of the dwellers or occupiers would not be sufficient to pay any taxes. Therefore, local governments do not see any value in incurring costs for assessing such properties in addition to facing public protests. Extending property tax to such properties may also be opposed by influential land developers who are holding land for speculative purposes. In view of these difficulties, local governments do not find it expedient to extend the coverage of property tax to such properties. But such a neglect perpetuates urban blight. Extending services to such informal urban settlements and also bringing them under the property tax net realizing fully well that revenue gains will be small but main objective will be orderly development of urban areas and getting rid of eyesores. Regarding the vacant private land under informal occupation, higher tax rates on vacant land would bring in additional revenues in addition to increase in supply of land and dampening land prices. Illegal use of the properties should be forced to comply with legal use by imposing heavy penalties for violating local land use controls (*see* also Smolka and De Cesare 2013).

3.5 Property Tax Relief to Advance Tax Equity, Social Policy and Economic Development Objectives

Property tax relief of one form or other is provided by most taxing jurisdictions to advance tax equity, social policy and economic development objectives as discussed below.

3.5.1 Tax Equity Objectives

Property tax is commonly perceived to be a regressive tax with a disproportionate burden of taxation borne by lower-income classes. While this conclusion is open to question on conceptual and empirical grounds, policy makers are keen to safeguard the interests of low-income and other needy individuals and groups (senior citizens, persons with disabilities, war veterans, single mothers etc.). This is done by providing the following types of reliefs.

Tax exemptions: This entails exempting certain group of individuals, for example, senior citizens, persons with disabilities, war veterans and single mothers, from property tax liability. For example, several Canadian provinces provide partial rebates or property tax deferrals for senior citizens (elderly over 65 years of age) from property tax liability on their principal residences (see Kitchen et al. 2019b). A number of countries specify a value threshold under which properties would not be taxed. The principal drawback of exemption based upon age and other characteristics is that ability to pay of the individual concerned is not taken into consideration. Therefore, some high-income individuals with high-valued properties would enjoy a windfall gain from such an exemption.

Property tax credits: Property tax credits whereby a defined credit is made available against property tax liability are frequently used to target needy groups. These credits may wipe out fully or partially the property tax liability of such individuals while eliminating any tax relief for properties valued higher than a defined threshold. Property tax credits are widely used in OECD countries and serve to enhance equity of the property tax.

Property assessment allowances: Property assessment allowances, whereby a non-taxable lump-sum allowance is given to reduce taxable assessment, are not practiced. However, these have been advocated to exempt properties below a certain threshold. Under this scheme all properties are assessed and then a fixed amount of assessment is deducted from each property leading to full or partial tax exemption (*see* Kitchen 2013).

Property tax deferral: Property tax deferrals whereby an individual may be authorized to defer his current tax liability to future years are made available to provide temporary relief to individuals with temporary cash flow or income deficiency problems on a case-by-case basis. Several Canadian and US jurisdictions operate such programs. Another form of tax deferral program is motivated by alleviating the enhanced tax burden associated with property re-evaluations for senior citizens and disabled persons. This program is available on demand to all senior citizens and people with disabilities in the province of Ontario, Canada. Several developing countries, for example Ghana, and Singapore also offer tax deferral programs on individual application basis.

Tax reduction, cancellation and refunds: Some jurisdictions allow such relief on a means tested basis. Means tested relief is also available in some developing countries, for example, in Burundi, Congo, Gambia, Lesotho, and Czech Republic (*see* Almy 2013).

Grants: Cash grants are also used by some jurisdictions to reduce or eliminate tax burdens for eligible, typically senior citizens or the needy, homeowners or renters. Grants are more difficult and costlier to administer and offer potential for fraud and abuse and therefore may offer a less desirable alternative in developing countries.

Multiple relief measures: A large number of countries (about 50) offer more than one of the tax relief options listed above.

3.5.2 Social Policy Objectives

Property tax design often underpins social policy objectives. These include (a) protection of vulnerable groups; (b) enhancing redistributive impact of the local public sector; (c) facilitating home ownership; and (d) enhancing public service provision through network governance. How these considerations are incorporated in property tax design are discussed below.

Protection of Vulnerable Groups: Some senior citizens, subsistence farmers, disabled persons, the poor and families on social welfare may not have the ability to pay property taxes. Imposition of property tax burden on these groups may force them to seek public housing leading to a greater strain on local public resources. In view of this considerations, these groups are often targeted for property tax relief.

Enhancing the redistributive role of the local public sector: Several studies have shown that property tax burdens and public services benefits are capitalized into property values with former reducing property values and the latter leading to an increase in these values. Therefore, the net impact by income class matters for fiscal incidence of the local public sector. Various property tax relief mechanisms are intended to make the net impact positive for lower income groups. Property assessment play a critical role in determining the overall redistributive impact of the local public sector. For example, a capitalization study for the city of Edmonton, Alberta (*see* Shah 1983), showed that the overall impact of the local public sector in Edmonton was to redistribute income from the middle classes to the poor and the rich homeowners. This happened because of a consistent over-assessment bias for middle-income households and underassessment bias for housing for the rich and the poor.

Financing higher quality and quantity of social welfare services and poverty programs: Local government sometimes tax business more heavily to finance higher level of social welfare services for the needy and the poor.

Such policies present a potential peril for local fiscal health and economic development as heavier tax burdens drive business out and generous menu of social services attract an increasing number of needy, poor and the unemployed leading to a shrinking tax base but higher needs of revenues for social welfare services. In the United States, the city of St. Louis, Missouri, experienced decline as a result of such policies and the New York City went bankrupt and had to abandon such policies to restore fiscal health (*see* Inman 2008). An important lesson emerging from these experiences is that local government must not tax business to subsidize services to people and vice versa. Social services are better financed through higher-level grants.

Facilitating home ownership: Home ownership strengthens civic participation leading to better public governance. In view of this, facilitating home ownership is a universal public policy priority. This policy also suggests relief mechanism to reduce property tax burdens on lower-income individuals to reduce the cost of home ownership and thereby facilitate home ownership.

Enhancing public service provision through network governance: An important role for a local government is to act as a catalyst for collective action through participation of private non-profit hope-based (religious groups) or interest-based groups, citizens with Good Samaritan values. This rationale calls for exemption of places of religious services and worship, self-help groups and associations, organizations providing community and social welfare services, libraries, educational institutions, nursing homes, museums, community halls, recreation facilities for seniors and physically challenged individuals, charities, women and youth groups/clubs, agricultural societies, chambers of commerce from property taxes. These groups and facilities typically serves to expand social and welfare services and thereby reduce citizens' dependence on the public sector. This leads to greater access to public services at lower tax costs, and therefore, an indirect public subsidy through property tax exemption serves public interest. It is important though that these decisions on exemption must not be on a case-by-case basis but guided by commonly agreed principles. For example, property tax exemption regulation in the province of Alberta, Canada, is guided by the following principles (Alberta 2015, p. 3):

Advancement of 'public benefit' in terms of charitable and benevolent purposes, community games, sports, athletics, recreation and educational purposes;

Recognition of the 'volunteer contribution and fund raising component' that most often characterizes 'not for profit' status organizations;

Advancement of youth programs and community care for the disadvantaged; and

Appropriate access to non-profit facilities and programs.

3.5.3 Economic Development Objectives

Real property taxes are often used to advance local economic development objectives. These objectives include (a) providing incentives for local economic development; (b) dealing with urban blight; (c) business improvement districts or specific area development; (d) facilitating capital market access; and (e) facilitating harmonized urban-rural development.

Incentives for Local Economic Development. Local governments frequently use property tax relief (tax holidays for defined periods, tax credits, tax allowances, tax deferrals and other tax rate relief and other measures) to attract capital to local area from other jurisdictions. These incentives can be helpful in promoting investment but care must be taken to ensure that investment stimulation impact exceeds loss in local government revenues otherwise such incentives will result in a race to the bottom in local service quality due to loss in revenue due to capital flight. An important lesson emerges from empirical studies on the effectiveness of such incentives (*see* Shah 1988, 1989, 1992). Tax credits and tax allowances typically serve as cost effective tools for investment promotion whereas tax holidays result in greater loss of public revenues than new fixed capital investment generated.

Dealing with urban blight: To deal with urban blight, one option is to create the so-called *tax increment financing* (TIF) *districts.* This requires designating an area for redevelopment with the consent of property owners of the area. Local government freezes annual property tax revenues at pre-revitalization levels. For a specified period of usually 15–30 years, all tax revenues above the pre-revitalization base are made available to private sector partners to defray project costs. Some TIFs stipulate declining share of incremental revenues returned to the project over the life of the project. Capacity improvement in the area done either through municipal borrowing or issuing revenue bonds against expected revenue increments. TIFs have been used in Canada, United States, United Kingdom and Australia for redevelopment. In Canada, though, TIFs have been used very sparingly—only in Edmonton, Calgary, Winnipeg and two times in the Toronto area, although consideration is being given to expanding their use in Toronto for a smart track development, in particular (for a good discussion of TIFs and potential problems, see Merk et al. 2012), TIFs in practice have been effective tool dealing with blighted areas but may or may not advance overall development objectives for the local jurisdiction as a whole.

Business improvement district or special area development: Sometimes local government is interested in promoting business investment in a specific already developed area (so-called Business Improvement Districts—BIDS) or to develop and underserviced area (so-called special area development—SAD) or to facilitate faster growth of certain industries by encouraging them to agglomerate in a special zone (Special Economic Zone—SEZ). Local Council decides on the designation of a geographic area for such development and makes plans for upgrading services. Businesses locating in the BIDS, SADs and SEZs are assured that additional property tax revenues (including development charges and frontage fees) generated with upgrading of services will be utilized only in the local area to provide better services to them.

Facilitating capital market access: Property taxes serve as important tools for facilitating capital market access for municipal infrastructure finance. Such revenue capacity is a major factor in credit ratings and serve as collateral in issuing both the general obligation and revenue bonds as well as in short-term bank borrowing.

Facilitating harmonized urban-rural development: This role of property tax has not yet figured in the design of property taxes worldwide but potentially could be very important for economies experiencing rapid urbanization as the PRC. A properly designed property tax would create incentives for compact development of urban areas and thereby limiting urban sprawl and urban encroachment of productive agricultural land. A graduated split mill property tax would achieve such objectives. A higher graduated tax rate on land with the land tax rate rising as one moves from central business district to periphery accompanied by a much lower fixed/constant tax rate on structures and equipment would provide the incentives for compact urban development as well as investment promotion. It would further discourage the use of vacant land for speculative purposes.

3.6 Property Tax Assignment

Taxes on real property are usually the mainstays of municipal finance, and with good reason. Real property is immobile across jurisdictions so the efficiency costs of using it as a tax base are low. Moreover, it can be argued that many benefits of local public services accrue to property owners, so the tax serves as a sort of benefit tax. Of course, there are costs incurred in administering property taxes, and considerable discretion is involved in arriving at property values for the purposes of taxation. Thus, there is an argument for having the states play a coordinating role in administering property taxes, though not necessarily in setting local rates. In Canada responsibility for assessment rests with the provincial government in some provinces; in others, it is the responsibility of an independent provincial agency whereas local government set their own rates (Boadway 2007). These agencies include, for example, the BC Assessment Authority (BCAA) in British Columbia; the Saskatchewan Assessment Management Authority (SAMA) in Saskatchewan (except for Saskatoon and Regina and a few other municipalities, which are responsible for their own assessments); the Municipal Property Assessment Corporation (MPAC) in Ontario; and the Property Valuation Services Corporation (PVSC) in Nova Scotia. In Quebec and Alberta, local governments are responsible for assessment, but they operate under a standard provincial assessment manual. In Newfoundland and Labrador, there are local assessors in St. John's; the rest of the province relies on provincial assessors. In Manitoba, local assessors are in Winnipeg and provincial assessors elsewhere (see Kitchen et al. 2019b).

In the United States, property taxes are primarily a local government levy, and generate nearly three-quarters of local revenues. States have intervened when sharply rising property values increase the tax burden. Michigan, for example, lowered property taxes in 1994 and replaced the revenues with a 2% increase in the state sales tax. Texas and New Jersey are among the states currently evaluating alternative sources of local funding, to reduce reliance on property taxation (Fox 2007). These concerns are primarily motivated by equalizing the tax burden of school taxes with little concern for differential burden of municipal taxation. In South Africa, on the other hand, national legislation was proposed to harmonize municipal property tax rates through the Property Rates Act of 2004.

Just as different states may have different fiscal capacities and can provide different levels of NFBs to their citizens, so municipalities have different fiscal capacities, particularly with respect to real property tax bases. The case for equalizing transfers among municipalities within states is as strong as that for similar transfers across states. Of course, it is likely to be the states that make the transfer, rather than the federal government. In industrial countries, a common practice regarding property development is for local governments to require developers to provide basic infrastructure in a new subdivision—the so-called practice of gold plating or exactions. Such a practice has potential applications in developing countries as well.

The assignment of property taxes varies across developing countries. In Indonesia, property taxes administration responsibility has recently been devolved from central to local governments (Kelly 2013a, b). In Brazil, China and the Philippines, the responsibility is shared among federal, state and local governments. In China, for example, local governments set the tax rate on urban land use subject to centrally legislated maximums and minimums. In Russia, real estate taxes and taxes on the property of organizations are regional levies. The revenues from the tax on organizational property are shared between the regional and local budgets. Local governments can tax land, individual property and the acquisition of property. In all cases, the taxes are collected by the federal Tax Ministry. Property taxation is a provincial-local responsibility in Argentina, Malaysia and Pakistan. In most other developing countries, such as Bangladesh, Colombia, Mexico, Nigeria, Papua New Guinea and Thailand, it is a solely local responsibility. Only municipalities collect real property taxes in Mexico, although arrangements can be made to have the state administer and collect the tax in exchange for a share of the revenues. Thus, significant potential exists for the decentralization of property taxes in developing countries. Colombia has successfully experimented with a tax on urban property value increases (valorization tax) to finance infrastructure investment projects that were responsible for the improvements in property values. The city of Jakarta, Indonesia, is experimenting with a betterment levy to finance urban infrastructure improvement projects.

Developing countries also frequently levy agricultural land taxes. Taxes based on land area, the market value of agricultural land, the productivity potential and market access of the land have been used as a source of central government revenues in many developing countries. These taxes are more suitable for assignment to local governments.

3.7 The Respective Roles of the Legislature and the Executive

While there is no guidance in the literature on the respective roles of the legislature and executive in the property tax design and administration, a few guiding principles should help in this determination.

Tax legislation should provide a framework for tax fairness, definition of the tax base, assign responsibility for tax policy, tax administration, accountability, transparency, compliance and redress mechanisms.

Executive should have the flexibility to design methods of valuation, setting tax rates, organization and management of tax administration, tax payers awareness mechanisms, methods of valuation, frequency of revaluations to ensure fairness of the tax system and to raise adequate revenues.

Following these principles, the following stylized view of executive and legislative roles is developed in Table 3.11.

The above described stylized view would require adaptation to individual country circumstances based on local context and path dependencies.

3.8 Institutional Arrangements for Property Tax Administration

Property tax administration involves valuation of property, setting tax rates, billing, collection and enforcement. The division of responsibility among various orders of government should be based on having revenue autonomy and adequacy for local governments, fair and comparable valuations across jurisdictions, having full coverage of all properties, ensuring valuations are consistent with legal requirements if any in relation to market value, ensuring full collection of assessed taxes, keeping the cost of collection and compliance low and having a fair and transparent redress and appeal mechanisms.

3.8.1 Property Valuation

A pre-requisite for property valuation is having a geographical information system that captures all properties, their physical site and public services characteristics. This is typically done by establishing a fiscal cadaster and linking it to other geographical, topographical and real estate states data bases. The task of establishing, maintaining and updating could be assigned to a private agency for a fee or to a governmental agency or department

Table 3.11 Stylized view of respective roles of the executive and the legislature in property tax administration

Legislature	*Executive*
Provide specific or as part of the local government act or other acts legislative authorization for the imposition of the real property tax system.	The authorized assessing agency to Issue detailed regulations on property valuations
Also grant authority to the assessing government/agency to collect data from taxpayers and to ensure the confidentiality of any subset of personal information that may be protected by law	Establish systems of land and property records, title registration and geographical information management (GIS) system and designate government or independent agencies responsible for record keeping and dissemination
Define (by central legislation) roles of various orders of government (in central legislation) for property tax policy, design and administration	Establish the precise method of assessment and publish an assessment manual to guide valuation of properties including guidance on whether or not mass appraisal methods are to be used
Provide a precise definition of the tax base—land, building, fixed assets, linear properties etc.	Designate agency to conduct such valuation and establish agency oversight mechanisms
Authorization as to who is liable to pay the tax e.g. owner, occupier, both, etc.	Establish processes and frequency for revaluation of properties
Provides the choice of the principle for valuation (e.g., market value, capital value, rental value, physical characteristics based, area based or hybrid etc.) and provides a legal definition of the chosen principle, e.g., what is meant by market value etc., and designate authority for choosing specific valuation methods and the valuation of properties	Publish citizen's guide to property taxes
Provide guidance on the frequency of revaluations	Determine property tax rates for various classes of properties
Authorize institutional mechanism for ensuring inter and intra-jurisdictional equity in assessments, e.g., an equalization assessment board	Send annual notices of assessment and tax liability to individual taxpayers
Provide listing of properties to be exempt from taxation but allow local governments limited flexibility to adjust this list subject to consultation with the central government	Assess and request GILOT/PILOT payments from otherwise tax exempt entities
Provide tax relief measures for various taxpayers	Establish administrative and compliance processes for tax collection

Provide authorization to request grants-in-lieu of taxes (GILOT) from government entities and payments-in-lieu of taxes (PILOT) from non-profits	Establish administrative procedures for tax relief
Provide a classification of properties for differential taxation and provide guidance on principles for such differentiation, e.g., various types of properties to be taxed according to the service benefits received and no cross subsidization of business and residences	Establish administrative procedures for appeal and redress
Designate authority for determination of tax rates	Establish mechanisms for compliance enforcement
Authorize mechanisms to collect and enforce taxation	Publish periodic reports on property tax collection and compliance
Provide penalties for non-compliance	Conduct analysis on equity of the property tax system
Specify taxpayers' bill of rights including the right to object or appeal, reasons for appealing and who can object/appeal	Continuously strive to reduce assessment errors
Designate institutional mechanisms and processes for appeal and redress and clarify the role of the judiciary	Establish equalization assessment board and facilitate its work
Designate independent authority for disputes resolutions	Conduct citizens and staff education and training
Specify transparency requirements to ensure availability of clear, detailed as well as concise information was readily accessible to all stakeholders	Establish intergovernmental coordination mechanisms on tax policy and administration
Identify institutions and agencies responsible for land and property records as well as tax records	Submit an annual report to the legislature on property tax collection, compliance, appeals, and compliance with legislation
Provide general guidance on land and property information management systems	
Impose tax limitations	

Source: Author's perspectives

that reports to the relevant government or to joint agency of various orders of governments.

In small unitary countries, central government role in property valuation is justified due to better fiscal and administrative capacity and ensuring uniformity and fairness of these valuations. Table 3.12 shows that out of a sample of 169 countries, 54 unitary countries assign such role to the central government. Regional government assume this role in five (mostly federal) countries. Local governments exercise this responsibility in 30 countries whereas in 31 countries responsibility is shared among the central, regional and local governments. In such cases typically the center for unitary countries and the regions for federal countries establish a legal framework for valuation and local governments conduct valuation of individual properties. Twenty-seven sample countries allow owners self-valuation of properties, with a few instances as in Bombay, India, the local government having the option to purchase property at assessed value to discourage low assessments. Twenty-two sample countries contract out valuation to private sector agencies.

Table 3.12 Responsibility for property assessment and valuation

Responsible government or agency	*Africa*	*Asia & Middle East*	*Australia & Oceania*	*Europe*	*North America and the Caribbean*	*South America*	*World*
	Number of countries						
Central government	14	7	5	15	11	2	54
Regional government		1		2	2		5
Local government	9	4	3	6	4	4	30
Shared/mixed/joint responsibility	5	7	3	6	5	5	31
Self-valuation by property owners	7	7		6	3	4	27
Private sector agency	10	2	2	4	4		22
All	45	28	13	39	29	15	169

Source: Tabulated from basic data provided by Almy (2013)

The responsibility for valuation does matter for tax performance as shown in Fig. 3.6. In Fig. 3.6, boxes represent 25–76% range of value with median value indicated by a bold line in the box. The figure shows that local government valuation systems lead to better revenue performance than central or mixed systems.

3.8.2 *Local Discretion in Rate Setting*

Local discretion in rate settings also varies across countries (*see* Table 3.13). Some countries, for example Australia, Canada, United States, South Africa, allow home rule in property tax rate setting by local governments, whereas in some countries local governments enjoy this discretion within bands defined by central or provincial governments; for example, Indonesia and Philippines and still other countries do not permit any local discretion in rate such as in China and Thailand.

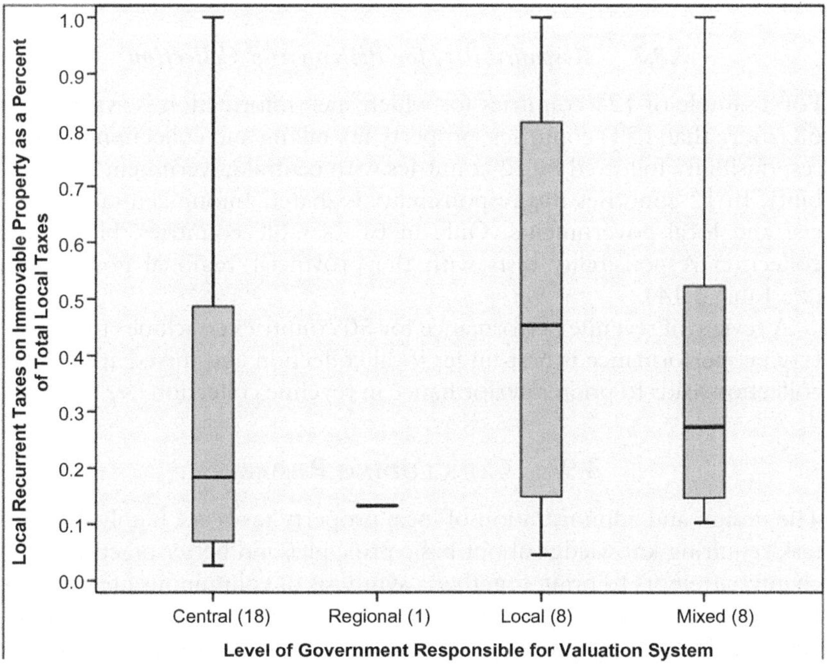

Fig. 3.6 Local valuation leads to better tax performance. (Source: Almy 2013)

Table 3.13 Local discretion over municipal property tax rates—worldwide examples

Local discretion	*Africa*	*Asia & Middle East*	*Australia & Oceania*	*Europe*	*North America*	*South America*
Full	Kenya, South Africa, Tanzania	–	Australia	Hungary	Canada, USA	Argentina, Mexico, Brazil
Within limits specified by the center or the province	–	Japan Indonesia India, Pakistan Philippines	–	Germany UK, Poland, Russia,	–	Colombia
None	Guinea, Tunisia	China Thailand	–	Latvia, Ukraine	–	Chile, Nicaragua

Source: Slack and Bird (2014, 2015)

3.8.3 *Responsibility for Billing and Collection*

For a sample of 124 countries for which such information is available, in 68 (more than half) countries, property tax billing and collection is a local responsibility followed by 42 countries with central government responsibility. In 12 countries this responsibility is shared among central, provincial and local governments. Only in two sample countries, billing and collection responsibility rests with the provincial/regional government (*see* Table 3.14).

A review of revenue performance for 50 countries concludes that property tax performance is best under local collection and mixed and central collection leads to poorer performance in revenue collection (*see* Fig. 3.7).

3.9 Concluding Remarks

The design and administration of local property taxes is a highly complex task requiring knowledge about basic principles and better practices. This chapter attempts to bring together a synthesis of voluminous literature on this subject to assist practitioners and scholars in their efforts to redesign and reform these taxes to enhance their potential as an important source of local revenues as well as useful tools to incentivize better urban

Table 3.14 Responsibility for billing and collection

Responsible government or agency	*Africa*	*Asia & Middle East*	*Australia & Oceania*	*Europe*	*North America and the Caribbean*	*South America*	*World*
	(Number of countries)						
Central government	11	9	3	10	8	1	42
Regional government					1	1	2
Local government	16	16	3	19	7	7	68
Shared/mixed/ joint responsibility	2	1		5	2	2	12
All	29	26	6	34	18	11	124

Source: Tabulated from basic data provided by Almy (2013)

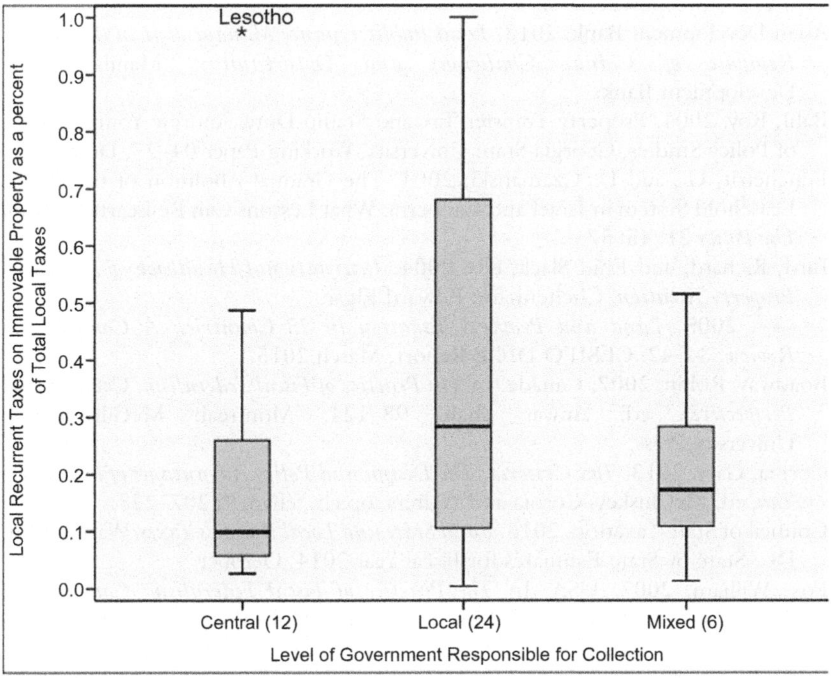

Fig. 3.7 Local responsibility for collection results in better revenue performance. (Source: Almy 2013)

planning and management. Such reforms are expected to build taxpayers' trust and confidence in local governance and enhance tax compliance and revenue performance to enable local governments to serve their residents better.

References

Alberta, Municipal Affairs. 2004. *Detailed Assessment Audit Manual.* Edmonton: Alberta Government.

———. 2010. *Guide to Equalized Assessments in Alberta*. Edmonton: Alberta Government.

———. 2015. *Guide to Property Assessment and Taxation in Alberta*. Edmonton: Alberta Government.

Almy, Richard. 2013. A Global Compendium and Meta-Analysis of Property Tax Systems. Lincoln Institute of Land Policy Working Paper.

———. 2014. Valuation and Assessment of Immovable Property. OECD Working Papers on Fiscal Federalism, No. 19, OECD Publishing. https://doi.org/10.1787/5jz5pzvr28hk-en

Asian Development Bank. 2013. *Local Public Finance Management in the People's Republic of China: Challenges and Opportunities.* Manila: Asian Development Bank.

Bahl, Roy. 2004. Property Transfer Tax and Stamp Duty. Andrew Young School of Policy Studies, Georgia State University, Working Paper 04–27, December.

Benchetrit, G., and D. Czamanski. 2004. The Gradual Abolition of the Public Leasehold System in Israel and Canberra: What Lessons Can Be Learned? *Land Use Policy* 21: 45–57.

Bird, Richard, and Enid Slack, eds. 2004. *International Handbook of Land and Property Taxation*. Cheltenham: Edward Elgar.

———. 2005. *Land and Property Taxation in 25 Countries: A Comparative Review*, 34–42. CESIFO DICE Report, March 2015.

Boadway, Robin. 2007. Canada. In *The Practice of Fiscal Federalism: Comparative Perspectives*, ed. Anwar Shah, 98–124. Montreal: McGill-Queen's University Press.

Cornia, Gary. 2013. *Tax Criteria: The Design and Policy Advantages of a Property Tax*, ed. McCluskey, Cornia and Walters, op.cit., chap. 9: 207–228.

Council of State Taxation. 2015. *Total State and Local Business Taxes.* Washington, DC: State by State Estimates for Fiscal Year 2014, October.

Fox, William. 2007. USA. In *The Practice of Fiscal Federalism: Comparative Perspectives*, ed. Anwar Shah. Montreal: McGill-Queen's University Press.

Fung, Esther. 2013. China Property Tax Facing Opposition. *The Wall Street Journal*, 19–21 July.

Galaty, Fillmore, Wellington Allaway, and Robert Kyle. 2000. *Modern Real Estate Practice*. Chicago: Dearborn.

Grabar, Henry. 2016. *These Graphs Explain Why California's Property Tax Regime Is the Worst*. Money Box, A Blog About Business and Economics, September 22.

Hong, Yu-Hung. 2013. *Taxing Public Leasehold Land in Transition Countries*, ed. McCluskey, Cornia and Walters, op.cit., chap. 11: 249–264.

Inman, Robert. 2008. *Financing Cities*. NBER Working Paper Series.

International Monetary Fund. 2013. *Government Finance Statistics*. Washington, DC: IMF.

Kelly, Roy. 2013a. Making Property Tax Work. International Center for Public Policy Working Paper 13–11, Georgia State University.

———. 2013b. *Property Tax Collection and Enforcement*, ed. McCluskey, Cornia and Walters, op.cit., chap. 6: 141–170.

Kenyon, Daphne, and Adam Langley. 2019. *Payments in Lieu of Taxes. Balancing Municipal and Nonprofits Interests*. Cambridge, MA: Lincoln Institute of Land Policy.

Kitchen, Harry. 2013. *Property Tax: A Situation Analysis and Overview*, ed. McCluskey, Cornia and Walters, op.cit., chap. 1: 1–40.

Kitchen, Harry, Melville McMillan, and Anwar Shah. 2019a. *Local Public Finance and Economics: An International Perspective*. New York: Palgrave Macmillan Press.

Kitchen, Harry, Enid Slack, and Tomas Hachard. 2019b. *Property Taxes in Canada – Current Issues and Future Prospects*. IMFG Perspective Series Number 26. Available at http://munkschool.utoronto.ca/imfg/resources/

Langley, Adam, Daphne Kenyon, and Patricia Bailin. 2012. Payments in Lieu of Taxes By Nonprofits: Which Nonprofits Make PILOTs and Which Localities Receive Them. Lincoln Institute Working Paper.

Lincoln Institute of Land Policy. 2015. *50-State Property Tax Comparison Study*. Cambridge, MA: Lincoln Institute of Land Policy.

McCluskey, William, and Riel Franzsen. 2013. *Non-market Value and Hybrid Approaches to Property Taxation*, ed. McCluskey, Cornia and Walters, op.cit., chap. 13: 287–303.

McCluskey, William, Gary Cornia, and Lawrence Walters, eds. 2013a. *A Primer on Property Tax Administration and Policy*. West Sussex: Wiley.

McCluskey, William, David Tretton, and Caireen M. McCluskey. 2013b. The Rating of Crown Properties in the UK: The Issues Past and Present. Working Paper. Lincoln Institute of Land Policy, Cambridge, MA.

McMillan, Melville. 2008. A Local Perspective on Fiscal Federalism: Practices, Experiences and Lessons from Industrial Countries. In *Macro Federalism and Local Finance*, chapter 7, ed. Anwar Shah, 245–290. Washington, DC: World Bank.

———. 2016. *Municipal Revenue Generation and Sprawl: Implications for the Calgary and Edmonton Metropolitan Regions Derived from an Extension of "Causes of Sprawl"*. University of Calgary School of Public Policy, SPP Technical Paper volume 9, no. 40, December.

———. 2017. *"Causes of Sprawl": A (Further) Public Finance Extension*. Lincoln Institute for Land Policy, Cambridge, MA.

Merk, Olaf, Stéphane Saussier, Carine Starapoli, Enid Slack, and Jay-Hyung Kim. 2012. Financing Green Urban Infrastructure. OECD Regional Development Working Papers 2012/10, OECD Publishing. https://doi.org/10.1787/5k92p0c6j6r0-en.

Mikesell, John. 2013. *Administration of Land Taxes: An International Review of Practices and Issues for Enhancing Fiscal Autonomy*, ed. McCluskey, Cornia and Walters, op.cit., chap. 4: 89–122.

Muniscope. 2010. *Grants in Lieu of Property Taxes*. Canada.

New York, State of. 2011. *Guidelines for Effective Assessment Administration in New York State. A Self-Review Guide for Assessing Units*. New York State Office of Real Property Services, Albany, September.

OECD. 2015. *Revenue Statistics Database*. Paris: OECD.

Saskatchewan, Ministry of Government Relations. 2012. *The Assessment System in Saskatchewan – An Overview*.

Sexton, Terri. 2010. Taxing Property Transactions Versus Taxing Property Ownership. In *Challenging the Conventional Wisdom of the Property Tax*, chap. 9, ed. R.J. Martinez-Vasquez Bah and Joan Youngman, 207–240. Cambridge, MA: Lincoln Institute of Land Policy.

Shah, Anwar. 1983. *Capitalization of Local Property Taxes and Public Services with Applications to Efficiency and Equity Issues*. Ph.D. dissertation, University of Alberta, Edmonton.

———. 1988. Capitalization and the Theory of Local Public Finance: An Interpretative Essay. *Journal of Economic Surveys* 2 (3): 209–243.

———. 1989. A Capitalization Approach to Fiscal Incidence at the Local Level. *Land Economics* 65 (4): 359–375.

———. 1992. Empirical Tests for Allocative Efficiency in the Local Public Sector. *Public Finance Quarterly* 20 (3): 359–377.

———. 2016. *The Practice of Real Property Taxation in the World and Pathways to Their Reform in the People's Republic of China*. ADB Technical Assistance Report, 26 September.

Slack, Enid, and Richard Bird. 2014. The Political Economy of Property Tax Reform. OECD Working Papers on Fiscal Federalism No. 18.

———. 2015. How to Reform the Property Tax: Lessons from Around the World. IMFG papers on Municipal Finance and Governance No. 21. University of Toronto.

Smolka, Martim, and Claudia De Cesare. 2013. *Property Tax and Informal Property: The Challenge of Third World Cities*, ed. McCluskey, Cornia and Walters, op.cit., chap. 12: 265–284.

UN-Habitat. 2011. *Land and Property Tax: A Policy Guide*. Nairobi: UN-Habitat.

———. 2013. *Property Tax Regimes in Europe*. Nairobi: UN-Habitat.

Youngman, Joan. 2016. *A Good Tax. Legal and Policy Issues for the Property Tax in the United States*. Cambridge, MA: Lincoln Institute of Land Policy.

CHAPTER 4

Municipal Budgeting and Accounting

4.1 Introduction

Over the past few decades, municipalities in every country have become more and more vigilant in searching for efficiencies and cost savings in the way in which local services are provided. At the core of these initiatives has been a movement to improve the role played by municipal budgeting and accounting systems.

Budgets have always been important as a means of controlling municipal expenditures and identifying revenues, but the way they are structured, the information they provide, and their importance in managerial decision-making has grown significantly and is certain to increase as they face increasingly critical expenditure and revenue decisions in the future. In addition to serving as a necessary management and planning tool, properly designed municipal budgetary and accounting systems contribute to the accountability and transparency of the overall municipal finance system and reduce the possibility of corruption and misappropriation of funds. In short, properly structured municipal budgets and accounting systems provide invaluable information for most decisions that local councilors make.

The remainder of this chapter is divided into five sections. Section 4.2 discusses the importance of municipal budgets including its role as an instrument for financial control, operational management, financial planning, risk management and monitoring financial behavior. This section also covers the formation of the budget cycle and the role of elected versus

B. Dollery et al., *Local Public, Fiscal and Financial Governance*,
https://doi.org/10.1007/978-3-030-36725-1_4

staff officials. Section 4.3 discusses budget formation issues. Section 4.4 concentrates on capital budgets. Section 4.5 covers accounting and reporting information as it applies to municipalities. Here, accounting standards and objectives are noted, as is the type of information required by the many users of accounting reports; different accounting systems are compared; and financial reporting practices are reviewed. Section 4.6 summarizes the chapter.

4.2 Municipal Budgets

Because municipalities are responsible for a range of services, budgets plan for and control the receipt and expenditure of monies. As for the budgetary process, it may be affected by a number of variables, including the constitutional relationship with senior levels of government, the revenue importance of intergovernmental transfers, the type of services for which municipalities are responsible, and the personalities of the principal decision-makers. In the presence of these differences, it should be noted that municipal governments in every country are controlled by a senior level of government (province/canton/state/laender). These controls require, amongst other things, the provisions of annual budgets which generally involves the preparation of two budgets—an annual operating or current budget (recurrent) that consists of projected revenues and expenditures plus relevant capital asset transactions for the upcoming fiscal year plus a capital budget that lays out future capital expenditure projects and anticipated revenues. As well, the two budgets may be consolidated for certain purposes. The consolidated budget indicates the amount of total estimated revenues available for the current period and the source of additional revenue for financing current and future capital projects (see Dachis 2018, ch. 2 and Dafflon 2018 for more detail).

Budgeted operating expenditures include wages and salaries, pension contributions, purchase cost of short-life equipment, cost of purchasing services from other agencies, materials and supplies, and expenditures on repair and maintenance. They may also include recurring financial transactions such as servicing long-term debt (annual interest cost and principal repayment) and contributions to reserve funds established for specific purposes. Current funds may also be transferred to the capital budget to 'up-front' finance a portion of capital projects. In Canada and a number of other countries, municipalities are authorized to set up reserves to fund contingencies or other obligations that may or may not become due or are difficult to estimate precisely.

The capital budget details the local government's acquisition or rehabilitation of long-term assets (roads, water/sewer lines and treatment plants, public buildings, and sanitary landfills). Often, it is for a period of at least five years and it outlines the public facilities, infrastructure, and land purchases that the jurisdiction intends to implement during this period given the availability of funds. At the same time, this plan should indicate how all capital expenditures are to be financed (own source revenues, borrowing, grants and so on).

4.2.1 Roles or Objectives

Municipal budgets should be designed to achieve the following (Solano and Brams 1996, at 163–164): (1) to provide for the maintenance of financial control; (2) to provide information essential for useful and efficient management decisions; and (3) to improve program and financial planning (Tassonyi 2002).

4.2.1.1 Financial Control

Historically, financial control has been the primary and sole concern of municipal budgets. The fact that local officials have control over local funds has necessitated the implementation of certain controls (statutory or otherwise) so as to regulate and monitor expenditures on particular functions and at particular times throughout the year.

Control budgeting tends to be input oriented, as opposed to goal or output oriented, and is frequently negative in its approach. Emphasis is placed on restricting expenditure increases with very little attention, if any, being devoted to the benefits accruing as a result of the programs or services affected. While this may be a laudable objective, especially in times of restraint, it is far from obvious that it is the most desirable or effective approach. A line-by-line or item-by-item assessment of expenditures usually ensues when inputs are identified and budgeted figures established on an incremental basis.

Incrementalism in the budgeting process has been, and still is, fairly common, particularly in countries or municipalities with a less specialized and relatively small managerial staff. Although there are some noticeable problems with using one year's expenditures as a base on which to add an incremental value in determining the budgeted figures for the following year, it is defended by local officials when there is a lack of other information relevant to the budgetary decision-making process. Their argument suggests that in the absence of useful 'other information' on existing programs and services, there is no basis for reducing or eliminating ongoing expenditures since costs alone do not provide a sufficient rationale for that exercise.

In addition, the incrementalist approach creates some further problems; for example, it provides no mechanism for assessing the benefits from existing expenditures and, therefore, no rationale for encouraging local officials to allocate their resources in an efficient manner. As well, the information provided (see discussion on accounting below) is frequently incomprehensible to all but the most sophisticated readers.

In essence, control budgeting is important but it often creates a narrow and cumbersome financial management system, characterized by, detail, duplication, complexity, and inflexibility. It also lacks the truly relevant information necessary for proper planning and efficient management of local government activities.

4.2.1.2 Operational Management

To improve managerial decision-making at the local level, budgets should be designed to reflect both past and projected expenditures on outputs or goals achieved or to be achieved rather than on the cost of inputs as has been accepted traditionally. This involves the establishment of workloads or targets; for example, a council may set as one of its targets a 5% reduction in crime rates at an average cost of X man-hours per investigation or it may state that all garbage must be collected with a minimum amount of inconvenience to all residents at an average cost of $Y per ton. Similar targets may involve a reduction in per capita fire losses of a fixed percentage at an average cost of $Z per alarm or the completion of road maintenance that ensures smooth riding at a cost of $K per mile/kilometre.

The establishment of targets or workloads allows local officials to make decisions on budgeted expenditures on the basis of costs (efficiency) and returns (effectiveness). Budgets, therefore, should be built around the kind of work to be undertaken in the next fiscal year. These workload targets dictate the programming part of budget preparation, which involves scheduling work, developing an organizational structure, and establishing procedures to reach the proposed plans. Alternative methods of achieving the volume of work to be undertaken should also be considered. This budgeting arrangement allows local budgeters faced with scarce resources to allocate their funds among the various services in a managerially efficient and effective manner.

Once such targets or objectives have been established, the task of achieving them begins. Workloads or targets must be defined in quantifiable terms. Such quantification requires data on both inputs and outputs for it is the ratio of inputs to outputs that generally defines the target.

Estimates of workload and other performance indicators ought to be measured, established, and monitored periodically to make certain that targets are adhered to or that actual changes of a justifiable nature are being incorporated into the budget. Such periodic reporting also provides a basis for evaluating improvements or discovering deviations that must be corrected. These deviations might exist because of unplanned inflationary cost pressures, inadequate financial control, unrealistic revenue or expenditure estimates, and/or simply because of foolish management decisions. Once the reason for the deviation has been determined, local officials should either alter the targets or adjust their operation to achieve the previously stated objective. Finally, an independent external audit by an individual or firm not employed directly by the municipality is necessary in order to guarantee that the objectives or goals have been achieved in an effective, efficient, and transparent manner.

Once performance measures have been implemented, it is critical that this information be linked to the budgetary process (Tassonyi 2002). The tighter financial environment facing local governments along with greater pressure for public accountability provides an impetus for municipalities to outline clearly their targets, goals or objectives and to relate these to performance measures. At the same time, municipalities should employ cost-benefit analysis in evaluating alternative means of achieving their stated objectives in order to provide those services yielding the greatest return given their revenue constraints.

4.2.1.3 Financial Planning

Financial plans are used to shape the future by forecasting the type of expenditures that will be made and the revenue sources that will be tapped. Each annual budget represents a one-year installment in a longer-range plan with the goal ultimately being reached sometime in the future. As well, financial planning should assess the impact of current expenditure decisions on future revenue sources. These impact studies are an invaluable input into the budgetary allocation process. All too often, local governments commit themselves to current programs without considering the financial requirements that these programs will impose on future revenues.

Forecasting

In the not too distant past and still in some countries and smaller municipalities, municipal forecasts consist of little more than simple straight-line projections of revenues and expenditures for the upcoming year. The importance of forecasting and its accuracy, however, has increased dramatically over the past few decades, primarily in response to rising municipal concerns and legislative changes by senior levels of government. For example, the heavy dependence on development charges or lot levies in Canada and the United States requires detailed capital budget forecasts for periods much longer than one year. Increasing emphasis on risk management programs requires carefully drawn up operational budgets to predict the possibility of future losses or damages. The need for detailed and careful budgeting procedures and practices is made all the greater by the growing urgency among municipalities to predict the fiscal impact on future budgets of current decisions to implement new programs or services, expand existing programs or services, or evaluate alternative means of achieving specific municipal goals or objectives.

Because forecasting is such an important managerial tool, each municipality should devise a means of forecasting that is appropriate for its own use. In a world without constraints such as the cost of undertaking the forecast, a rational municipality would aim for the highest degree of accuracy that it can possibly achieve. In practice, of course, generating a forecast involves costs that vary with the availability of data and with the level of expertise that the development and use of the forecast model requires. As such, each municipality must make a trade-off between the degree of accuracy and complexity of the forecast and the cost of operating the forecasting system. Many communities, particularly small- and medium-sized ones, may settle for forecasts that are simpler and potentially less accurate than they would be if the municipality could afford the cost of collecting additional data or raising the level of expertise. For other, mainly larger cities and in the presence of 'big data', the improvement in the accuracy and the completeness of information likely justifies the cost of a more fully developed and sophisticated forecasting model.

This ongoing interest in improving information systems has led to the development and expansion of a set of analytical techniques useful for municipal forecasting. In general, these include time-series techniques, deterministic techniques, and econometric forecasting.

Time-series techniques yield forecasts that are based on the projection of past events; for example, expenditures will increase over the next few years by the same absolute amount as they increased over the past few years, or that the growth rate will be an extension of the growth rate in the recent past. In order to predict changes in local public expenditures, times-series forecasting divides the percentage change in the public expenditures over the past few years by the percentage change in the level of national income or provincial income or municipal income over the same period. It then uses the resultant elasticity coefficient, as it is called, to predict the change in local public expenditures, given that it is possible to predict future changes in national, provincial, or municipal incomes.

Time-series techniques may be useful in deriving short-range forecasts, but they suffer from the weakness that they cannot predict a turning point. Their only basis of projection is the trend of past events. In any case, it does not necessarily follow that changes in income generate changes in local public expenditures. What is needed is a careful determination of the reasons why expenditures (individually and collectively) change in the predicted fashion, rather than an assumption that the change is caused by changes in income.

Deterministic techniques are similar to time-series techniques, except for the base for estimating future expenditures or revenues. It is not past changes in expenditures or revenues but rather some variable such as projected changes in the demographic characteristics of the population. The deterministic approach will use this change to estimate changes in expenditures on, say, police protection or recreation and parks, for example. The weakness of this approach lies in assumptions implicit in the estimation procedure: to predict, for example, that spending on police, or on parks or on recreation will decline if the population ages requires the assumption that the current level of service is the appropriate one.

It is difficult to say how much use different municipalities have made of different forecasting techniques. Nevertheless, deterministic methods are popular. Municipalities often use them to project expenditures and revenues associated with property-related services. If a municipality can project the number of additional residential and commercial/industrial dwellings with reasonable accuracy, a reasonable projection of property-related expenditures will follow. At the same time, knowledge of tax rates permits projections of increases in property tax revenues associated with the expanded assessment base. Finally, considerable scope exists for the imaginative employment of this method to project expenditures on additional resources in order to provide people-related services of a specified level and quality.

Econometric forecasting is a more complex method of prediction. In essence, this approach estimates the effects on local expenditures or revenues arising from simultaneous changes in a number of independent variables that are hypothesized to have some effect on municipal expenditures and revenues. Alternatively, one can use this approach to estimate the effect on local expenditures or revenues of a change in only one of the independent variables while holding all other variables constant. The potential for accurate estimates and for information about the relative importance of each of several causal (independent) factors suggests that this approach is superior to either time-series or deterministic techniques, which almost always measure the effect of only one causal factor (income, population, or time) on local expenditures or revenues. Under the econometric approach, a municipality can, for example, measure the effect of population density on the average unit cost of collecting refuse from residential units while holding constant output, pickup location, annual snowfall, collection frequency, number of multi-unit dwellings, labor costs, type of collection vehicles, size of family per dwelling unit, and private versus public collection constant. The municipality can also estimate the effect on average cost of simultaneously changing all or some of these variables.

Another important advantage of econometric forecasting is that it rests on behavioral relationships that have a theoretical basis and that the user of the forecast can evaluate. The other forecasting techniques lack this attribute. Econometric forecasting also allows for changes in direction of expenditures or revenues—a claim that, by definition, cannot be made for any forecast dependent on past trends. Finally, one can use the econometric approach to determine whether the observed relationship between each causal factor and the level of local revenues or expenditures (the dependent variable) is statistically significant, another advantage that the other approaches lack.

Risk Management

Almost all governmental activities carry elements of risk: fires, automobile accidents, on-the-job accidents, embezzlement, and public liability are a few examples. Until the early 1980s, municipal governments tended to protect themselves by relying on commercial insurance and employee safety programs. Since then, however, municipal officials have gained a clearer understanding of the rising costs of risk and have become more concerned about prevention measures and the importance of obtaining expert advice. This has led to an increasing reliance on risk management programs which, in turn, has heightened the importance of proper accounting techniques and improved budgetary records.

Risk management is the process of analyzing exposure to risk and determining how best to handle this exposure. It involves the identification of risks facing a municipality; it measures the potential impact of these risks on the municipality's financial well-being; and it develops and administers programs of risk control and risk financing. Among other things, this includes the maintenance of safe working conditions for employees and the provision of municipal services in a manner that minimizes user damages and possible financial claims on the municipality. Risk management programs enhance the efficiency of municipal operations and reduce operational costs through lower insurance premiums because of reduced liability and injury-induced losses of work time.

Most large municipalities, especially in developed countries, have risk management programs. They are less common in small municipalities and in developing countries. Risk management is actively promoted by municipal associations, through manuals and educational programs, and by insurance companies.

A risk management program determines the best method of handling the risks encountered by a municipality. It may be that the best method of dealing with a particular risk is to buy insurance, but before the municipality commits itself to this, it should undertake a systematic review of its options. These are described in a variety of manuals or 'how to do' pamphlets produced by municipal government associations such as the Municipal Finance Officers Association in the United States and elsewhere. The municipality's first step is to identify all programs and work areas that may result in accidental losses. It should then evaluate each area in which a loss could occur in terms of the potential frequency and severity of the loss. This assessment will permit the municipality to determine what resources it should devote to either preventing losses or paying for them. Once the municipality has identified and measured the risks, it should seek to reduce or eliminate them through safety and risk control programs. Of course, even the most successful programs of this kind cannot wholly eliminate risk: the municipality must also have a plan for covering the losses it will inevitably incur. In addition to the purchase of insurance, the choices include self-financing of losses in a variety of ways, including the use of reserves, direct expensing to the relevant department, the retention of part of the risk through higher deductibles on existing insurance policies, and the pooling of risk with other municipalities.

4.3 The Budget as a Monitoring Instrument

Municipal budgets, accounting systems, and financial reports are all necessary ingredients for monitoring a municipality's behavior. Of particular importance is performance-based budgeting (see Chap. 7 for more detail). Local governments in some countries (Australia, New Zealand to name only two) are required to provide performance measures for a wide range of municipal services.

Further restrictions have been placed on the behavior of local governments through legislation that requires municipalities to enter into competitive tendering for the provision of municipal services. This has happened in Great Britain and New Zealand.

In the province of Ontario (Canada), the *Public Sector Accountability Act* requires that public sector agencies (municipalities, hospitals, school boards, universities and social services agencies and other large public institutions) consider contracting out to lower costs.

4.3.1 Budget Formation

The preparation or formation of the budget generally passes through a series of stages and involves both elected and appointed officials and sometimes, the taxpaying public.

4.3.1.1 Budget Cycle

Preparation of the budget begins with a policy direction from the locally elected council; for example, a focus on water and sewers, transit, roads, zero tax increase and so on. The first stage of the budgetary cycle involves the preparation of initial requests for funds on a department-by-department basis. This is driven by a number of factors, including the size of the municipality's budget, the degree of sophistication involved in providing and evaluating local programs or services, the importance attached to budgeting, the size of the department and even the style of the department head. If departments are reasonably large, there may be an identifiable department budget staff. In smaller municipalities, budget requests may be made by department heads or staff members on an 'ad hoc' or a part-time basis. The adoption of performance measures and cost/benefit techniques as a basis for making budgetary decisions tends to be correlated positively with the size of the municipal budget.

During the second stage of the budget cycle, departments or individuals responsible for administering local programs and services submit their requests to the chief administrative or financial officer. This officer and/or staff compile, combine, and coordinate all requests for funds. Since municipal governments in many countries are required by law to approve a balanced budget for their annual operating activities, it is the responsibility of the local staff to develop a budget that is generally presented to the budget committee of the municipal council or the council itself.

The third stage is the adoption of the budget. At the local level, and particularly for smaller communities, this exercise may be much less sophisticated than in larger cities. In many municipalities, the public (taxpayers) are invited to comment (at public meetings and in written presentations) on the proposed budget prior to council approval. This public participation is designed to add transparency and accountability to the budgetary process and to gain public acceptance of the budget.

The execution and monitoring of the budget throughout the fiscal year constitutes the fourth stage of the budget cycle. The responsibility for these activities along with the presentation of an updated picture of the municipality's financial position to the local council rests with the chief financial officer and/or his staff.

Finally, legislation generally requires that municipalities have their financial records audited by an independent auditor after the completion of the fiscal year. This ensures that the municipality has adhered to legal requirements regarding local expenditures and that local officials have not misappropriated (deliberately or accidentally) local funds.

4.3.1.2 Role of Elected Versus Appointed Officials

Throughout the budgetary process, there are a number of participants, each performing different roles. Elected officials should play a different role than appointed officials. Elected officials should be responsible for setting policy and establishing the strategic directions of council. As a representative of a local constituency, they play a major role in the communication process between the council and local taxpayers and through this process are responsible for translating the desires and needs of the local constituents into appropriate budgetary polices. Local input is frequently solicited through public meetings. As well, the media and the internet play a role in informing the public about ongoing budget deliberations. Ultimately, the elected councilors must approve the budget and accept responsibility for monitoring the overall financial performance and transferring this responsibility to service delivery performance.

Elected officials should not, however, be involved in the day-to-day management activities of the municipality or its special purpose bodies. This should be left to appointed officials. In this regard, New Zealand has gone as far as any country, maybe farther, because it has legislation that decouples local council decision-making from day-today management. In this environment, the council's job is to set policy and monitor the performance of the chief administrative or chief executive officer. In New Zealand, this officer is on a performance-based contract for up to five years and is the employer of all other staff. His responsibility is to manage the municipality within policies set by the local council.

4.4 Capital Budgets

In most countries, annual capital budgeting practices and techniques suffer from greater inadequacies and deficiencies than do annual operating budgets. For example, municipalities frequently fail to consider future operating and maintenance costs in making decisions on the wisdom of spending on capital projects. This happens most often when municipalities undertake capital projects in response to the availability of grants from senior levels of government or when they make decisions without the aid of a carefully developed and detailed capital budget. As well, very few municipalities consider opportunity costs (the value of forgone alternatives if a municipality chooses this project) in their capital budget, although almost all of them take into consideration debt costs. Finally, municipalities all too frequently ignore depreciation or asset replacement costs in calculating annual operating costs. This is especially important for those projects that are funded from user fees (water, sewers and so on) and whose fee should cover all costs (including those to replace the asset or facility) associated with the operation of the facility.

An important policy objective of municipal decision-makers should include the integration of capital infrastructure programs and growth management objectives. The latter are generally designed to control 'urban sprawl' and promote 'infilling' or higher density development. The availability of (or lack of) local infrastructure including water and sewer lines, roads and streets can control the type of development (Slack 2002).

Unfortunately, this integration is often less than it should be. First, capital programs and budgets are frequently drawn up or altered without the consent or involvement of all local departments or officials. This, when combined with decisions of special purpose bodies such as utility commissions creates situations where capital maintenance or construction of a specific project may not be coordinated with other capital projects in the same years. For example, one frequently observes the construction or maintenance of sidewalks or roadways and shortly afterward the tearing up of these facilities to construct or replace sewers or water mains. Such uncoordinated efforts prove to be costly and difficult to justify. Second, further problems exist if capital projects represent political compromise and compliance with legal approval dates (calendar) rather than well thought-out plans for community improvement. The notion that capital projects flow smoothly from well-organized community plans to implementation is often not borne out. Among the reasons for this is the likelihood that a number of development or management decisions are made in a public forum (public meetings, for example) or influenced by public input from special interest groups. These forums or the public input, however, seldom cover all aspects of community planning such as the maintenance, renewal, and construction of new projects. While the overall policy may include an integrated approach to capital programs and growth management objectives, this objective is paid only lip-service. The sheer numbers of people involved and their interest in only selected aspects of the overall plan place constraints on the actual achievement of this objective.

Finally, much of the capital spending tends to be devoted to short-term rehabilitation and renewal projects even though longer-term projects may generate greater net gains. Emphasis on short-term projects arises for at least two reasons. First, the relatively short term of office for municipal politicians means that they are generally more interested in short-term projects because they coincide with their term of office and provide visible signs of political initiatives. Second, municipal decision-makers are reluctant to become locked into long-term projects without guarantees of future funding and concern about the impact of future annual interest and debt repayment charges on local budgets.

A carefully developed capital budget should, at a minimum, include the following five steps (Schaeffer 2000a, pp. 20–24).

1. *Inventory of Capital Assets.* An inventory of capital assets provides information on the capacity of existing infrastructure and the appropriate timing for its replacement. Surprisingly, a large number of municipalities do not have detailed or accurate records on the age and condition of much of their important infrastructure, especially that which is underground (water and sewer pipes, hydro-lines and so on).
2. *Development of a Capital Investment Plan (CIP).* This would include information on the urgency of building or rehabilitating a capital project, the benefits derived from it, the cost and financial impact of the project, and its acceptability to the local constituency.
3. *Development of a Multi-Year CIP.* This plan establishes the time schedule and all costs for capital investment projects being considered. This would permit the municipality to choose the most cost-effective option and it would provide the municipality with information that would assist it in developing a prudent financial plan for funding the project. This multi-year plan should be integrated with a multi-year operating budget to avoid the common problem of failing to provide information on future operating and maintenance costs. As well, integrating these two budgets would lead to better decisions over the optimal size of potential capital assets or facilities.
4. *Developing the Financial Plan.* For each capital project, the municipality should develop a detailed financial plan that includes information on the municipality's capacity and ability to finance the project, sources of funds for the project (user fees, local revenues, grants, borrowing and so on), and procedures to be followed if revenues fall short of the target or if surpluses are generated.
5. *Implementing the Capital Budget.* The success of any capital budgeting process is highly dependent on public participation and acceptance of the proposed projects (Tassonyi 2002). Public acceptance may depend on the urgency of the project; for example, crumbling underground sewers that have caused basement backups or leaky water pipes that produce insufficient water pressure to fight fires may be deemed to be more urgent than repairing roads or sidewalks that have deteriorated over the winter.

4.4.1 Restrictions or Controls on Borrowing for Capital Projects

Municipalities in a number of countries are permitted to engage in long-term borrowing for capital projects only. This, however, is not so in many cities in the United Sates where many have borrowed to cover operating expenditures as well. Where capital projects provide services that benefit future generations, borrowing is an ideal financing instrument because the annual repayment of principal and interest charges can be recovered through taxes or user fees collected from future users or beneficiaries of the projects. In other words, those who benefit are those who pay.

While borrowing is important for financing municipal capital projects and is used frequently, local borrowing in most countries is subject to a variety of restrictions or controls imposed by senior levels of government. These are in place because municipalities are creatures of the province/state/canton/laender and the latter do not wish to be responsible for unlimited municipal borrowing and possible repayment of municipal debt. As well, unrestricted municipal access to capital markets may in some circumstances crowd out private sector borrowing or have an impact on borrowing by more senior levels of government. Finally, controls minimize the possibility of municipalities going bankrupt.

Local borrowing is monitored in a variety of ways. Table 4.1 lists the types of restrictions imposed on local borrowing in a selection of countries. In general, restrictions relate to the dollar value of outstanding debt

Table 4.1 Local borrowing restrictions in selected countries

Type of restriction	*Description*	*Countries*
Affordability Formulae	Ceilings on (i) debt service/local revenues; (ii) debt service/local current spending	Argentina, Brazil, Italy, Japan, Spain, Lithuania, Poland, Columbia, Canada
Indebtedness Formulae	Limit on outstanding debt/net revenues	Brazil, Columbia, Italy, Canada
"Golden Rule" Provision[a]	Borrowing for capital expenditures	Brazil, Canada, USA, Austria, South Africa, Switzerland, India
Balanced Budget	Local councils are required to pass balanced operating budgets	Brazil, Canada, Germany, Netherlands, USA
Local Approval	Local councils are required to approve borrowing for individual projects	Canada, Switzerland, USA
"No Bailout" Provision	National government does not guarantee subnational debt	South Africa, Mexico

Source: Dana Weist, "Borrowing and Capital Financing", a power point presentation on Intergovernmental Fiscal Relations in East Asia, ASEM Sponsored Workshop (World Bank), Bali, Indonesia, January 10–11, 2002

[a]Local government borrowing cannot exceed the amount spent on investment

that is permitted and/or annual debt service charges as a percentage of own-source revenue or operating (current) expenditures.

Since Canadian restrictions are not unlike those in many developed and developing countries and tend to vary from province to province, it may be worth hilighting them (Amborski 2013). One type of restriction is based on a formula related to the level of debt or debt-servicing costs (Table 4.2: Panel A); the other requires specific approval (Table 4.2: Panel B).

A general question that emerges in discussions of local borrowing is whether or not controls should exist or whether municipalities should be free to borrow and, hence, be subjected to the discipline of the market. As long as municipalities are creatures of a senior level of government, an argument exists for controlling their borrowing behavior primarily to prevent bankruptcy and a potential need to be 'bailed-out'. Where municipalities are creatures of a senior level of government with the latter

Table 4.2 Local borrowing in Canada

Province/Territory	*Restrictions*
Panel A: Based on a formula: Debt or debt service	
Nova Scotia	30% of own source revenue
New Brunswick	2% of assessed real property value
Prince Edward Island	10% of assessed real property value
Ontario	Debt servicing costs (principle and interest) can't exceed 25% of own source revenue
Manitoba	Total debt—maximum 7% of municipal assessment; annual debt servicing costs—maximum 20% of annual own source revenue
Alberta	Debt limit is 1.5 times annual revenue; debt servicing limit is 25% of annual own source revenue
Yukon	3% of assessed real property value
Northwest Territories	Debt servicing costs restricted to 20% of municipal revenue; for villages, the limit is 10%
Panel B: Based on restrictions requiring specific approval	
Newfoundland	None for municipalities; service districts are set by the Minister
Saskatchewan	Must be approved by the Saskatchewan Municipal Board
British Columbia	Must be approved by the Inspector of Municipalities based on a formula
Nunavut	Set by Municipal Regulation

Source: Amborski, David, 2013, "The Context of Municipal Borrowing in Canada", A Presentation at the Institute of Municipal Finance and Governance, University of Toronto, 2013.

ultimately responsible for all outstanding liabilities/debts of the municipal sector, failure to impose controls provides an incentive for municipal officials to borrow more than they should.

Controls that restrict annual debt servicing charges to a fixed percentage of own-source revenues with provisions for additional borrowing approved by a senior level of government have been appropriate and effective in countries where it has been used. It has permitted municipalities to remain solvent and to function in a normal and expected manner.

4.4.1.1 Issuance of Municipal Debt

The way in which long-term municipal debt is issued varies from country to country. In some countries, a provincial or state organized authority or agency may borrow on behalf of all municipalities; in other countries, municipalities borrow on their own. The advantages of a state-wide, region-wide, or province-wide body are significant. Municipalities borrow from the authority who, in turn, totals up all requests for local funds and issues long-term debentures against the authority itself. In some countries, debentures are guaranteed by a senior level of government. When the proceeds are received from the sale of these debentures, the funds are dispersed to the requesting municipalities usually under a loan agreement with the borrowing municipality.

Pooling of municipal debt through a provincial or state-wide organization can produce significant benefits for many municipalities, especially the smaller ones. These organizations or authorities generally issue bonds on a regular basis; some only for municipal units but others include schools, hospitals, utilities, and other municipal bodies. The administration costs may be funded by a senior level of government or by earnings on reserve funds, participants, or a combination of these.

Borrowing costs are lowered by the ability to issue debt in national and international markets and from lower administration costs in issuing debt. A large finance authority substitutes one contract with an underwriter for separate contracts between each borrower and debt issuer. It economizes on transactions costs because it issues debentures more frequently than individual municipalities would if they had to borrow themselves and it provides stability in volatile capital markets that are subject to uncertainty. It can exercise a greater degree of flexibility over issue terms and costs to municipal clients.

One study (Gilbert and Pike 1999) compared the cost of municipal funds for pooled versus stand-alone issues using data from the province of

Ontario, Canada. The findings show that pooled financing through a hypothetical municipal financing corporation or province-wide authority would significantly lower costs to municipalities when compared with the actual cost of capital for municipal issues. The authors concluded that the benefits of municipalities participating in a municipal finance authority that issues ten-year debentures through investment dealers varied inversely with population size and credit rating (a measure of the credit worthiness of a municipality). Issue size was not a factor. In other words, the largest savings would accrue to municipalities with smaller populations, those that are un-rated (no bond rating for debt purposes), and those that borrow for longer periods of time.

4.5 Accounting and Reporting

The budget is the heart of municipal resource administration with municipal accounting systems, practices and their subsequent reports being central to the budget-making process. For example, past accounting records furnish important data for revenue and expenditure forecasts used to construct the budget. Accounting records provide information on debt and debt service charges and serve as a basis for estimating a municipality's ability to carry further debt. Sound accounting reports provide timely information on whether budget plans are on target or amiss; when capital funds are diverted to operating expenditures; when expenditures are outpacing revenues; and when the municipality is incurring financial obligations beyond its fiscal capacity (Holder 1996). The focus of reporting and accounting, then, is to document, classify and summarize transactions so users of the resulting financial reports are able to understand and evaluate municipal operations.

4.5.1 Standards

Internationally, accounting and financial reporting standards are often established by independent standards setting authorities or boards. In the United States, for example, the Government Accounting Standards Board (GASB) establishes financial reporting standards for the public sector. In Canada, public sector accounting standards are set by the Public Sector Accounting Board (PSAB) of the Canadian Institute of Chartered Accountants. Many other countries have established similar Public Accounting Standards.

Municipal accounting often differs from private sector accounting because the emphasis in the former is on cash flow and transparency and accountability to the local constituency while the emphasis in the latter is on profit or loss reporting. More specifically, the following practices have become the norm for most public sector accounting (Schaeffer 2000a, at 5).

- Fund accounting should be used to ensure legal compliance with restrictions on the use of revenues and to enhance sound financial administration of diverse governmental operations.
- Fixed asset accounts should be maintained separately from current assets. All tangible assets should be depreciated.
- Long-term obligation bonds (debt) should be recorded in a separate group of accounts as obligations of the entire governmental unit. Revenue bonds are obligations of specific funds and should be recorded as such.
- Different accounting methods are used for matching revenues and expenditures over a specific time period. On a cash basis, revenues are recorded when cash is received and expenditures are recorded when cash payments are actually completed. On a full accrual basis, revenues are recorded when earned and expenses are recorded when liability is incurred. The modified accrual basis records expenditures when liability is incurred but does not record most revenues until cash is received (discussed below in more detail).
- Financial reports should be issued regularly and an annual report covering all funds and operations should be published.

4.5.2 Objectives

Public sector accounting standards are generally designed to achieve a number of objectives. As an example, municipal financial statements should:

- Provide reliable, understandable, timely, and consistent information that meets the needs of persons for whom the statements are prepared.
- Provide an accounting of the full nature and extent of the financial affairs and resources for which the municipal government is responsible.
- Demonstrate the accountability of the municipal government for the financial affairs and resources entrusted to it.

- Account for the sources, allocation, and uses of financial resources in the period.
- Provide information that shows the state of the municipal government's finances.

A number of financial management functions have to be fulfilled to meet these objectives. Municipalities need to have in place systems for accounting, auditing and analysis of financial information. Accounting systems are needed to record revenues and expenditures in a consistent way that permits comparisons between budgets and actual figures. Financial audits are needed to determine whether the municipality's financial statements provide an accurate and reasonable picture of the municipality's financial position and activities for the reporting period. The financial audit is designed to detect deficiencies in the system of internal financial control, failures to comply with accounting principles and standards or with reporting requirements of senior levels of government and instances of errors or misappropriation of funds. In that the focus of the financial audit is on the financial statements, these audits do not address the issues of efficient resource utilization and the achievement of performance standards. Issues of efficiency and performance are addressed in management and performance audits, or special audits such as an environmental audit.

4.5.3 Users of Accounting Information

To facilitate the discussion of users and their respective financial information needs, it may be useful to categorize these users into the following groups: external users, internal users, and senior governments.

4.5.3.1 External Users

External users include constituents, creditors, suppliers, and others engaged in business transactions with the government. This group is external to the government and generally lacks any effective control over the type of financial information available. The kind of information of greatest use to these users includes information on performance measures. This permits an intermunicipal comparison of unit costs, efficiency and effectiveness of local programs or services. It permits users to assess the financial health and fiscal viability of their community. In addition, external users benefit greatly from the provision of information on such things as the impact of current capital projects on future operating budgets; the ability of local governments to be able to draw on future resources (taxes, grants, and user charges) and the extent to which these revenue sources may be substituted for each other; and the impact of inflation on future expenditures and revenue requirements.

4.5.3.2 Internal Users

This category includes all individuals engaged in the managerial and administrative functions of local government. Specifically, it includes policymakers, managers and administrators. Their functions involve the planning, organization, execution and evaluation of the diverse programs and services provided by local governments.

The financial information needs of these users are more comprehensive than those of external users. Not only do policymakers and administrators require the same information as external users, they also require cost estimates for alternative ways of achieving specific goals. Cost-benefit analyses of proposed and existing programs, forecasts of current and capital expenditures, and the impact these will have on local revenue sources both in terms of the effect on tax rates or charges and their distributional impact on local residents are important. With the exception of some larger urban or regional municipalities, impact studies, cost-benefit analyses, and careful revenue and expenditure forecasts are seldom attempted. As pressures mount for more transparency, accountability and cost-efficient programs, however, increased emphasis should be placed on more useful and relevant financial information—information that will assist in making local administrators and policymakers more responsive to users' desires and needs.

4.5.3.3 Senior Levels of Government

Since local governments are almost always creatures of a senior level of government and since they often receive grant support from their senior counterparts, there is both an expectation and a requirement that local governments provide financial, economic, and statistical information to the donor government in a consistent and uniform manner. Much of this information may be of little use to external users. Indeed, in its initial stages it may be of limited use even to the municipality actually supplying it. Once collected and compiled by the senior level government, however, it is useful because it indicates different trends in expenditure and revenue categories over time; differences in the extent to which municipalities support different expenditure programs; and differences in the dependency of municipalities on their various sources of revenue. Such intermunicipal comparisons on a uniform basis will allow municipalities, senior government analysts and others to assess the feasibility, cost, level and quality of current programs. If specific expenditures, costs or dependence on a particular revenue source tend to be out of line for some municipalities, this information may provide a base for pursuing a more in-depth analysis of the reasons for this difference—reasons that may generate improvements in the quantity and/or quality of local services or programs or improvements in the funding of these services or programs.

Senior levels of government in exercising their legal and statutory responsibilities also require information that will allow them to oversee and control certain activities of local governments. These governments, for instance, may require detailed information on capital budgets and debt capacities to ensure that local governments do not commit themselves to future excessive financial burdens and risk bankruptcy. As well, other information is required as a basis for determining the recipients of many grant programs. Equalization grants, for example, are established only after economic, financial, and statistical data have been supplied, compiled, and evaluated.

4.5.4 *Accounting Bases*

The basic difference between municipal (and other levels of government) accounting systems and personal/business accounting is the use of fund accounts (Schaeffer 2000b, p. 15). In conventional accounting systems, all monies go into one account from which all expenses are paid. A single set of accounts is usually sufficient to disclose transactions and details of financial conditions. Legal restrictions on the use of government monies, on the other hand, make co-mingling of monies an obstacle to a clear demonstration of compliance with prescribed rules and conditions.

Under fund accounting, a separate fund is used to report financial transactions for a particular aspect or activity of government such as water or sewage operations. Fund accounting features self-balancing double entry accounts from which a balance sheet and statement of operations can be prepared. Separate budgets are prepared for each fund.

The fund basis of accounting has two important advantages. First, it recognizes that a considerable amount of government revenue is not fungible—that is, available for purposes other than those budgeted—and that data on budgeting compliance are an important part of the stewardship responsibility of government. Second, distinct fund accounting and reporting is necessary to control resources for their designated use and to demonstrate compliance with legal and budgeting constraints affecting municipal governments. The funds that are used may be categorized into three basic types: (i) governmental, (ii) proprietary and (iii) fiduciary. Table 4.3 offers a definition of these funds and their respective categories.

In essence, commonly used funds are those for general municipal activities, revenue funds for special activities, utility operations, sinking funds, capital funds, reserves, trusts and agency funds.

Since financial transactions associated with a specific fund are subject to legal or administrative restrictions, a reserve fund should be used to record the proceeds from, for example, charges on specific properties or users and their application to designated capital works, while a utility fund would be used to report the transactions of a municipal service that has been set up as a self-financing department.

Table 4.3 Municipal funds

Fund	*Definition*
Government Funds:	
General Fund	Consists of general revenue sources such as taxes, fines, licenses and fees. The general fund is usually the largest municipal fund.
Special Revenue Fund	Consists of revenues that are resources for special purposes. Examples include transportation trust funds or senior government grants.
Debt Service Fund	Consists of resources used to repay long-term general obligation debt (general obligation bonds).
Capital Project Funds	Consists of resources restricted for construction and acquisition of capital facilities.
Special Assessment Funds	Consists of resources received from special charges or fees levied on persons that benefit from a particular capital improvement project.
Proprietary Funds:	Proprietary funds account for records of operation.
Enterprise Fund	Contain financial records of self-supporting operations (water and sewer funds).
Internal Service Fund	Account for the financing of goods and services provided by one department or agency to other departments or agencies on a cost reimbursement basis (building maintenance).
Fiduciary Fund:	Account for assets held by a governmental unit in a trustee capacity (law enforcement fund).

Source: Susan L. Riley and Peter W. Colby, *Practical Government Budgeting*, State University Press, 1991

Cash, accrual, and modified accrual accounting form the three possible accounting bases that can be used for municipalities and their enterprises. As noted above, *cash accounting* involves the recording of expenditures and revenues when funds are actually disbursed or received. It is the simplest of the accounting bases but it is not recommended under generally accepted public sector accounting principles because it gives a misleading picture of municipal accounts. For example, cash received as a loan would be reported as revenue in the operating statement but not as a liability on the balance sheet.

Accrual accounting is the more commonly accepted approach internationally. It records transactions when they occur regardless of when expenditures are made or funds received. For example, the cash expenditure to finance an investment in a fixed asset may take place within one year but the associated expenses reported in the financial statement of operations takes the form of annual depreciation charges incurred over the life of the asset. Since depreciation is a charge that is used to recover the original cost of an asset and associates the annual flow of benefits with costs, it is incorrect to interpret depreciation as a charge to cover replacement costs since this would entail double counting. Moreover, the cost of asset maintenance and repair is recovered directly as an expense (Dachis 2018, ch. 2).

Modified accrual accounting is somewhat different. It adopts the same principles and approach as accrual accounting with the exception that depreciation and a return on capital are not included as costs. Instead, interest costs and principal repayments on debt are recovered directly in the year in which they are due through user fees and local taxes. These are generally set to generate revenues in excess of expected operating and maintenance costs and debt service costs, thus resulting in operating surpluses which are transferred to a capital fund to finance ongoing investments or into reserves or reserve funds to finance planned future investments. Because principal repayments are recovered directly each year as chargeable expenses, municipalities are less likely to face cash flow problems. Capital financing does not therefore depend on the flow of funds from a depreciation charge and a return on equity.

The adoption of accrual or modified accrual accounting does not suggest that absolutely every revenue source or expenditure item be accrued. For very small revenue and expenditure items, a simple recording on a cash basis along with proper notation of the approach followed may be sufficient.

Under both the full accrual and modified accrual accounting systems, the treatment of operating and maintenance costs is identical. As well, both systems can accommodate capital contributions from outside sources. In the modified accrual system, these take the form of grants from senior governments or transfers from the municipality's general revenue or reserve funds (such transfers are not customary where municipalities run utility operations on a self-financing basis). Under the full accrual-based system, capital contributions are normally equity injections from private or public sector investors.

The main difference between the two methods lies in the treatment of capital. As well, whether a municipality uses the modified or full accrual method of accounting can affect the timing and amount of costs that are written off as expenses in a given year, and hence the timing and size of capital costs passed on to customers.

At the same time, the sum of principal repayments and the operating surplus in the modified accrual system can be equated to the sum of depreciation charges and retained earnings in the accrual system. These two sources of funds are similar and both accounting methods can be made to work effectively given the appropriate level of financial management.

Table 4.4 provides an overview of differences in accrual and modified accrual accounting. The ability to match benefits with costs over the service life of assets and the importance of fully recovering costs each fiscal year suggests that the full accrual method presents a greater opportunity to achieve the objective of service delivery related to equity.

4.5.4.1 International Experience

Accrual accounting, however, has not been universally supported for local governments, but it is growing in importance and usefulness. In New Zealand, Australia (Pallot 2001) and the United States, it has been required for some time. Similarly, with municipalities in Switzerland where they have also been required to balance their budgets annually (Dafflon 2018). More recently, municipalities in Canada have moved to accrual-based accounting.

Interest in full accrual-based accounting for municipalities is generally motivated by concerns over the state of aging infrastructure and a lack of reliable information that could be used to evaluate this concern. In New Zealand and the United States, these concerns led to reforms in accounting standards for local government.

Table 4.4 Comparison of accounting approaches

Item	*Accrual basis*	*Modified accrual basis*
Treatment of investment costs in statement of operations	An annual depreciation expense is included in costs over the expected life of the asset. The sum of depreciation expenses should equal the original cost of the asset less its scrap value. The annual depreciation charge does not correspond to any expenditure in the year for the asset in question.	The statement of operations will show actual capital expenditures for the asset drawn from the capital fund. Money in the capital fund is transferred from the revenue fund or a capital reserve fund, or it comes from newly issued debt or a capital contribution such as a grant.
Treatment of fixed assets in balance sheet	The original cost of the fixed asset is recorded when the asset is commissioned and this value is then reduced each year by the amount of the corresponding depreciation charge. At the end of its service life, the assets value goes to zero.	The value of the fixed asset does not appear in the balance sheet. Only current assets are reported (e.g., inventories, cash, accounts payable).
Treatment of long-term debt in statement of operations	Only the interest portion of debt service cost is reported as a cost but not the principal repayment. Principal is repaid using cash originating from depreciation charges and profit.	Both the interest and principal portion of debt service cost are reported as costs.
Treatment of long-term debt in balance sheet	Reported as a liability and diminished as principal is repaid.	Reported as a liability and diminished as principal is repaid.
Cost recovery through user fees and taxes (assuming no grants)	All of it in the form of depreciation charges. The period of recovery extends over the service life of the asset, which may be considerably longer than the repayment period of debt to finance the investment.	All of it in the form of principal repayments and transfers from the revenue fund to capital and reserve funds to finance the investment. The period of recovery matches the period of debt repayment and revenue fund transfers and actually commence prior to the investment when reserves built in advance.
Financing costs	Interest charges on debt and a return on the equity portion of the investment including retained earnings (if any).	Interest charges on debt.

Source: "Financing Water Infrastructure", by Strategic Alternatives et al., Issue Paper 14 commissioned by the Walkerton Inquiry, Toronto, Ontario, Canada, May 2001, chapter 8

In 1993, for example, the New Zealand Audit Office reported to parliament that it could not vouch for the long-term financial viability of local governments because there was no information on the condition of assets and inadequate strategic planning for future investment requirements. In response, the *Local Government Amendment Act* (no. 3) was passed in 1996. Among other things, this Act required local government to adopt fixed asset accounting and to prepare and approve a long-term financial strategy every three years providing long-term financial and asset management plans (Pallot 2001). Under the Act, depreciation charges are estimated and funded through local taxes and user charges. The depreciation charge provides an estimate of the decline in service potential of assets, while its funding assures that "users of the service pay the real cost" (Office of the Controller and Auditor General of New Zealand 1999).

Accounting reforms in the United States were similar (ICMA 2000). The requirement for full accrual accounting by local government was established by the U.S. Government Accounting Standards Board (GASB 2001), which concluded that reporting infrastructure assets is essential to provide information for assessing financial position and changes in financial position, and for reporting the costs of programs or functions (Johnson and Bean 1999).

Asset management planning is mandatory in many countries (New Zealand, Canada and the United States to name three). As a source of information on the condition of infrastructure, asset management planning goes well beyond fixed asset accounting in that it requires an assessment of the physical condition of the infrastructure. Fixed asset accounting uses accounting standards and conventions as a basis for estimating depreciation charges, and, therefore, provides only a proxy measure of the condition of physical assets. Asset management planning develops a strategy and financing plan for asset maintenance and replacement. In contrast, fixed asset accounting generates cash funds that are available for capital finance, but this doesn't mean that they will be used for that purpose or that they are needed when received. Asset management planning is therefore a more effective tool than fixed asset accounting as a means of providing information on the condition of infrastructure and the funding required for its maintenance.

4.5.5 *Financial Reporting Practices*

In general, the following three objectives should be met in the financial reports produced by municipal governments (Reny 1983, p. 120; and Schaeffer 2000b, p. 15).

- Financial reporting practices should provide information to determine whether current revenues are sufficient to pay for current year expenditures. This improves transparency and provides an incentive for municipal officials to be accountable for their actions.
- Municipal financial reporting should provide information about the sources and uses of financial resources and the way in which it finances its activities and meets its cash requirements. Financial reporting should also provide information necessary to determine whether the jurisdiction's financial position has improved or deteriorated as a result of the current year's operation.
- Financial reports should provide enough information for users to assess the ability of the municipality to meet future commitments. This should include information about the financial position and condition of the municipal government, about the physical and non-financial resources that have useful lives that extend beyond the current fiscal year.

Requirements that municipalities report all budgetary information, the extent to which their budgetary goals are met and information on performance measures to the local citizens on an annual basis should improve the efficiency, accountability and transparency of local government activities. This reporting could take a variety of forms including mail outs to all residents; through tax and/or utility bills; notices in local newspapers; and postings on the municipality's website.

4.6 Summary

Because municipalities are responsible for a range of services, budgets are necessary for planning and controlling the receipt and expenditure of monies. In practice, there are generally two budgets—an annual operating or current budget that consists of projected revenues and expenditures and a capital budget that lays out future capital expenditures and anticipated revenues. As distinct from senior levels of government, municipalities in many countries are not permitted to budget for operating deficits but they are permitted to borrow for capital purposes; however, this is often subject to a variety of controls and restrictions.

In recent years, municipal budgets have become more sophisticated and comprehensive in their design and hence, more useful as a management tool for controlling municipal expenditures and for assisting in municipal decision-making. More emphasis is now placed on the importance and usefulness of designing budgets to reflect past and projected expenditures on outputs or goals to be achieved rather than on the cost of inputs. The establishment of targets or workloads (goals) permits local decision-makers to make decisions on the basis of both efficiency (costs) and effectiveness (returns). Once these targets have been established, municipal spending activities must be monitored to ensure that targets are met or that changes of a justifiable nature are incorporated into the budget. This strengthens accountability because taxpayers are in a better position to evaluate the services provided by the municipality given the cost of producing these services and, therefore, in a better position to judge whether local service provision is effective and efficient.

While the budget is the heart of municipal resource administration, municipal accounting systems and practices and their subsequent reports are central to the budget-making process. For example, past accounting records furnish important data for revenue and expenditure forecasts used to construct the budget. Accounting records provide information on debt and debt service charges and serve as a basis for estimating a municipality's ability to carry further debt. Sound accounting reports provide timely information on whether budget plans are on target or amiss, when capital funds are diverted to operating expenditures, when expenditures are outpacing revenues, and when the municipality is incurring financial obligations beyond its fiscal capacity. The focus of reporting and accounting, then, is to document, classify and summarize transactions so users of the resulting financial reports are able to understand and evaluate municipal operations.

The basic difference between municipal accounting systems and personal/business accounting is the use of fund accounts. Under fund accounting, a separate fund is used to report financial transactions for a particular aspect or activity of government such as water or sewage operations. The fund basis of accounting recognizes that most government assets are not fungible—that is, available for purposes other than those budgeted—and that data on budgeting compliance are an important part of the stewardship responsibility of government. Distinct fund accounting and reporting is necessary to control resources for their designated use and to demonstrate compliance with legal and budgeting constraints affecting municipal governments.

Cash accounting, accrual accounting and modified accrual accounting form three possible accounting bases used by municipalities. Cash accounting, however, is the weakest of these alternatives because it often fails to provide a true or complete picture of the financial health and fiscal sustainability of the municipality. This, and a concern that municipalities do not have reliable information on the age and quality of much of the local infrastructure has motivated senior levels of government in some countries to pass legislation requiring municipalities to move to full accrual accounting or a version of it. This would provide local decision-makers with more reliable information for making efficient and effective decisions in managing municipal assets.

References

Amborski, David. 2013. The Context of Municipal Borrowing in Canada. A Presentation at the Institute of Municipal Finance and Governance, University of Toronto, 2013. Available at http://munkschool.utoronto.ca/imfg/resources/. Accessed 7 July 2019.

Dachis, Benjamin. 2018. *A Roadmap to Municipal Reform: Improving Life in Canadian Cities*. Toronto: CD Howe Institute.

Dafflon, Bernard. 2018. Returning to the Golden Rule of Balanced Budgets: Institutional and Political Economy of Restricting Public Deficits and Debt. IMFG Papers on Municipal Finance and Governance Series, University of Toronto, No 39. Available at http://munkschool.utoronto.ca/imfg/resources/

Gilbert, M., and R. Pike. 1999. Financing Local Government Debt in Canada: Pooled Versus Stand-Alone Issues – An Empirical Study. *Canadian Public Administration* 42: 529–552.

Government Accounting Standards Board (GASB). 2001. New Rules for Reporting Infrastructure Information Enacted for State and Local Governments. Available at www.rutgers.edu/Accounting/raw/gasb/repmodel/infrastructure.html

Holder, William W. 1996. Financial Accounting, Reporting and Auditing. In *Management Policies in Local Government Finance*, ed. J. Richard Aronson and Eli Schwartz, 4th ed., 169–200. Washington, DC: International City Management Association.

International City/County Management Association (ICMA). 2000. *GASB: What It Means For You*, Service Report, Vol. 332, No. 12. Washington, DC: International City/County Management Association.

Johnson, L.E., and D.R. Bean. 1999. GASB Statement No. 34: The Dawn of a New Governmental Financial Reporting Model. *The CPA Journal*. Available at archives.cpajournal.com/1999/1299/f141299a.html

Office of the Controller and Auditor General of New Zealand. 1999. *Reports to Parliament, Second Report for 1999*.

Pallot, June. 2001. Local Government Reform in New Zealand: Options for Public Management as Governance. A Paper Presented at the 1998 International Public Management Network Conference, Salem, Oregon. Available at http://www.impuma.net/research/papers/salem

Reny, Robert A. 1983. Municipal Accounting. In *Budget Management*, ed. Jack Rabin et al. Athens: Carl Vinson Institute of Government.

Riley, Susan L., and Peter W. Colby. 1991. *Practical Government Budgeting*. Albany: State University Press.

Schaeffer, Michael. 2000a. *Municipal Budgeting*. Washington: DC: World Bank Background Series, April.

———. 2000b. *The Budget and Public Sector Performance*. Washington, DC: World Bank, March.

Slack, Enid. 2002. Municipal Finance and The Pattern of Urban Growth. In *Commentary*. Toronto: C.D. Howe Institute.

Solano, Paul L., and Marvin A. Brams. 1996. Budgeting. In *Management Policies in Local Government Finance*, ed. J. Richard Aronson and Eli Schwartz, 4th ed., 125–168. Washington, DC: International City Management Association.

Strategic Alternatives et al. 2001. Financing Water Infrastructure. Issue Paper 14 Commissioned by the Walkerton Inquiry, Toronto, Ontario.

Tassonyi, Almos. 2002. Municipal Budgeting. *Canadian Tax Journal* 50 (1): 181–198.

Weist, Dana. 2002. Borrowing and Capital Financing. A Power Point Presentation on Intergovernmental Fiscal Relations in East Asia, ASEM Sponsored Workshop (World Bank), Bali.

CHAPTER 5

Local Fiscal Discipline

Ernesto Crivelli

5.1 Introduction

Fiscal discipline by various order of government remains an area of major concern in both industrial and developing countries alike. Lack of fiscal prudence by various governments during the past decade have destabilized global economic order and disrupted the lives of millions of ordinary citizens. Fiscal indiscipline at the local level disrupts delivery of basic services to residents and erodes trust in local governance. This chapter is concerned with policy responses to ensure fiscal discipline at the local and state/provincial orders of government. The chapter is organized as follows: Section 5.2 highlights principal features of a multi-order governmental system and other incentives in the public sector that motivate a lack of fiscal discipline and presents a conceptual framework for addressing these issues. Section 5.3 presents informal and non-legal alternatives that may advance fiscal discipline. Section 5.4 describes piecemeal legislative or regulatory or administrative self-imposed or higher-order government-imposed controls. Section 5.5 details comprehensive legislative approaches to such controls. Section 5.6 reviews

This chapter is a revised version of Ernesto Crivelli and Anwar Shah (2009). Promoting Subnational Fiscal Discipline: A Review of Budget Institutions and Their Impact on Fiscal Performance. Unpublished Working Paper, World Bank Institute, Washington, DC.

B. Dollery et al., *Local Public, Fiscal and Financial Governance*,
https://doi.org/10.1007/978-3-030-36725-1_5

evidence on the impact of fiscal rules on subnational fiscal performance. A final section provides concluding remarks.

5.2 Incentives and Motivations for Fiscal Indiscipline at the Local Level

Institutional incentives and information asymmetries play a major part in motivating local governments not to observe prudent fiscal management. Some of the major sources are noted below:

a. *Incomplete contracts and weak citizen-based accountability*. Citizen-residents in numerous countries do not have complete information on local government operations to hold them to account due to a lack of fiscal transparency. Such a situation creates information asymmetries between the citizens and local government. Such a situation also contributes to fiscal illusion by residents as they perceive cost of local government operations to be lower than it actually is. This leads to incomplete contracts as citizens do not have adequate information to hold the local government to account.
b. *Lack of local fiscal and administrative autonomy*. Local governments work best when they are mostly self-financed for municipal services as they must justify any incremental spending by seeking from the local electorate authority to raise additional revenues. This is, however, not the case in the real world as higher-order transfers provide two-thirds of financing in developing countries and one-third of financing in industrial countries. In the absence of revenue autonomy, local governments depend upon higher-order transfers for local finances. This weakens local accountability as it separates local spending and taxing decisions. Under such circumstances, local accountability depends upon the design of transfers. These transfers typically either come as mostly unconditional transfers with little accountability or as highly intrusive regimes that undermine local autonomy. Furthermore, higher-order financing of local governments have also the potential of accentuating the tragedy of the commons where local governments face perverse incentives to indulge in fiscal imprudence by running higher and higher deficit over time to demonstrate higher relative needs for higher-order financing. Such a situation also creates a moral hazard as local

governments expect higher-order bailouts in the event of default and higher-order governments lack the political will to uphold no bailout provisions of the law due to disruption of essential services and their economic, social and political consequences (von Hagen and Eichengreen 1996). These perverse incentives are often compounded by unfunded mandates and lack of administrative discretion in spending and human resource management at the local level.

c. *Weak budgetary institutions and a lack of culture of budget responsibility.* In a majority of developing countries local government budget methods and processes are in their infancy and budgetary institutions are not well developed to promote prudent fiscal management. Political interventions in the budget process make matters worse. This is especially true about public investments as fiscal risks associated with level and methods of financing are not properly assessed.
d. *Lack of separation of legislative and executive functions.* In most local governments legislative council is not able to exercise oversight on the executive as typically the mayor performs dual role of head of both the legislative council and the executive. Further, legislative members typically are elected on a neighborhood basis as opposed to at-large basis and they face strong incentives to seek higher level of financing for their own constituents and in the process place a lower priority on their oversight roles.
e. *Interest group capture.* Interest groups especially land developers play an important role in financing local elections and in the process policy makers become beholden to their agenda to ensure re-election. This capture is compounded when there are no term limits for elected officials.

5.2.1 Conceptual Framework for Fiscal Discipline

Prudent local public expenditure management is considered as a prerequisite to realize good local governance. Basic elements of good public expenditure management are aggregate fiscal discipline, allocative efficiency, operational efficiency, equity and accountability to local residents (see Table 5.1 for elaboration of these concepts). This chapter is focused on aggregate fiscal discipline at the local level.

Table 5.1 Basic elements of local public expenditure management

Aggregate Fiscal Discipline	Aggregate expenditure should be based on deliberative choices made by taking into account revenue including debt constraints and menu of public services to be provided and should be sustainable over the medium and long runs.
Allocative efficiency	Expenditure should be based on a considered view of local priorities and programs that would be most cost effective in delivering those priorities.
Operational efficiency	Government providers should deliver goods and services at least cost and where applicable at competitive prices with market and beyond-government providers.
Equity	Access to local public services should be fair.
Accountability to local residents	Public financial operations should be fully transparent to enable local residents to evaluate the net benefits of these programs.

Source: Authors. See also Schick (1998)

Aggregate fiscal discipline requires that external and internal controls are in place. External controls refer to state and national government and independent audit and inspection agencies and actors that are empowered to examine local government accounts. Internal controls refer to rules and procedures established by local government administration as to how public monies are used and internal auditors that are responsible for checking the adequacy and effectiveness of those controls. Schick (1998) has argued that good public expenditure management requires a number of principles to be followed to ensure aggregate fiscal discipline. These are: Aggregate budget envelope is established in advance of spending decisions and sustainable over the medium and long terms. Local revenue means are consistent with local expenditure needs. Fiscal gap is minimized by exploring additional own source revenues. Operating budget is financed by current revenues and capital budget from borrowing and reserves. Budgeting is linked with planning through medium-term expenditure framework. Debt management framework with associated restraints is finalized and possibly legislatively enacted. In this context, sole reliance on external assessment for credit worthiness such as Standard and Poor's or Moody's may not be prudent as those assessments can place too heavy reliance on broader national macroeconomic considerations rather than local factors. Table 5.2 shows that Moody's assessment places 60% weight on national macroeconomic environment and national government effectiveness.

Table 5.2 Moody's rating criteria for credit worthiness

Aggregate Indicators and sub-indicators (with weights)	*Weights*
Operating environment	60%
GDP per capita (50%	
GDP volatility (25%)	
Government effectiveness index (25%)	
Institutional framework on powers and responsibilities	
Predictability, stability and responsiveness (50%)	
Fiscal flexibility (33.4%)	
Fiscal adequacy (16.6%)	
Financial position and performance	7.5%
Interest payments/operating revenues (25%)	
Cash surplus/total revenues (25%)	
Gross operating balance/operating revenues (25%)	
Net working capital/total expenditures (25%)	
Debt profile	7.5%
Net direct and indirect debt/operating revenues (50%)	
Short-term direct debt/direct debt (25%)	
Four-year trend in net direct and indirect debt/operating revenues (25%)	
Governance and management practices	7.5%
Fiscal management (40%)	
Investment and debt management (20%)	
Transparency and disclosure—Financial statement disclosure (15%	
Transparency and disclosure—Audit (15%)	
Institutional capacity (10%)	
Economic fundamentals	7.5%
GDP per capita	

Source: Qiao et al. (2010)

Ex ante fiscal rules regarding deficit and debt and sanctions for non-compliance are clearly established in laws and regulations. Local government exposures to sources of explicit and implicit fiscal risks as suggested by Brixi (2005) are frequently and rigorously analyzed (see Table 5.3) and methods and processes are in place to detect and deal with early warning signs of fiscal distress as practiced by several countries and a few of the US states (see Table 5.4 for examples).

Table 5.3 Fiscal risk matrix—local government exposures

Sources of risk	*Direct obligation in any event*	*Contingent obligation only if a particular event occurs*
Explicit		
Govt. liability as recognized by a law or contract	Local govt. debt (loans contracted and securities issued by the local government) Arrears in wage and benefits payments (if legal responsibility of the local govt.) Nondiscretionary budgetary spending Expenditures legally binding in the long term (civil service salaries and pensions)	Local govt. guarantees for debt and other obligations of public sector entities Local govt. guarantees for debt and other obligations of non-public sector entities Local govt. guarantees on private investments (infrastructure) Local govt. insurance (crop insurance)
Implicit		
A moral obligation of the government that reflects public and interest group pressures	Remaining capital and future recurrent costs of public investment projects The cost of future benefits under the local social security schemes Future spending on public health and disease control and on goods and services that the local govt. is expected to deliver	Claims related to local govt. letters of comfort Claims to failing financial institutions Claims by various entities to assist on their non-guaranteed debt and their own guarantees, arrears, letters of comfort and other possible obligations Claims related to enterprise restructuring and privatizations Claims by beneficiaries of failed local pension fund, employment fund, or social security fund – Beyond any guaranteed limits Claims related to local crisis management (public health environment, disaster relief, etc.)

Source: Brixi (2005)

Table 5.4 Early warning systems of fiscal stress

Indicators used by several countries

- Debt/revenues (Russia <30% for oblasts and <15% for rayons)
- Debt service/revenues (<25% Italy, Spain; <20% Japan; <15% Russia)
- Deficit/revenue contingent liabilities adjusted for risk as a ratio of total revenues
- Liquid assets/spending needs
- Borrowing requirements/revenues
- Ratio of short-term debt to total debt
- Guarantees to revenue ratio
- Debt dependency ratio: Debt income/total expenditure
- Debt burden ratio = debt to GDP ratio

State of Michigan, United States: 10-point scale fiscal stress indicators for local governments

1. Population growth (2 years)
2. Real taxable value growth (2 years)
3. Large decrease in real taxable value
4. General fund expenditures as a percentage of taxable value
5. General fund operating deficit
6. Prior general fund operating deficits
7. General fund operating balances as percentage of general fund revenues
8. Current year deficit in a major fund
9. Previous year deficit in a major fund
10. General long-term debt as a percentage of real taxable value

State of Ohio, United States, fiscal watch program

- *Fiscal watch*: Local government placed under fiscal watch if deficit exceeds 8.3% of revenue. Requires state auditor to suggest a workout.
- *Fiscal Emergency*: More than 30 days default on debt obligation and/or payment of salaries or deficit or overdue amounts exceed one-sixth of the previous year revenues. Local government placed under a state-appointed control board (planning and supervisory commission).

Columbia's traffic light system for local debt

Indicator	Green light	Yellow light	Red light
Interest payments /savings (liquidity indicator)	<40%	40–60%	>60%
Debt/current income (solvency indicator)	<80%		>80%

Source: Ma et al. (2012), Qiao et al. (2010)

5.3 Alternatives to Fiscal Rules

Fiscal rules are neither necessary nor sufficient to address fiscal indiscipline. Other local institutional factors may play a critical role in ensuring fiscal discipline. These factors are explored in the following paragraphs.

5.3.1 Societal Fiscal Conservatism

A society that places high premium on minimization of economic risk acts as a strong deterrent to fiscal imprudence. This explains the high degree of fiscal prudence shown by local governments in most Western societies.

5.3.2 Citizen-Centric Local Governance

Local governments with high degree of local engagement and local accountability will have strong incentives to minimize fiscal risks.

5.3.3 Strong Budgetary Institutions

Budgetary institutions play an important role in ensuring fiscal discipline. If budgetary institutions work well then fiscal risks are minimized. Von Hagen (2005), based on a review of EU experiences with fiscal rules, concludes that budgetary institutions matter more than fiscal rules. The EU fiscal rules may have encouraged European countries to strengthen budgetary institutions, which in turn had welcome effects on fiscal discipline and fiscal outcomes.

5.3.4 Local Governments Are Self-Financed at the Margin

For local self-discipline, Boadway (2007) has emphasized the need for local governments to be self-financed at the margin. If local governments are primarily self-financed at the margin, they must justify any additional spending by seeking mandate from local electorate for additional taxation commensurate with additional spending. This introduces strong restraints on expansion in local spending.

5.3.5 Reliance on Market Discipline

The greater the discipline that markets can impose on subnational governments (e.g., via financing and credit ratings), the lesser the need for budget constraints imposed from the center (Ter-Minassian 2006). As Lane (1993) points out, however, there are a number of preconditions for effectiveness of market discipline on subnational governments. First, market participants need access to all the information required to evaluate the financial soundness of each government. Second, markets should be free and open, with no regulation on financial intermediaries that could place subnational governments in a privileged-borrower position. Third, there should not be a history or expectation of bailouts by subnational governments. Otherwise, the incentives for discipline faced by local authorities are weakened. Finally, subnational governments need to have an adequate base of own resources. Subnational governments should be able to finance additional spending by rising own revenue, as this increases accountability to local constituencies.

These conditions are difficult to attain and unlikely to apply simultaneously. Subnational governments may rely on "creative accounting" and "window dressing" to create ambiguity regarding the true assessment of the government finances (Balassone et al. 2003). The hard budget constraint condition may lack credibility, especially in those countries where the public sector plays an important role in providing public services and goods (Wildasin 1997). In addition, the reaction time of decentralized fiscal authorities may be excessively long (Blondal 1999).

Market discipline is, however, the main form of control is some countries. In Finland, for example, no administrative or legal restrains apply to domestic or foreign borrowing. Moreover, there are no budget balance requirements for subnational governments (state governments). The provincial governments in Canada have no constitutional or legal limits on their borrowing (both domestic and external), and are not subject to central government controls on it. Their debt and debt-servicing capacity are closely monitored by financial markets, in particular by major debt-rating agencies. However, most provinces require balanced budget on annual basis. Moreover, there are strict limits on borrowing by local governments. These include prior approval by the provincial government or restrictions to specific purposes, like capital spending.

Among developing countries, Mexico has established ex ante, market-based mechanisms in order to prevent excessive subnational borrowing. The new regulatory framework of year 2000 has four main components (Braun and Tommasi 2002): (i) the federal government gave up its role in securing debt, (ii) subnational debt is subject to normal credit exposure ceilings, (iii) bank's capital risk weighting of loans to subnational governments is linked to the international rating of the borrowing government's creditworthiness, and (iv) the federal government has restricted the use of discretionary transfers (Webb 2004). Note, however, that central government's approval is still required for borrowing by local governments.

5.3.6 *Cooperative Arrangements*

With cooperative solutions, all levels of government must be involved in formulating the objectives of economic policy and be responsible for their attainment. In these cases, the incentive problem, namely how to make politicians accountable is addressed through moral suasion and peer pressure. The main advantage of this approach is that it promotes dialogue across levels of governments, while enhancing local policy makers' awareness about the macroeconomic implications of their budgetary choices (Ter-Minassian 2006).

Commonwealth-state fiscal coordination in Australia offers important lessons for federal countries. Australia established a loan council in 1927 as an instrument of credit allocation since it restricted state governments to borrow only from the commonwealth. An important exception to this rule was that states could, however, use borrowing by autonomous agencies and local government for own purposes. This exception proved to be the Achilles' heel for the Commonwealth Loan Council, as states used this exception extensively in their attempt to by-pass the cumbersome procedures and control over their capital spending plans by the Council. The Commonwealth Government ultimately recognized in 1993 that central credit allocation policy was a flawed and ineffective instrument. It lifted restrictions on state borrowing and reconstituted the Loan Council so that it could serve as a coordinating agency for information exchange so as to ensure greater market accountability. The New Australian Loan Council attempts to provide a greater flexibility to states to determine their own borrowing requirements and attempts to coordinate borrowing with fiscal needs and overall macro strategy. It further instills a greater understanding of the budgetary process and provides timely and valuable information to the financial markets on public sector borrowing plans. The process seems to be working well so far (see Shah 2006).

Some European countries have also adopted cooperative solutions. In Austria, the Domestic Stability Pact of 2001 establishes a national committee, which represents all levels of government, and eight regional committees. These have advisory, coordination, supervision, planning, and implementation responsibilities and are the main information channel among governments. The pact requires all authorities involved to provide proper flows of information concerning their budgetary positions. In Belgium, the High Finance Council (Conseil Superieur des Finances, CSF) sets yearly guidelines for the expenditure growth and the deficit level of each level of government (federal, regions, communities). The regions can levy supplements on national taxes, but they have to consult the federal government and the other regions. In Denmark, bilateral discussions are held with subnational governments, and rules are both set and enforced cooperatively by the association of regional governments. In Spain, a supervisory Council for Fiscal and Financial Policy, composed by officials from central government's Ministry of Finance and subnational governments, monitors implementation and is required to ratify delinquent governments' action plans.

5.4 Rules-Based Control

Fiscal rules have attracted significant attention over the last three decades, as several countries have adopted them in an attempt to eliminate large deficits and reduce public sector debts. Kennedy and Robbins (2001) define "fiscal rule" as a statutory or constitutional restriction on fiscal policy that sets a specific limit on a fiscal indicator such as the budgetary balance, debt or spending.

Fiscal rules (and budgetary institutions in general) have been emphasized in the literature because of their impact on the fiscal results.[1] Fiscal rules refer to *numerical* fiscal rules but also to procedural and transparency rules. Numerical fiscal rules introduce ceilings (numerical restrictions) on certain fiscal indicators and limitations on contracting debt. These restrictions can differ according to the fiscal performance indicator to which they relate, to the legal hierarchy of the rule that establishes them, or to their coverage (Filc and Scartascini 2007). Procedural and transparency rules aim to enhance transparency, accountability, and fiscal management. They typically require the government to commit up front to a monitorable fiscal policy strategy, usually for a multi-year period, and to routinely report and publish fiscal outcomes and strategy changes (Ter-Minassian 2006).

[1] See, for example, Alesina et al. (1998), Poterba and von Hagen (1999), von Hagen and Harden (1995), Hallerberg et al. (2004).

Fiscal rules can be adopted by governments at the national or subnational level. The aim of this chapter is to review fiscal rules implemented at subnational level. Subnational fiscal rules may be imposed by a higher level of government, or subnational governments may adopt them themselves, where constitutional arrangements grant them the autonomy to do so. In cases where subnational governments enjoy great autonomy (legal or de facto), the central government can find it difficult to enforce effective budget constraints on them.

A number of reasons make the adoption of fiscal rules at subnational level particularly important and distinguish them from the adoption of fiscal rules at national level. In particular, subnational fiscal rules can help mitigate the "common pool problem" in a federation, which results from the fact that the costs of fiscal indiscipline by one or more subnational governments are likely to spill over to the others. Fiscal rules are also crucial to avoid moral hazard created by the expectation of bailouts. Subnational governments facing soft budget constraints face weak incentives for fiscal responsibility since the costs of indiscipline are transferred to the national budget (Wildasin 1997; Crivelli and Staal 2013).

Fiscal rules and their adoption at subnational level have evolved over the time. The first wave acknowledges the adoption of fiscal rules in some federal systems, where subnational governments implemented limits on borrowing up to the level of capital spending. This so-called golden rule, that is, borrowing only for capital spending and not for operating expenditures (operating budget must be in balance), was adopted by most states and local governments in the United States since the mid-nineteenth century and several cantons in Switzerland since the 1920s. A second wave, starting with New Zealand's Fiscal Responsibility Act of 1994, gives particular importance to procedural rules, including high accounting and reporting standards, increased transparency, and a medium-term macro-budgetary framework. In recent years, a number of legislations, most prominently Brazil's Fiscal Responsibility Law of 2000, have attempted to set a framework of budgetary planning, execution and reporting, with strong emphasis on procedural and transparency rules, but also containing numerical ceilings on selected fiscal indicators and sanctions for non-compliance of the rules.

5.4.1 *Numerical Fiscal Rules*

Numerical rules are a permanent constraint on fiscal policy generally defined in terms of an indicator of overall fiscal performance. They refer to specific quantitative limits. Numerical rules can help contain a deficit or expenditure bias, and address time inconsistency problems. However, they also introduce policy inflexibility and may create incentives to resort to low-quality measures to meet numerical targets. For example, in some countries the application of numerical rules has led to creative accounting practices aimed at circumventing the rules, including reclassification of expenditures, accumulation of arrears, and the use of off-budget public entities to perform government operations (Ter-Minassian 2006). The following paragraphs discuss numerical fiscal rules in terms of balance budget requirements and borrowing constraints.

5.4.1.1 Budget Balance Requirements

At the subnational government level, budget balance requirements can vary across several dimensions. The first relates to the targeted aggregate such as the current budget, the current budget and capital account and the off-budget items. Note that targeting the current budget alone allows sub-central governments to borrow for public investment. The second important dimension refers to the time horizon for budget balance requirements. Although usually annual, in some countries the budget periods have moved to a multi-annual basis. Table 5.5 presents a summary of the budget balance requirements for selected countries.

Budget balance requirements can be targeted to specific types of spending. Targeting current spending alone, which allows subnational government borrowing to finance public investment, is common in some industrial countries. This is, for example, the case in the German states (Laender), Switzerland, regions in Italy, and municipalities in Denmark. In the United States, all but two states have provisions requiring a balanced budget, in most cases targeting current spending only. In Canada, self-imposed fiscal rules cover the operating budget in every local and provincial jurisdiction (Kennedy and Robbins 2001). In Austria, the consolidated state governments accounts have to reach a surplus of 0.75% of GDP, and financially stronger states have agreed to contribute more to the overall target. In the Czech Republic, Korea, Poland, and Turkey, the balance budget requirement for local governments also applies to capital spending. In China, the Budget Law of 1994 requires local governments to have balanced budgets and restricts subnational governments from borrowing in financial markets and issuing bonds.

Budget balance requirements are frequently set on an annual basis. In some countries, however, the provisions estipulate a multi-annual

Table 5.5 Budget balance requirements in selected countries

	Covered budget			*Duration*		*Carry-over*	*Application/Implementation*		
	Only current	*Current + capital*	*+Off-budget items*	*Annual*	*Multi-annual*	*Allowed*	*Imposed*	*Negotiated binding*	*Self-imposed*
Advanced countries									
Australia					x			x	
Austria		x	x (state)		x			DSP	
Canada	X				x (local)	x	x (local)		x (state)
Denmark	x (local)			x			x		
Finland	x (local)				x		x		
France	X			x			x		
Germany	x (state)			x			x (local)		x (state)
Italy	x (region)			x		x	DSP		
Japan	x (local)			x					x
Netherlands	x (local)				x	x (local)	x (local)		
New Zealand	x (local)				x			x	
Norway	x (local)				x		x		
Portugal		x (local)		x			x		
Spain		x	x		x	x	x (local)	DSP	
Sweden	x (local)			x			x		
Switzerland	X			x					x
United Kingdom	X				x		x		
United States	X			x					x
Developing countries									
Argentina	X				x				FRL
Brazil	X						FRL		

Chile	X				x	x		x	
Colombia	X			x			FRL		
Ecuador	X				x		FRL		
India	X				x				FRL
Korea		x		x			x		
Peru	x				x	x	FRL		
Turkey		x (local)					x		
Transition countries									
China	x								
Croatia	x								
Czech Republic		x		x			x		
Estonia	x								
Hungary	x (local)								
Kazakhstan	x								
Poland		x	x	x			x		
Russia	x								
Slovenia	x								

Source: Crivelli and Shah (2009). Notes: *DSP* Domestic Stability Pact, *FRL* Fiscal Responsibility Law

balanced budget. This is the case, for example, in Australia, Austria, local governments in Canada, Finland, Norway, and Spain. In the Netherlands and Spain, the budget period is three years, with specified annual targets. In Canada, the provinces of New Brunswick and Saskatchewan are required to balance their budgets over a four-year period. Carry-over rules are considered in some countries. In the Netherlands, a municipality can be allowed to run a deficit in a given year as long as the budget is balanced over the three-year period. In Spain, if a subnational government runs a deficit, it must submit an action plan to resolve the situation within four years. In Canada, deficits are permitted in the provinces of Nova Scotia, Quebec, and Ontario as long as they are offset in the next fiscal year.

5.4.1.2 Borrowing Constraints

Both federal and unitary countries have relied on rules specified in the constitution or in laws to control subnational government's borrowing. Instead of relying on market discipline or cooperative arrangements, the constraints analyzed here include clear limits on the level of indebtedness of subnational governments (in absolute terms or limiting borrowing to specific purposes). We also consider cases of direct control of the central government over subnational borrowing (approval, review, and authorization or prohibition). Table 5.6 presents a summary of these controls internationally, and Table 5.7 presents as to how selected US states assess local government debt affordability.

Several countries impose specific limits on the level of indebtedness. Regions in Italy are allowed to borrow domestically only if debt service does not exceed 25% of the sum of regional own revenue, net of health contributions and the Common Fund. Municipal and local governments are subject to ex ante ceilings on borrowing. The central government in Bolivia can set annual limits on borrowing and debt service for the municipalities. In the Philippines, debt servicing must not exceed 20% of regular income. Most of the Fiscal Responsibility Legislations (Argentina, Brazil, Colombia, Ecuador, India, and Peru) establish limits on either the level of indebtedness or debt service of state and municipal governments (see Sect. 5.5). In Poland, no borrowing is allowed if general government debt exceeds 60% of GDP. Upper limits on the total amount of debt and debt service were introduced in Albania, Estonia, Hungary, Slovakia, Russia, and Kazakhstan.[2] In Estonia, for example, for borrowing in excess of

[2] For a survey of the rules on subnational borrowing in transition economies, see, for example, Wetzel and Dunn (2001) and Dabla-Norris and Wade (2002).

Table 5.6 Subnational borrowing controls in selected countries

	Market discipline	*Rule based control*			*Administrative control/prior approval*	*Prohibition*	
		Limit on debt	*Limit on debt service*	*Specific purpose*		*Domestic*	*Foreign/Abroad*
Industrial countries							
Austria				X	X		
Canada	X			X (local)	X (local)		
Denmark				X		X (local)	
Finland	X						
France				X (local)			
Germany				X	X		
Greece					X (local)		
Ireland					X (local)		
Italy		X	X	X			X
Japan					X		
Norway				X (local)	X		
Portugal				X (local)			
Spain			X	X	X		
Sweden				X			
Switzerland				X			
UK				X (local)	X (local)		
USA				X			
Developing countries							
Argentina		X		X			
Bahamas						X	X
Bolivia		X	X	X	X		

(*continued*)

Table 5.6 (continued)

	Market discipline	*Rule based control*			*Administrative control/prior approval*	*Prohibition*	
		Limit on debt	*Limit on debt service*	*Specific purpose*		*Domestic*	*Foreign/Abroad*
Brazil		X	X	X			
Chile				X	X		
Colombia		X	X	X			
Costa Rica				X	X		
Ecuador		X	X	X	X		
El Salvador				X	X		
Ethiopia					X		X
Guatemala				X	X		
Guyana				X	X		
Honduras				X	X		
India		X	X	X			
Jamaica					X		
Korea				X	X		
Mexico	X				X (local)		
Panama				X	X		
Paraguay				X	X		
Peru		X	X	X	X		
Surinam						X	X
Thailand						X	X
Trinidad and Tobago				X	X		
Turkey					X (local)		
Transition countries							
Albania		X					

Armenia			X				X
Azerbaijan						X	X
Belarus			X				
Bosnia						X	X
Bulgaria		X					
People's Republic of China				X			
Croatia				X	X		
Czech Republic	X						
Estonia		X	X	X			
Georgia					X		X
Hungary			X	X (local)			
Kazakhstan		X	X	X			X
Kyrgyz Republic		X			X		
Latvia		X			X		
Lithuania		X			X		
Poland			X		X		
Romania			X				
Russian Federation		X	X	X			X
Slovakia	X						
Slovenia		X		X			
Tajikistan						X	X
Ukraine					X		X
Uzbekistan						X	X

Source: Crivelli and Shah (2009)

Table 5.7 How US states assess local government debt affordability

Indicators	*Number of states*	*Alaska*	*California*	*Florida*	*Louisiana*	*Maine*	*Maryland*	*North Carolina*	*Oregon*	*Vermont*	*Virginia*	*Washington*	*West Virgina*
Direct debt as % of assessed value of taxable property	1												X
Direct debt per capita	7		X	X		X			X	X	X		X
Direct debt as % of personal income (also per capita)	9		X	X		X	X	X	X	X	X		X
GO debt as % of market value of taxable property	1					X							
Debt service as a% general fund and special revenues	12	X	X	X	X	X	X	X	X	X	X	X	X
Budget revenues as % of general revenues	1			X									
% of net debt paid in 10 years	2					X		X					
New debt authorization not greater than redemptions	1						X						
Estimated market capacity	1		X										

Source: Ma et al. (2012)

12 months, the stock of debt must not exceed 75% of projected last year's revenues and debt service payments not exceed 20% of projected revenues. In Kazakhstan, borrowing in any year cannot exceed 10% of local revenue, total debt cannot exceed 25% of local revenue and expenditure on debt service must not exceed 10% of local revenues in that year. Additionally, Romania and Bulgaria have established limits on the annual amount of short-term loans. In Armenia, the annual interest payments for earlier borrowing should not exceed 20% of local budget's reserve fund. In Belarus, debt obligations must be repayable within a year.

Borrowing constraints are typically imposed on certain types of spending. Rules that limit subnational governments' borrowing to investment purposes (the so-called golden rule) are quite common in industrial countries. This is, for example, the case in the German states (Laender), Switzerland, regions in Italy, municipalities in Denmark, and in the majority of the state constitutions in the United States.[3] In Spain, local authorities can borrow up to 30% of current revenues to cover short-term liquidity needs, while long-term borrowing is restricted to capital investment. Among developing countries, subnational borrowing is limited to investment purposes in the majority of Latin American countries (Daughters and Harper 2007), and several Eastern European countries.

Prior approval of subnational borrowing from higher levels of government is also quite widespread (Sutherland et al. 2005). In Norway and Spain, prior authorization can be imposed when subnational governments breach agreed deficits, or the proposed borrowing is substantial. In Belgium, regions and communities can issue bonds, but they must have the approval of central government. In Germany, borrowing by the communities (local governments) is subject to approval by the Laender authorities. Local governments in the United Kingdom and Canada need to obtain central and provincial government approval respectively before borrowing. The limit is based on the amounts required to meet capital expenditure needs less available funds from own sources for such expenditures. Also in Japan, the Ministry of Home Affairs supervises and controls all local authority borrowing and it is generally approved only to finance investment needs or emergency expenditure. Turkey requires permission to borrow in foreign currency. Prior approval is required in most Latin American countries, either at provincial

[3] In practice, however, there are weaknesses in both the formulation and application of the law. The investment requirements are specified ex ante rather than ex post, and the interpretation of what constitutes investments is flexible. At the same time, the extent of market discipline is muted by the fact that the federal government has provided assistance to Laender experiencing debt-service problems. For an empirical assessment, see Heppke-Falk and Wolff (2008).

or local level. In Korea, all borrowing proposals require the prior approval of local councils and the Ministry of Home Affairs. The procedures specify which local governments can borrow and which projects are eligible (usually capital investment). In Ethiopia, state governments are legally empowered to borrow domestically subject to terms and conditions set by the center.

Subnational borrowing is prohibited in some countries. Foreign borrowing is not permitted to subnational governments in Italy. Thailand, The Bahamas, and Suriname legally prohibit subnational (provincial, district, town, and village) governments from foreign or domestic borrowing. In Ethiopia, state and local governments are not allowed to borrow abroad. The same prohibition applies to Bosnia and Herzegovina, Macedonia, and most countries in the Commonwealth of Independent States.

5.4.2 *Procedural Rules*

Procedural rules are aimed to enhance transparency, accountability and fiscal management. The key elements of this approach are increased transparency and greater accountability, based on high accounting and statistical standards, monitoring by higher levels of government or independent councils, and periodic reporting. They typically require the government to commit up front to a monitorable fiscal policy strategy, usually for a multi-year period, and to report and publish fiscal outcomes and strategy changes on a routine basis. The successful implementation of procedural rules requires modern budget systems and a high degree of fiscal transparency, and a substantial constituency for fiscal discipline and responsibility (Ter-Minassian 2006).

New Zealand pioneered this approach. Its Fiscal Responsibility Act of 1994 mainly focuses on procedures. It dictates a set of principles that governments must follow to achieve responsible fiscal management. The government has to publish a budget policy statement with long-term objectives, strategic priorities and fiscal goals for the next three months before the start of each financial year. Additionally, the government has to present in May–June a Fiscal Strategy Report assessing the consistency of the budget with the budget policy statement, a ten-year outlook and three-year economic and fiscal update, as well as half-year and current-year updates. Governments may temporarily depart from the principles but must do so publicly, explain why they have departed, and reveal how and when they intend to conform to the principles. The FRA does not include any sanctions for non-compliance, but accountability rules are very precise, establishing the responsibilities of the public officials.

The UK Code for Fiscal Stability of 1998 sets principles of responsible fiscal management that must be adhered to in the formulation and implementation of fiscal policy. An independent Audit Commission is in charge of monitoring local governments and making the results public in annual audit letters. Additionally, it contemplates a set of Best Value performance indicators to assess the quality of local service provision. The Code for Fiscal Stability is supported by numerical rules not contained in the Code.

As noted by Sutherland et al. (2005), most of the industrial countries and some developing and transition countries have been making great efforts to increase accountability by including requirements for transparency in financial accounting and improving the quality of monitoring and reporting of budget accounts at subnational level. Some countries have established reporting standards (Denmark, Finland, Czech Republic, the German states, the Netherlands, Norway, Poland, Portugal, Turkey). Almost all countries have implemented independent auditing (by the central government or an independent council) and submission deadlines for subnational budgets.

In some cases, as in Austria and Spain, it was during the negotiations concerning the implementation of a Domestic Stability Pact that a great deal of attention was focused on how to evaluate budgetary outcomes. This decision goes in the direction of setting common accounting standards for all levels of government and of harmonizing accounting standards in a way which makes national rules compatible with those applied at the European level. In some other cases, procedural rules were contemplated in Fiscal Responsibility Laws (Argentina, Brazil, Colombia, Ecuador, Peru, India). In Australia, procedural rules are part of cooperative arrangements between different levels of government.

5.5 Fiscal Responsibility Legislation

Recognizing the limited scope for improvement that stand-alone fiscal rules can provide, and the frequent lack of immediate results from enhanced transparency alone, fiscal responsibility laws (FRLs) have been enacted in many countries as permanent institutional devices to promote fiscal discipline in a credible, predictable, and transparent manner. It refers to cases where FRL provisions are contained in a single law and does not cover other public finance legislation, such as budget laws or stand-alone legislated fiscal rules.

Provisions for subnational governments can be adopted either with a top-down or a bottom-up approach. In a top-down approach, FRLs are national laws that also apply to subnational levels of government. In a bottom-up approach, the national government passes a FRL only for itself, setting incentives for subnational governments to follow. Brazil, Colombia and Peru are examples of a top-down approach, while India and Argentina have followed a bottom-up approach.

The main distinguishing features of FRLs are (Corbacho and Schwartz 2007):

- combine procedural rules with numerical rules (see Sect. 5.4)
- set up transparent mechanisms by which others can judge if the government is complying with established goals and priorities
- include sanctions for non-compliance, escape clauses—that limit the application of the FRLs during exceptional circumstances—and cyclical considerations (e.g., stabilization funds, multi-annual horizons)

We consider the main characteristics and implications of Fiscal Responsibility Rules for subnational governments in Argentina, Brazil, Colombia, Ecuador, Peru and India.

Argentina first adopted a FRL in 1999 to help maintain confidence in the currency board arrangement in an environment of significant fiscal pressures and poor growth prospects. The FRL followed a bottom-up approach, inviting subnational governments to pass their own fiscal responsibility legislation. The law was modified twice in 2000 and 2004 to provide for a longer period of convergence to fiscal balance. The revised law of 2004 (called the Federal Regime of Fiscal Responsibility) has been ratified by 20 provinces (out of 23) and the city of Buenos Aires. India's Fiscal Responsibility and Budget Management Act (FRBMA) was enacted in 2003. As in Argentina, it follows a bottom-up approach and, therefore, it is applicable to the national government only. Before the Twelfth Finance Commission, five states passed fiscal responsibility legislation and after that, fiscal responsibility legislation has become mandatory for states, with incentives being offered to states to pass FRLs. All states are in the process of putting the required legislation in place (Liu and Waibel 2008).

Within a top-down approach, Brazil passed the FRL in May 2000. It is considered the most comprehensive and effective stabilization program implemented to date. This law applies to all orders of government and sets limits on current spending, ceilings on borrowing, multi-year budget targets, and limits on loan guarantees, as well as explicitly defined sanctions for non-compliance (Shah 2006). In a new attempt to stabilize subnational finances, Colombia passed two Laws, the first in 2000 called Subnational Fiscal Responsibility Law (Oliva 2001), and the second applicable to all levels of government (the Organic Law of Fiscal Transparency and Responsibility) in 2003, containing both procedural and numerical rules. Ecuador's FRL was passed in late 2002, with the main goals of establishing numerical rules limiting expenditure growth, dictating the saving of fiscal revenues from the new oil pipeline, and improving the transparency of the budget process. Several modifications of the law were introduced in 2005, mainly changing the numerical targets specified previously. Finally, Peru enacted the Fiscal Responsibility and Transparency Law in 2003 and the General Debt Law in 2005, while embarking on decentralization, with the main objective to avoid a subnational debt crisis as experienced by other countries in the region.

The main implications of the FRLs for subnational governments are analyzed in terms of (i) the type of numerical rules implemented, (ii) the procedural rules established, and (iii) the sanctions for non-compliance.

5.5.1 FRL Numerical Rules

Argentina (Corbacho and Schwartz 2007): (i) all jurisdictions are required to balanced revenue and expenditure, excluding investment in basic social and economic infrastructure,[4] (ii) debt service cannot exceed 15% of net revenues for states and the city of Buenos Aires.

Brazil: (i) outlays on payroll (including social security benefits, pensions, and payments to subcontractors) cannot exceed 60% of net revenues, (ii) the ratio of net public debt-to-net revenues cannot exceed 2 for states, and 1.2 for municipalities, (iii) if the ceilings are exceeded, measures must be taken within 12 months, (iv) credit operations cannot exceed capital expenses.

Colombia: (i) the ratio of primary surplus to interest payments has to be equal or higher than 100%, (ii) the ratio of interest payments to operational savings should not exceed 40%, (iii) the ratio of debt stock to current revenues should not exceed 80%, (iv) upper limit on the expenditure of state's legislatures, local councils, and municipal comptroller offices, and caps on wages of legislators and comptroller officials. Additionally, primary current expenditure must be exclusively financed by non-earmarked current revenues, and should not exceed a fixed percentage, depending on the state or municipality category.

[4] However, capital spending and current spending financed by international financial institutions (IFIs) are not covered by the limits.

Ecuador: (i) the ratio of debt service to total revenues cannot exceed 40%, (ii) the ratio of total liabilities to total revenues should not exceed 100%, (iii) explicit multi-year targets for debt reduction.

India (Liu and Waibel 2008): (i) a state with debt service ratio exceeding 20% is classified as having a debt-stress status, triggering the central government's close monitoring of additional borrowing by the state, (ii) revenue deficit should be eliminated, (iii) the fiscal deficit has to be reduced to 3% of gross state domestic product by fiscal year 2009, (iv) borrowing is allowed only for long-term public capital investments.

Additionally, the laws establish annual intermediate deficit reduction targets. The Debt Restructuring and Relief Facility, covering 2005–2009, rewards states for revenue deficit reduction with debt restructuring and relief.

Peru: (i) the three-year average primary balance must be positive, (ii) the total debt service-to-current revenues ratio must be below 25%, (iii) the total debt-to-current revenues ratio must be below 100%, and (iv) subnational governments need central government's guarantee to contract external debt, which must be allocated to finance infrastructure.

5.5.2 FRL Procedural Rules

In general, all FRLs set detailed provisions on the formulation and implementation of the budget and regulates intergovernmental relations. The laws define minimum reporting requirements for the budgets of all levels of government.

In Argentina, the law of 2004 established a Federal Council for Fiscal Responsibility. The federal government must send to the council the targets and debt limits for each level of government, wage and tax policy and revenue projections for the budget year. The law also requires transparent fiscal reporting, which have to be published on the website, along with quarterly budget execution and debt reports. The budget balance requirements are set on a multi-annual basis. In Brazil, the government has to present a brief account of budget execution every two months and report on budget management every four months, identifying remedial policies to achieve fiscal targets if needed. The targets for revenue, expenditures, and indebtedness are set on a three-year basis. In Colombia, the government must present a medium-term fiscal framework stating fiscal and macroeconomic objectives and explanations and deviations from previously set targets. In Ecuador, a four-year plan with goals and strategies must be presented by the government and periodical report on the progress of the plan is required. The central government in India has to present a Medium-Term Fiscal Policy Statement containing three-year rolling targets for key fiscal parameters that underpin the government's fiscal correction trajectory. According to Peru Fiscal Decentralization Law (2004), regional and local governments are required to prepare detailed multi-year budgetary frameworks that are consistent with the national government's multi-year budget framework.

5.5.3 FRL Sanctions

In Argentina, the Federal government has some discretion in the application of sanctions that may include: (i) restriction from voting in the Federal Council of Fiscal Responsibility, (ii) limits on guarantees and new credit operations from the national government, and (iii) limits on discretionary transfers from the national government.

Enforcement mechanism in Brazil include fiscal sanctions, fines, imprisonment and impeachment, but also nullifications of contracts or administrative decisions and prison terms ranging from three months to four years. Among the fiscal sanctions, if the wage expenditures reach 95% of the ceiling, wage increases, overtime, and new hiring (except in health, education or social security) are suspended (see Annex A1 for details).

In Colombia, non-compliance with the rules implies that the debt level of this subnational government is classified as non-sustainable and any new debt issuance must be approved by the ministry of finance. An adjustment program to seek eventual compliance with all indicators is required. Personal sanctions for public officials also apply according to the Disciplinary Law. Colombia also fosters market enforcement mechanisms by applying bankruptcy procedures to municipalities and requiring main municipalities and departments to obtain credit ratings from private companies.

In Ecuador, subnational governments that fail to maintain updated information cannot access domestic or external credit and failure to provide information within 15 days of the deadline imposed by the FRL will result in the suspension of the transfer of budget appropriations. Depending on the official's rank, the FRL determines administrative sanctions, in addition to the civil and criminal penalties that derive from other laws.

In case of non-compliance, subnational governments in Peru are restricted from access to intergovernmental funds. The National

Decentralization Council can deny access for 90 days to conditional transfers to regions not complying with the fiscal rules during two consecutive years. The central government can intervene with a regional government that is placing in danger the non-financial public sector finances.

5.6 The Impact of Fiscal Rules on Subnational Fiscal Performance

5.6.1 Empirical Evidence

In this section, we review the impact of fiscal rules on subnational fiscal management. In a survey of recent empirical studies, Kennedy and Robbins (2001) argue that for industrial countries, the evidence is not conclusive. Fiscal consolidation, they argue, has occurred in countries with and without fiscal rules, implying that these rules are not a necessary condition for fiscal adjustment. Using a panel of 31 countries, Fornasari et al. (2000) find that constraining subnational borrowing does not seem to have any consistent effect on subnational fiscal deficits. In contrast, Rodden (2002) concluded that the largest deficits are run by subnational governments that rely heavily on federal transfers and at the same time are free to borrow. Singh and Plekhanov (2005) used data from 44 countries (industrial, developing and transition countries) for the period 1982–2000. They find that fiscal rules adopted by subnational governments themselves seem to lead to better fiscal outcomes at low levels of vertical fiscal imbalance. As vertical fiscal imbalances widen, however, they find that centrally imposed rules are the best option to control subnational borrowing. Moreover, they find that the existence of a bailout history significantly erodes the effectiveness of centrally imposed fiscal rules.

In the following, we describe some experiences with subnational fiscal rules and its impact on fiscal management.

In Norway, 18% of municipalities had a deficit each year during the period 1980–1998, on average, and by 2006, 95 out of 434 municipalities and 5 out of 19 counties are facing administrative sanctions due to non-compliance with the balance-budget requirement. Likewise, in Sweden and Finland, only approximately two-thirds and three-quarters of the municipalities, respectively, achieved balance in 2001. In Spain, fiscal outcomes remained strong after the introduction of the Domestic Stability Pact. However, 11 out of 17 regional governments ran a deficit in 2003, despite the requirement of balanced budget or surplus at subnational government level. The consolidated regional deficit remained relatively contained in terms of national GDP, but the relatively widespread violation of the budget target in the first year of application of the law raised questions regarding the effectiveness of the framework in promoting fiscal discipline.

Fiscal rules have in some cases been circumvented by creative accounting techniques. In Italy, local deficits have been partly financed by arrears to suppliers. Similarly, in China, subnational governments have borrowed from local banks and enterprises, although they are not, in principle, allowed to borrow for current spending on their own account (see Shah 2013 for local borrowing crisis in China and associated policy responses).

In Australia, the cooperative framework was redesigned in the mid-1990s in response to the increased use of sophisticated financing techniques, such as financial leases, to circumvent Loan Council borrowing limits. In New Zealand, fiscal outcomes improved markedly after the adoption of the FRA of 1994, although they had started to improve a few years before the enactment of the law. The fiscal balance has remained in surplus since 1994, reaching nearly 3% of GDP in 2003, and net debt declined to 12% of GDP, from over 50% a decade earlier.

Although many provinces have balanced budget legislations in Canada, provincial debt loads have only decreased somewhat in aggregate—the largest province, Ontario is, however, operating with a large deficit after suspending its balanced budget rules used for several years since 1999. Similarly, the oil-rich province of Alberta has run deficits in all but one year since 2008–2009 and its net financial assets have declined more or less steadily since $35 billion in 2007–2008 to become net debt in 2016–2017 and the net debt is continuing to grow as the province continues to run deficits and is expected to do so for a few more years.

Poterba and Reuben (1999) find that in the United States, those states with weak anti-deficit provisions face borrowing costs 10 to 15 basis points higher than similar states with stricter anti-deficit rules. Furthermore, a state with binding tax limitation rules would face, on average, a borrowing rate 15 to 20 basis points higher than those which do not have a tax limitation law. A state with an expenditure limitation law in contrast, will face a borrowing rate several basis points lower than that of states without any fiscal limits (Joumard and Kongsrud 2003). Also Poterba (1994) finds that more restrictive state fiscal institutions, particularly annual balanced budget requirements and tax and expenditure limits, are correlated with more rapid fiscal adjustment to unexpected deficits. An interesting feature of Poterba's findings is that more stringent state constraints are related to the state putting more responsibility on its local governments. von Hagen (1991) examines the effectiveness of debt limits and balanced budget requirements in the states by comparing fiscal performance indicators in states with and without debt limits and in states with varying degrees of strictness in terms of their balanced budget requirements. He finds that there is a higher percentage of states with high ratios of non-guaranteed to guaranteed debt in the state groups with debt limits or with more stringent budget requirements (debt limits routinely restrict only guaranteed debt and balanced budget requirements only target on-budget or general account activities). This assertion is, however, refuted by Bohn and Inman (1996), who find that tighter balanced budget rules are associated with higher state surpluses.

5.6.2 *The Experience with Fiscal Responsibility Legislation*

Fiscal responsibility legislation covering Canadian local governments is extensive and quite successful (at least in avoiding serious financial problems).

In Argentina, the numerical rules established in the subnational FRLs of 1999 were never respected, and fiscal performance continued to deteriorate. By the end of 2001, Argentina faced the deepest crisis in its history and the FRL became completely non-operational. The law was modified in 2001 and again in 2004.

Fiscal performance in Brazil remained strong after adopting the FRL, although it had already started to improve before the implementation of the law. The fiscal performance of subnational governments has improved markedly over the last few years. The average ratio of debt to net revenue declined from 3.8 in 1998 to 1.9 in 2001. From year 2000 to 2002, 18 states improved their primary surplus, 8 states turned from deficit to surplus, and only 3 states reported primary deficits in 2002. By 2005, all states had achieved primary surplus, all had restrained personnel expenditures to 50% of current revenues, and all states and municipalities had reduced debt burdens. Only 5 of 27 states (including the federal district) are still above the ceiling of 200% of revenues, owing to the 2002 currency devaluation. Of municipalities, 92% have reduced debt below 1.2 times revenue levels, and only a handful of large municipalities have unsustainable debt levels (Shah 2008).

In Colombia, local governments ran deficits through the 1990s, but posted a small surplus in 2001 and achieved a surplus of 1.3% of GPD in

2004 after the FRL was passed in 2003. In Peru, fiscal performance improved in the most recent periods, but the numerical target on the real growth of non-financial expenditures was breached in 2003 and in 2004. Although it is too early to judge the effects of the FRL in India, initial results appear promising, and several states have been successful in reducing operative deficits. More important, this legislation is creating new political dynamics. For example, the chief minister of the state of Orissa has used the legislated fiscal rules to restrain spending demands by his cabinet colleagues and by state legislators (Shah 2008).

5.7 Concluding Remarks

This chapter has provided a review of budget institutions at subnational levels in developed, as well as developing and transition countries. The focus is placed on evaluating the role played by fiscal rules in fiscal consolidation at subnational level. A review of the experiences suggests that, when properly designed and implemented, fiscal rules can be useful tools for fiscal performance.

A closer look at country experiences suggests that successful fiscal adjustment requires sustained political commitment. Such a commitment is easier to obtain in countries with traditions of fiscal conservatism, self-financed local governments, well-developed budgetary institutions, strong budgetary institutions and well-functioning institutions of executive and legislative federalism. Under such circumstances, reliance on fiscal rules may not be needed for fiscal discipline.

In countries where budgetary institutions are weak and a reputation for fiscal prudence is lacking, fiscal rules can help restrain pork barrel politics. Fiscal rules may take a wide variety of forms. In this chapter we have discussed the use of numerical fiscal rules, such as budget balance requirements, borrowing constraints, and also procedural and transparency rules, such as the adoption of common standards in budgetary reporting or the setting of medium-term policy frameworks. Furthermore, we have analyzed the recent implementation and impact of fiscal responsibility legislation on subnational fiscal performance. This evidence points to a positive impact of fiscal rules on local fiscal discipline but less so on provincial/state levels. Broader fiscal responsibility legislation binding on all orders of government points to even stronger positive influence on fiscal discipline in countries adopting such a legislation.

Annex A1: Brazilian Fiscal Responsibility Legislation 2000

The Brazilian Federal Government adopted a Fiscal Responsibility Law (Lei de Responsibilidade Fiscal—LRF) in May 2000 and its companion law (Lei 10028/2000) binding for federal, state and municipal/local governments (see Table 5.8 for a summary view). The LRF prohibits intergovernmental and government-controlled bank debt financing, imposes limits on total debt and personnel expenditures, establishes rules for the last year in office, requires compensatory measures for tax expenditures and new entitlements, establishes verifiable fiscal limits, mandates transparency of national and subnational fiscal data and fiscal administration reports and dissemination to public on a timely basis, correction mechanisms and intra-year adjustment rules to meet fiscal limits and institutes enforcement mechanisms and penalties for non-compliance. The escape clauses are few and specific and related to economic slowdown.

The LRF is likely the most significant reform after 1988 constitution in terms of its impact on the dynamics of federalism in Brazil; as subsequent compromises between states and the federal government have continuously increased the negotiation leverage of the latter increasing also its effectiveness in macroeconomic management. The LRF requires that no program can be funded unless part of a multi-year (4-year) plan and the annual budget must evaluate fiscal risks from contingent liabilities. The LRF establishes *ex ante* institutions such as a threshold state debt, deficit, and personnel spending ceilings. According to the LRF federal government, states and municipalities must maintain debt stock levels below ceilings (3.5, 2.0 and 1.2 times own net current revenues for federal government, states and municipalities respectively) determined by the Federal Senate regulations. If a subnational government exceeds this debt ceiling, the exceeding amount must be reduced within one-year period, during which the state or municipality is prohibited of incurring any new debt and becomes ineligible for receiving discretionary transfers. The LRF also regulates that all new borrowing requires the technical approval of the Central Bank and the approval of the Senate. Borrowing operations are prohibited all together during a period of 180-days before the end of incumbents' government mandate. In terms of personnel management, the LRF provisions define ceilings on payroll spending. This should not exceed 50% of federal government's net revenues while this ceiling equals 60% at the subnational level. The LRF also institutionalized a variety of

Table 5.8 Brazil fiscal responsibility law 2000 at a glance

Political unit and main features	Applicable to all orders (tiers) and branches of government with Prohibition of intergovernmental debt financing and government-controlled bank lending Limits on total debt and personnel expenditures, compensatory measures for tax expenditures and new entitlements Verifiable fiscal targets and transparency rules Borrowing and expenditure limits for the last year in government Adjustment rules and personal and institutional penalties and sanctions.
Procedural rules and transparency requirements	The law sets minimum standards for state budgeting, personnel management and debt management. The annual budget of each SNG has to be consistent with its multi-year budget plan and with the federal fiscal and monetary program. The law explicitly prohibits debt refinancing operations between different levels of government. Strengthened transparency rules for all levels of government. Proposals, laws and accounts must be widely distributed including through electronic media. Forecasts, objectives as well as targets and results need to be periodically published. The executive branch of each municipal government must consolidate its accounts and send to the Federal Government. The Federal Government compiles the accounts for the entire federation. A bi-monthly budget execution report should be published, containing budget balance sheet as well as a summary of expenditures and revenues. The heads of government branches must issue a fiscal management report every four months and make it available to the public. Any bill that creates new expenditures including tax expenditures has to show how these will be financed. Budget neutrality requirement: Any new tax expenditure or continued mandatory expenditures can be approved only if new tax revenues are secured or expenditures of similar nature are reduced. Time limited correction mechanisms
Fiscal targets	Public debt limits as percentage of net current revenues: Federal 3.5%; states 2.0%; municipalities 1.2% Personnel expenditure limits as % of net current revenues: Federal: executive 40.9%; legislative 0.5%; judiciary 6.0%; prosecutor 0.6% States: executive 49.0%; legislative 3.0%; judiciary 6.0%; prosecutor 2.0% Municipalities: executive 54.0%; legislative 6.0%

(*continued*)

Table 5.8 (continued)

Escape clauses	Natural calamities GDP growth rate below 1% in last 4 quarters
Sanctions for non-compliance	Can be imposed by executive, legislature (audit courts), public prosecutor. Further a citizen can bring suit *Institutional sanctions*: Withholding of federal transfers and guarantees; suspension of National Treasury endorsement of credit operations; suspension of bank operations if exposure to public sector borrowing exceeds 45% of bank capital; if total personnel expenditures exceed 95% of the ceiling, new hiring, wage increases and contracting overtime work are suspended. *Personal sanctions*: Imprisonment (1–4 years); fine of 30% of annual salary; removal from office; ineligibility to be appointed or to run for office for 5 years

Source: Authors and Liu and Webb (2011)

ex post provisions aimed at the enforcement of its regulations. For governments, violations to personnel or debt ceiling can lead to fines up to 30% of annual salary of the responsible officer; impeachment and removal from office of mayors or governors and ineligibility to run for office for five years; and even prison terms (1–4 years) in case of violation of mandates regarding election years. For capital markets, the LRF declares that financing operations in violation of debt ceilings would not be legally valid and amounts borrowed should be repaid fully without interest and the Bank officials involved could be criminally prosecuted. This provision is aimed at discouraging such lending behavior by the financial institutions. Sanctions can be imposed by the Executive (institutional sanctions), legislature (Audit Council) or by the independent Public Prosecutor. Citizens are also empowered to file suit against governments for a breach of any provisions of this act.

The Brazilian Federation had a remarkable success in ensuring fiscal policy coordination and fiscal discipline at all levels in recent years. By June 2005, the LRF (2000) had significant positive impacts on fiscal performance in Brazil. All states and the federal government have complied with the ceiling on personnel expenditures (50% of current revenues). On debt, only 5 states out of 27 states (inclusive of Federal District) are still above the ceiling of 200% of revenues, owing to 2002 currency devaluation. Ninety-two percent of municipalities have reduced debts below 1.2 times revenue levels and only a handful of large municipalities have

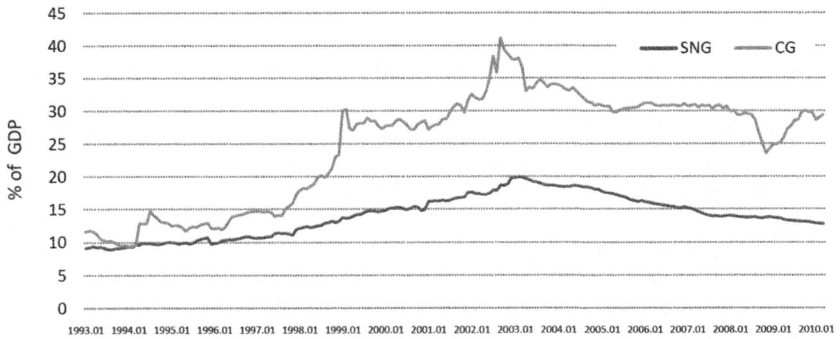

Fig. 5.1 Brazil net government debt as share of GDP. (Source: Liu and Webb (2011). Notes: *SNG* Subnational Governments, *CG* Central Government)

unsustainable debt levels. Primary surplus was achieved by all states by 2004 (Levy 2005; Boadway and Shah 2009). A recent study by Liu and Webb (2011) reaffirms positive impact of the FRL on fiscal management in Brazil. Liu and Webb note that the rate of growth of sovereign gross debt as a share of GDP slowed from 15.13% in the pre-LRF period to 2.39% in the post-LRF whereas the rate of growth of the subnational debt fell from 4.99% in the pre-FRL to 1.31 in the post-FRL period. Figure 5.1 shows the positive impact of the LRF on the trend in net government debt as a share of GDP for both federal and subnational governments.

References

Alesina, A., R. Hausmann, R. Hommes, and E. Stein. 1998. Budget Institutions and Fiscal Performance in Latin America. Research Department Working Paper 394. Inter-American Development Bank, Washington, DC.

Balassone, F., D. Franco, and S. Zotteri 2003. Fiscal Rules for Subnational Governments in the EMU Context. Società Italiana di Economia Pubblica, Working Papers 196.

Blondal, J. 1999. Fiscal Federalism in OECD Member Countries. In *Fiscal Decentralization in Emerging Economies: Governance Issues*, ed. K. Fukusaku and L. de Mello. Paris: Organization for Economic Cooperation and Development.

Boadway, Robin. 2007. Grants in a Federal Economy. In *Intergovernmental Fiscal Transfers*, Chapter 2, ed. Robin Boadway and Anwar Shah, 55–74. Washington, DC: World Bank.

Boadway, Robin, and Anwar Shah. 2009. *Fiscal Federalism. Principles and Practice of Multiorder Governance*. London: Cambridge University Press.

Bohn, H., and R. Inman. 1996. Balanced-Budget Rules and Public Deficits: Evidence from the U.S. States. *Carnegie-Rochester Conference Series on Public Policy* 45 (1–4): 13–76.

Braun, M., and M. Tommasi. 2002. Fiscal Rules for Subnational Governments: Some Organizing Principles and Latin American Experiences. Prepared for the IMF/World Bank Conference on Rules-Based Fiscal Policy Fiscal Policy in Emerging Economies. Oaxaca, Mexico, February 14–16.

Brixi, Hana Polackova. 2005. Addressing Contingent Liabilities and Fiscal Risk. In *Fiscal Management*, Chapter 7, ed. Anwar Shah, 163–188. Washington, DC: World Bank.

Corbacho, A., and G. Schwartz. 2007. Fiscal Responsibility Laws. In *Promoting Fiscal Discipline*, ed. M. Kumar and T. Ter-Minassian. Washington, DC: International Monetary Fund.

Crivelli, Ernesto, and Anwar Shah. 2009. Promoting Subnational Fiscal Discipline: A Review of Budget Institutions and Their Impact on Fiscal Performance. Working Paper. World Bank Institute, Washington, DC.

Crivelli, E., and K. Staal. 2013. Size, Spillovers, and Soft Budget Constraints. *International Tax and Public Finance* 20: 338–356.

Dabla-Norris, E., and P. Wade. 2002. The Challenge of Fiscal Decentralization in Transition Countries. IMF Working Paper 02/103. International Monetary Fund, Washington, DC.

Daughters, R., and L. Harper. 2007. Fiscal and Political Decentralization Reforms. In *The State of State Reform in Latin America*, ed. E. Lora. Washington, DC: Inter-American Development Bank.

Filc, G., and C. Scartascini. 2007. Budgetary Institutions. In *The State of State Reform in Latin America*, ed. E. Lora. Washington, DC: Inter-American Development Bank.

Fornasari, F., S. Webb, and H. Zou. 2000. The Macroeconomic Impact of Decentralized Spending and Deficits: International Evidence. CEMA Working Papers 28.

Hallerberg, M., R. Strauch, and J. von Hagen. 2004. The Design of Fiscal Rules and Forms of Governance in European Union Countries. Working Paper Series 419. European Central Bank, Frankfurt.

Heppke-Falk, K., and G. Wolff. 2008. Moral Hazard and Bail-Out in Fiscal Federations: Evidence for the German Laender. *Kyklos* 61 (3): 425–446.

Joumard, I., and P. Kongsrud. 2003. Fiscal Relations Across Government Levels. OECD Economics Department Working Paper 375. OECD, Paris.

Kennedy, S., and J. Robbins. 2001. The Role of Fiscal Rules in Determining Fiscal Performance. Department of Finance Working Paper 2001-16. Ministry of Finance, Canada.

Lane, T. D. 1993. Market Discipline. *Staff Papers – International Monetary Fund* 40 (1): 53.
Levy, Joaquim Vieira. 2005. Fiscal Rules and Fiscal Performance. Unpublished Manuscript. Ministry of Finance, Brazil.
Liu, L., and M. Waibel. 2008. Subnational Borrowing, Insolvency, and Regulation. In *Macro Federalism and Local Finance*, ed. A. Shah. Washington, DC: The World Bank.
Liu, Lili, and Steven Webb. 2011. Laws for Fiscal Responsibility for Subnational Discipline. International Experience. Policy Research Working Paper No. 5587. World Bank, Washington, DC.
Ma, Jun, Xiaorong Zheng, and Li Zhiguo. 2012. *A Study of China's National Balance Sheet*. Beijing: Social Science Academic Press.
Oliva, C. 2001. Fiscal Responsibility Laws: How Broad Should they Be? Paper Presented at the International Seminar on Transparency and Fiscal Responsibility, Rio de Janeiro, November 26–27.
Poterba, J. 1994. State Responses to Fiscal Crises: The Effects of Budgetary Institutions and Politics. *Journal of Political Economy* 102 (4): 799–821.
Poterba, J., and K. Reuben. 1999. State Fiscal Institutions and the U.S. Municipal Bond Market. In *Fiscal Institutions and Fiscal Performance*, ed. J. Poterba and J. von Hagen. Chicago: The University of Chicago Press.
Poterba, J., and J. von Hagen, eds. 1999. *Fiscal Institutions and Fiscal Performance*. Chicago: University of Chicago Press.
Qiao, Baoyun, Qian Chen, Lezheng Liu, Guo Shen, Jianmei Zhao, and Xiangyi Meng. 2010. Blueprint for Better Management of Subnational Government Impilicit and Explicit Debt. Unpublished Report, December, 2010.
Rodden, J. 2002. The Dilemma of Fiscal Federalism: Grants and Fiscal Performance around the World. American *Journal of Political Science* 46 (3): 670.
Schick, Allen. 1998. *A Contemporary Approach to Public Expenditure Management*. Washington, DC: Economic Development Institute, World Bank.
Shah, A. 2006. Fiscal Decentralization and Macroeconomic Management. *International Tax and Public Finance* 13: 437–462.
———. 2008. Federalism and Macroeconomic Performance. In *Macro Federalism and Local Finance*, ed. A. Shah. Washington, DC: The World Bank.
———. 2013. *Local Public Finance Management in the People's Republic of China: Challenges and Opportunities*. Manila: Asian Development Bank.
Singh, R., and A. Plekhanov. 2005. How Should Subnational Borrowing Be Regulated? Empirical Evidence from a Cross-Country Study. IMF Working Paper 05/54. International Monetary Fund, Washington, DC.
Sutherland, D., R. Price, and I. Joumard. 2005. Fiscal Rules for Sub-Central Governments: Design and Impact. OECD Economics Department Working Papers 465.

Ter-Minassian, T. 2006. Fiscal Rules for Subnational Governments: Can they Promote Fiscal Discipline? *OECD Journal on Budgeting* 6 (3): 111–121.

von Hagen, J. 1991. A Note on the Empirical Effectiveness of Formal Fiscal Restraints. *Journal of Public Economics* 44 (2): 199–210.

von Hagen, J. 2005. Fiscal Rules and Fiscal Performance in Europe and Japan. *SSRN Electronic Journal*.

von Hagen, J., and I. Harden. 1995. Budget Processes and Commitment to Fiscal Discipline. *European Economic Review* 39: 771–779.

von Hagen, J., and B. Eichengreen. 1996. Federalism, Fiscal Restraints, and European Monetary Union. *American Economic Review* 86 (2): 134–38.

Webb, S. 2004. Fiscal Responsibility Laws for Subnational Discipline: The Latin American Experience. WB Policy Research Working Paper 3309. The World Bank, Washington, DC.

Wetzel, D., and J. Dunn. 2001. Decentralization in the Transition Economies: Challenges and the Road Ahead. Poverty Reduction and Economic Management, Unit Europe and Central Asia. The World Bank, Washington, DC

Wildasin, D. 1997. Externalities and Bailouts: Hard and Soft Budget Constraints in Intergovernmental Fiscal Relations. WB Policy Research Working Papers Series 1843. The World Bank, Washington, DC.

PART III

Local Government Integrity and Performance Accountability

CHAPTER 6

Local Public Infrastructure and Corruption

6.1 Introduction

During the past two decades a silent revolution has swept the globe and a large number of industrial and developing countries have pursued decentralization reforms that attempt to move public decision-making closer to people. The reform agenda has been pursued through varying combinations of political, administrative and fiscal decentralization initiatives that aim to shift some traditional central government functions to intermediate or lower orders of government. These reforms have proven to be controversial. This is because decentralization is perceived as a solution to some problems such as a dysfunctional public sector with lack of voice and exit as well as a source of new problems such as capture by local elite, aggravation of macroeconomic management due to a lack of fiscal discipline, race to the bottom and potentially greater barriers to common economic and social union through beggar-thy-neighbor policies. The impact of decentralization on corruption (defined as the abuse of public office for private gain or exercise of official powers against public interest) is an area of growing interest inviting much controversy and debate. While this debate

This chapter is a revised version of Anwar Shah (2016), "Decentralized Provision of Public Infrastructure and Corruption". In Jonas Frank and Jorge Martinez-Vazquez, eds. *Decentralization and Infrastructure in the Global Economy*, Chapter 14: 418–454. New York, NY: Routledge Press. The permission of Routledge Press for this reprinting is gratefully acknowledged.

B. Dollery et al., *Local Public, Fiscal and Financial Governance*,
https://doi.org/10.1007/978-3-030-36725-1_6

has largely centered on the overall impact of decentralization, the focus of current chapter is to examine various arguments in this debate in the specific case of decentralized provision of infrastructure—a yet largely unexplored area of research.

6.1.1 What Is Special About Decentralized Provision of Infrastructure?

Infrastructure projects are typically lumpy, have long gestational periods and are long lived. This implies that a local government must have assured financing of capital and maintenance costs and a plan for recovering capital costs and recurring costs over the life of the project. Infrastructure projects are typically costly and since in most countries local governments have constrained tax autonomy and even more constrained access to capital market finance, higher-level financing and assistance for capital market access assumes critical importance for initiation of projects. Even if local governments may enjoy significant tax autonomy, poorer local jurisdictions would not have the revenue capacity to finance infrastructure provision from own revenue surpluses and would have typically no access to capital market finance due to a lack of credit worthiness even in the absence of prohibitions usually practiced against local bond finance. Higher-level capital grant financing without local matching funds create incentives for softer budget constraints as local governments do not have to justify these expenses to electorate to have buy in for additional taxation. Infrastructure projects may entail interjurisdictional externalities as the optimal size to reap economies of scale may be larger than required by one jurisdiction such as water purification and waste disposal plants or in the absence of user fees free ridership may be possible by residents of other jurisdictions such as for roads, bridges, mass transit and sports and recreation centers and libraries. Therefore, intermunicipal partnerships for cost sharing or higher-level transfers to compensate for benefit spill-outs may be required.

6.1.2 Why It Is Important to Examine the Implications of Decentralized Provision of Infrastructure for the Incidence of Corruption?

Decentralized provision of infrastructure is advocated for better matching of infrastructure services with local preferences and needs and for enhancing efficiency and equity of public provision. But if decentralized provision is seen to lead to a higher incidence of corruption especially with higher order grant financing then these advantages may be undermined. Corrupt practices in infrastructure affect the whole project investment and operations cycle and result in projects with roads and bridges to nowhere and creation of white elephants while a median voter is denied access to basic services such as clean water and sanitation. Potential of such corrupt practices is enhanced when these projects are mostly financed by higher-order governments which is often a necessity with decentralized provision of infrastructure or external donors. Since infrastructure projects are typically lumpy and have long gestational periods, corrupt strategic behavior of current regimes can tie hands of future regimes to the priorities set by the initiating regime. The times of fiscal stress offer even greater opportunities for corruption as projects must be approved, financed and implemented on an accelerated schedule. In view of the potential negative impact of corruption on good governance, it is important to analyze the implications of decentralized provision of infrastructure for good government both in theory and in practice with a view to examining options for limiting opportunities for corruption while enhancing possibilities of detection and punishment. This chapter takes an important first step in this direction by providing a synthesis of conceptual and empirical literature on this subject and highlighting the limits of our knowledge in this area especially the void in the area of empirical underpinnings of lessons in combating corruption.

The chapter is organized as follows. Section 6.2 provides an introductory review of fundamental concepts and concerns relating to corruption, its many facets and its drivers. Section 6.3 highlights corruption concerns with decentralized infrastructure provision. Section 6.4 presents counter-arguments and discusses the promise of decentralized provision of infrastructure for improved service delivery and reduced corruption. Section 6.5 synthesizes available evidence on the relationship between decentralized infrastructure provision and corruption. Section 6.6 draws overall tentative conclusions on the susceptibility of decentralized provision to corruption. Section 6.7 draws lessons for a strategy to combat corruption when infrastructure provision is decentralized. A final section provides concluding remarks.

6.2 Corruption and Its Drivers: Fundamental Concepts and Concerns

Corruption is defined as exercise of official powers against public interest or the abuse of public office for private gains. Public sector corruption is a symptom of failed governance. Here, we define "governance" as the norms, traditions and institutions by which power and authority in a country is exercised—including the institutions of participation and accountability in governance and mechanisms of citizens' voice and exit and norms and networks of civic engagement; the constitutional-legal framework and the nature of accountability relationships among citizens and governments; the process by which governments are selected, monitored, held accountable and renewed or replaced; and the legitimacy, credibility and efficacy of the institutions that govern political, economic, cultural and social interactions among citizens themselves and their governments.

Concern about corruption—the abuse of public office for private gain—is as old as the history of government. In the fourth century BCE, Kautilya, who served as an advisor, responded to the Indian king's concerns about corruption by arguing that corruption is inevitable. He wrote that "[j]ust as it is not possible to not to taste honey placed on the surface of the tongue, even so it is not possible for one dealing with the money of the king not to taste the money in however a small quantity". He further advised the king that corruption would be difficult to detect. He stated, "Just as fish moving under water cannot possibly be found out either as drinking or not drinking water, so government servants employed in the government work cannot be found out (while) taking money (for themselves)." In 350 BCE, Aristotle suggested in *The Politics* that "to protect the treasury from being defrauded, let all money be issued openly in front of the whole city, and let copies of the accounts be deposited in various wards".

In recent years, concerns about corruption have mounted in tandem with growing evidence of its detrimental impact on growth and development (see World Bank 2004; Abed and Davoodi 2000; Tanzi and Davoodi 1997; Tomaszewska and Shah 2000; Shah et al. 2004). As a result of this growing concern, there has been universal condemnation of corrupt practices, leading to the removal of some country leaders. Moreover, many governments and development agencies have devoted substantial resources and energies to fighting corruption in recent years. Even so, it is not yet clear that the incidence of corruption has declined perceptibly, especially in highly corrupt countries. The lack of significant progress can be attributed to the fact that many programs are simply folk remedies or "one-size-fits-all" approaches and offer little chance of success. For programs to work, they must identify the type of corruption they are targeting and tackle the underlying, country-specific causes, or "drivers", of dysfunctional governance. This calls for examination of structure of government among other factors.

6.2.1 The Many Forms of Corruption in Infrastructure

Corruption is not manifested in one single form; indeed, it typically takes at least four broad forms.

Petty, administrative or bureaucratic corruption. Many corrupt acts are isolated transactions by individual public officials who abuse their office, for example, by demanding bribes and kickbacks, diverting public funds, or awarding favors in return for personal considerations. Such acts are often referred to as petty corruption even though, in the aggregate, a substantial amount of public resources may be involved. For infrastructure provision, petty corruption is often observed for "greasing the wheels" in public-private interface in proposals, registration, procurement and access to public services.

Grand corruption. The theft or misuse of vast amounts of public resources by state officials—usually members of, or associated with, the political or administrative elite—constitutes grand corruption. For infrastructure provision, grand corruption occurs in the selection process for public procurement and in procurement itself and in public-private partnerships and interface. In developing countries, foreign private sector participation is considered a major source of such corruption.

State or regulatory capture and influence peddling. Collusion by private actors with public officials or politicians for their mutual, private benefit is referred to as state capture. That is, the private sector "captures" the state legislative, executive, and judicial apparatus for its own purposes. State capture coexists with the conventional (and opposite) view of corruption, in which public officials extort or otherwise exploit the private sector for private ends. This form of corruption is prevalent in both industrial and developing countries.

Patronage/paternalism and being a "team player". Using official position to provide assistance to clients having the same geographic, ethnic and cultural origin so that they receive preferential treatment in their dealings with the public sector including public sector employment. Also providing the same assistance on a quid pro quo basis to colleagues belonging to an informal network of friends and allies. Geographic, ethnic and culture-based patronage is commonplace in developing countries and "team player" form of corruption is fact of everyday life in industrial countries.

It is also known that corruption is country-specific; thus, approaches that apply common policies and tools (that is, one-size-fits-all approaches) to countries in which acts of corruption and the quality of governance vary widely are likely to fail. One needs to understand the local circumstances that encourage or permit public and private actors to be corrupt. Finally, we know that if corruption is about governance and governance is about the exercise of state power, then efforts to combat corruption demand strong local leadership and ownership if they are to be successful and sustainable.

6.2.2 *Many Facets of Corruption in the Provision of Infrastructure*

An important distinguishing aspect of infrastructure corruption is that mostly it comes in the form of grand corruption which is commonplace in both industrial and developing countries. OECD estimates that in OECD countries bribe rate in procurement for construction projects ranges from 5% to 25% of contract value (Ehlermann-Cache 2007). In developing countries guesstimates place these much higher. Industrial countries have largely been successful in eliminating petty corruption through higher wages which remains widespread and adversely affects billions of people in developing countries. Table 6.1 highlights the incidence of corruption in infrastructure provision at various decision points in the legislative-executive-private sector interface in provision of public infrastructure.

Vulnerability to corruption is significant regardless of centralization or decentralization of provision as described in Table 6.2. With decentralization, however, the probability of detection of corruption is significantly enhanced.

6.2.3 *What Drives Corruption?*

Public sector corruption, as a symptom of failed governance, depends on multitude of factors such as the quality of public sector management, the nature of accountability relations between the government and citizens, the legal framework and the degree to which public sector processes are accompanied by transparency and dissemination of information. Efforts to address corruption that fail to adequately account for these underlying "drivers" are unlikely to generate profound and sustainable results (Shah and Schacter 2004). To understand these drivers, a conceptual and

Table 6.1 Many facets of corruption in the provision of infrastructure—decentralized or not

Decision point	*Incidence of corruption*	*Type of corruption*
At appraisal/planning stage		
Legislative framework	Lobbying legislators for pet projects, log rolling, political campaign financing, perks and privileges in exchange for legislative favors, preparation of draft legislation by lobbyists	Grand corruption, state capture (universal phenomenon)
Policymaking	Policy framework to suit special interest groups and bribe payers	Executive capture, grand corruption, most countries
Regulation	Zoning and regulatory framework tailored to favor special interest groups. Extortion over licensing	Executive capture, grand corruption, most countries
Planning and budgeting	Rezoning and selection of projects based upon bribes received	Executive capture, grand corruption, most countries
At project financing stage		
External financing	Higher costs of externally financed projects, Donors favor PPPs especially with foreign participation. Kickbacks in return for favorable terms	Executive capture, grand corruption, most developing countries
Bond financing	Higher costs for floating bonds	Grand corruption, some developing countries
Grant financing	Pork barrel grants as quid pro quo for political finance	Grand corruption by financing pork projects such as "The Bridge to Nowhere in Alaska", most countries
Tax financing	Elite capture	Grand corruption though tax expenditures and financing of projects preferred by elites
At implementation stage		
Public-private partnerships	Collusion among public managers and private providers to give favorable terms to private participants in return for a bribe commonly practiced in energy and road projects, re-negotiation of contracts during and after execution	Grand corruption, most countries

(*continued*)

Table 6.1 (continued)

Decision point	*Incidence of corruption*	*Type of corruption*
Program and project management	Ghost projects, ghost employees, phantom expenditures	Mostly grand corruption, most developing countries
Public procurement	Kickbacks, rigged bidding and tendering. Mechanisms: intermediary collusion, consulting fees, false services, overpayment, payment to a front company, Swiss and Cayman Island bank accounts, collusion among competitors Procurement cycle: registration, manipulating specifications, insider info, quality reduction, clearance from inspectors, expediting payments	Mostly grand corruption, most countries
Construction	Use of low quality materials, theft of materials, false prices	Mostly grand corruption, most developing countries
At operations stage		
Operations and maintenance	False reporting, ghost workers	Mostly grand corruption, most developing countries
User charges	Theft and free ridership	Petty corruption, most developing countries
Public access	Delay or denial of access	Petty corruption, most developing countries
At ex post evaluation stage		
Evaluation	Project financing and selection of evaluators leads to lack of independence and biased evaluations	Patronage, most countries

Source: Shah (2016)

empirical perspective is needed to understand why corruption persists and what can be a useful antidote. At the conceptual level, a number of interesting ideas have been put forward. These ideas can be broadly grouped together in three categories: (a) principal-agent or agency models; (b) new public management perspectives; and (c) neo-institutional economics frameworks.

Table 6.2 Vulnerability to corruption observed in both centralized and decentralized provision of infrastructure in various sectors

Water and sanitation	Land acquisition, selection of contractors, bid rigging, compromising quality, bribes for connections, meter tampering, conflict of interest with officials involved in private provision, collusion with companies offering bottled water or tanker provision
Roads	Land acquisition at above market prices, rehabilitation, selection of contractors, false procurement and maintenance expenditures, certification of quality of construction
Electricity	Public utilities: land acquisition, rights of way, rehabilitation, equipment purchase and repair mark ups, patronage appointments, defective meters, meter tampering, theft of electricity by tapping distribution lines with side payments, connections delays, false billing, response to non-payment of bills, false subsidy payments, public sector guarantees for assured demand for supply at above market rates Private utilities: selection, regulatory regime, price hikes, regulators turning blind eye to capital deterioration
Hospitals	Ghost hospitals, bribes for admissions and drugs, false procurement and construction,
Schools	Ghost schools, bribes for admissions, ghost enrollments, false procurement and corruption
Fitness and recreation centers	Padding up cost of construction and purchase of equipment

Source: Shah (2016)

6.2.3.1 Conceptual Perspectives on Drivers of Corruption

Principal-Agent Models

This is the most widely used modeling strategy. A common thread in these models is that the government is led by a benevolent dictator, the principal, who aims to motivate government officials (agents) to act with integrity in the use of public resources (see Becker 1968; Becker and Stigler 1974; Banfield 1975; Rose Ackerman 1975, 1978; Klitgaard 1988, 1991; Becker 1983). One such view, the so-called crime and punishment model by Gary Becker (1968), states that self-interested public officials seek out or accept bribes so long as the expected gains from corruption exceed the expected costs (detection and punishment) associated with corrupt acts. Thus, according to this view, corruption could be mitigated by (a) reducing the number of transactions over which public officials have discretion; (b) reducing the scope of gains from each transaction; (c) increasing the probability for detection; and (d) increasing the penalty for corrupt activities. Moreover, since it is costly to increase detection, but not to increase penalties (at least assuming detection is accurate), the most efficient way to eliminate corruption is to impose very high penalties with a relatively low probability of detection. Klitgaard (1988) restates this model to emphasize the unrestrained monopoly power and discretionary authority of government officials. According to him, corruption equals monopoly plus discretion minus accountability. To curtail corruption under this framework, one has to have a rules-driven government with strong internal controls and with little discretion to public officials. This model gained wide acceptance in public policy circles and served as a foundation for empirical research and policy design to combat administrative, bureaucratic, or petty corruption. Experience in highly corrupt countries, however, contradicts the effectiveness of such an approach as the rules enforcers themselves add extra burden of corruption and lack of discretion is also thwarted by collusive behavior of corruptors. In fact, lack of discretion is often cited as a defense by corrupt officials who partake in corruption as part of a vertically well-knit network enjoying immunity from prosecution.

Another variant of principal-agent models integrates the role of legislators and elected officials in the analysis. In this variant, high-level government officials – represented by legislators or elected public officials – institute or manipulate existing policy and legislation in favor of particular interest groups – representing private sector interests and entities or individual units of public bureaucracy competing for higher budgets – in exchange of rents or side payments. In this framework, legislators weigh the personal monetary gains from corrupt practices and improved chances of re-election against the chance of being caught, punished and losing an election with a tarnished reputation. Factors affecting this decision include campaign financing mechanisms, information access by voters, the ability of citizens to vote out corrupt legislators, the degree of political contestability, electoral systems, democratic institutions and traditions and institutions of accountability in governance. Examples of such analyses include: Rose-Ackerman (1978), Advig and Moene (1990), Grossman and Helpman (1994), Flatters and Macleod (1995), Chand and Moene (1997), Van Rijckeghem and Weder (2001), Acconcia, D'Amato and Martina (2003). This conceptual framework is useful in analyzing political corruption or state capture.

There is a fine line dividing theoretical models that focus on the effects of localization on corruption and those that analyze the decentralization of corruption within a multi-tier hierarchy from an "industrial organization of corruption" type of framework. In the latter group a distinction is made between "top-down corruption" – where corrupt high levels buy lower levels by sharing a portion of gains – and "bottom-up corruption" – where low-level officials share their own collected bribes with superior levels to avoid detection or punishment. The former phenomenon is more likely to exist in a federal system of governance where powers may be shared among various orders of government and the alternate is more likely to prevail under unitary or centralized forms of governance or dictatorial regimes. The impact of governance on the corruption networks is an interesting yet unresearched topic. Tirole (1986) analyzed one aspect of this network by means of a three-tier principal-supervisor-agent model (see also Guriev 1999). This extension of a conventional principal-agent model assists in drawing inferences regarding the type of corrupt relations that could evolve under a three-tier unitary government structure. These inferences are highly sensitive to underlying assumptions regarding principal-agent relationships under a multi-tiered system of governance (four-tier hierarchies are modeled by Carillo 2000; Bac and Bag 1998). In Guriev's three-tier hierarchy model the mid-level bureaucrat supervises the agent and reports to the principal. In comparing the characteristics of equilibria with top-bottom and all-level corruption, Guriev concludes that top-level corruption "is not efficient, as it redistributes rents in favor of agents, and therefore makes it more attractive for potential entrants" (p. 2) and thereby leading to higher total corruption.

Shleifer and Vishny (1993) utilize conventional industrial organization theory model and conclude that decentralization is likely to increase corruption. In this model, government bureaucracies and agencies act as monopolists selling complimentary government-produced goods which are legally required for private sector activity. The main idea behind the model is that under centralized corruption bureaucracies act like a joint monopoly, whereas under decentralized corruption bureaucracies behave as independent monopolies. When bureaucracies act as independent monopolies, they ignore the effects of higher prices on the overall demand for a good and hence drive up the cumulative bribe burden.

Waller, Verdier and Gardner (2002) define decentralized corruption as a system in which higher-level officials collect a fixed amount of bribe income from each of the bureaucrats that take bribes, without mandating on the bribe size that the bureaucrats charge. In a centralized system, on the contrary, bribe size is determined by the higher level of government which collects them from bureaucrats and redistributes it among them after keeping a share. Waller et al. posit that decentralized corruption leads to lower levels of total corruption in the economy (lower spread), higher levels of bribe per entrepreneur (higher depth), and a smaller formal sector *vis-à-vis* a centralized corruption equilibrium. Yet, these results vary widely for specific 'regimes' in the model – when given parameters satisfy key conditions – for instance, for high-enough wages and monitoring systems, centralized corruption may reduce total corruption and expand the formal economy.

While previously discussed studies centered on the organizational structure of corruption, Ahlin (2001) differs by concentrating on the effects of bureaucratic decentralization. Under the assumption of no interregional mobility, corruption increases with the degree of bureaucratic decentralization but is independent of the degree of regional decentralization, whereas for perfect interregional mobility corruption decreases with regional decentralization and is independent of bureaucratic decentralization. A key intuition of the model is that corrupt bureaucrats fail to internalize the costs of increases in bribe-charges imposed on other bureaucrats. Arikan (2004) uses a tax competition framework to examine localization-corruption links and finds that higher degree of decentralization is expected to lead to lower levels of corruption. Bardhan and Mookherjee (2001) shed light upon the determinants of capture of the democratic process. Not surprisingly, they conclude that the extent of relative capture is ambiguous and context specific.

In conclusion, no definitive conclusions can be drawn regarding corruption and the centralization-decentralization nexus from the agency-type conceptual models. These models simply reaffirm that the incidence of corruption is context dependent and therefore cannot be uncovered by generalized models.

New Public Management Frameworks

The new public management (NPM) literature, on the other hand, points to a more fundamental discordance among the public sector mandate, its authorizing environment and the operational culture and capacity. According to NPM, this discordance contributes to government acting like a runaway train and government officials indulging in rent-seeking behaviors with little opportunity for citizens to constrain government behavior. This viewpoint calls for fundamental civil service and political reforms to create a government under contract and accountable for results. Public officials will no longer have permanent rotating appointments but instead they could keep their jobs as long as they fulfilled their contractual obligations (see Shah 1999, 2005).

The new public management (NPM) paradigms have clear implications for the study of localization and corruption as it argues for contractual arrangements in provision of public services. Such a contractual framework may encourage competitive service delivery through outsourcing, purchaser-provider split under a decentralized structure of governance. The NPM goals are harmonious with decentralization as greater accountability for results reinforces government accountability to citizens through voice and exit mechanisms. Conceptually, therefore, the NPM is expected to reduce opportunities for corruption (see Shah 1999, 2005). Andrews and Shah (2005) integrate these two ideas in a common framework of citizen-centered governance. They argue that citizen empowerment holds the key to enhanced accountability and reduced opportunities for corruption.

Others disagree with such conclusions and argue that the NPM could lead to higher corruption as opposed to greater accountability. This may happen because the tendering for service delivery and separation of purchasers from providers may lead to increased rent-seeking behavior and enhanced possibilities for corruption (Batley 1999; Von Maravic 2003). Further, some argue that decentralized management leads to weaker vertical supervision from higher levels and the inadequacy of mechanisms to exert controls over decentralized agencies (Scharpf 1997). This loss in vertical accountability is seen as a source of enhanced opportunities for corruption. Of course, this viewpoint simply neglects potential gains from higher horizontal accountability.

Neo-Institutional Economics (NIE) Frameworks

Finally, Shah (2006) has utilized the transactions costs approach of the neo-institutional economics (NIE) to present a newer perspective on the causes and cures of corruption. Shah argues that corruption results from opportunistic behavior of public officials (agents) given that citizens (as governors and principals) are either not empowered or face high transaction costs to hold public officials accountable for their corrupt acts. The principals have bounded rationality—they act rationally based upon the incomplete information they have. In order to have a more informed perspective on public sector operations, they face high transaction costs in acquiring and processing the information. On the other hand, agents (public officials) are better informed. This asymmetry of information allows agents to indulge in opportunistic behavior which goes unchecked due to high *transactions costs* faced by the principals and a lack of or inadequacy of countervailing institutions to enforce accountable governance. Thus, corrupt countries have inadequate mechanisms for contract enforcement, weak judicial systems and inadequate provision for public safety. This raises the transactions costs in the economy further raising the cost of private capital as well as the cost of public service provision. The problem is further compounded by path dependency (i.e., a major break with the past is difficult to achieve as any major reforms are likely to be blocked by influential interest groups), cultural and historical factors and mental models where those who are victimized by corruption feel that attempts to deal with corruption will lead to further victimization, with little hope of corrupt actors being brought to justice. These considerations lead principals to the conclusion that any attempt on their part to constrain corrupt behaviors will invite strong retaliation from powerful interests. Therefore, citizen empowerment (e.g., through decentralization, citizens' charter, bill of rights, elections and other forms of civic engagement) assumes critical importance in combating corruption because it may have a significant impact on the incentives faced by public officials to be responsive to public interest.

6.3 The Perils of Decentralized Provision of Infrastructure in Breeding Corruption

A number of arguments have been advanced to support the notion that corruption increases with localization. A few of these are summarized below.

a) *Personalism.* Tanzi (1995) argued that localization brings officials in close contact with citizens. This promotes personalism and reduces professionalism and arm's-length relationships. Personalism in his view breeds corruption as officials pay greater attention to individual citizen needs and disregard public interest. Further, a higher degree of discretion at the local level and long tenure of local officials make it easier to establish unethical relationships (Prud'homme 1994).
b) *Weak monitoring and vertical controls.* Impediments to corrupt practices also decrease as local politicians and bureaucrats collude to advance narrow self-interests while the effectiveness of auditing agencies and monitoring from the central level wanes (Prud'homme 1994). Localization may increase the motivation for corruption

among public officials by creating an impression that they are subject to lower monitoring, control and supervision.

c) *Fiscal decentralization and overgrazing.* Treisman argues that decentralized federal systems tend to have higher corruption ratings due to (a) their larger size; (b) more likely to have separate police forces at both central and subnational levels (which increases corruption due to overgrazing) and their greater propensity to have a regionally elected upper house of parliament with veto power (which also may increase corruption as regional governments may buy off these veto-players or have greater leverage to protect their ill-gotten gains). Using cross-country regression analysis, Treisman (1999, 2000) presents empirical evidence that support the existence of this negative relationship. Treisman's empirical results, however, are sensitive to the inclusion of other variables in the equation and may have omitted variables bias in view of a lack of underlying framework for corruption.

   A recent study by Fan, Lin and Treisman (2009) provides a more nuanced view of the impact of fiscal decentralization. Combining cross-sectional secondary data for 80 countries with a survey of 9000 business owners, it finds that "in countries with large number of government or administrative tiers and (given local revenues) a larger number of local public employees, reported bribery was more frequent. When local or central governments received a larger share of GDP in revenue, bribery was less frequent" (p. 1). These results suggest that while decentralization in general opens up possibilities for rent seeking by a larger number of individuals, tax decentralization limits such opportunities by bringing greater citizen oversight of local government operations.

d) *Political decentralization and lack of discipline.* Political decentralization is seen as a cascading system of bribes by Shleifer and Vishny (1993). They note that "to invest in a Russian company, a foreigner must bribe every agency involved in foreign investment including the foreign investment office, the relevant industrial ministry, the finance ministry, the executive branch of the local government, the legislative branch, the central bank, the state property bureau, and so on" (p. 615). In the same vein, Bardhan (1997) and Blanchard and Shleifer (2000) [B&S] have argued that political centralization leads to lower levels of corruption. B&S sustain that political decentralization is seen as a source of corruption in Russia but not China.

This conclusion emerges from the contrasting role of local governments in their relations with local enterprises observed in China and Russia. In China, local governments have provided a supporting role whereas in Russia, local governments have stymied the growth of new firms through taxation, regulation and corruption. The authors note that behavior of Russian local governments can be explained by (a) state capture by old firms, leading local governments to protect them from competition and (b) rent-seeking behavior of local officials discouraging new firms to enter. The authors attribute this contrasting experience to presence of political decentralization in Russia and its absence in China. They argue that political centralization in China contributes to party discipline which in turn reduces the risk of local capture and corruption. However, B&S analysis does not pay sufficient attention to local-enterprise relations in the two countries. Local enterprises in China are owned and run by local governments and even deliver local services such as education, health and transportation in addition to their economic functions. Thus local enterprises are part and parcel of the local government. In Russia, on the other hand, a mixed pattern of these relationships has begun to emerge. Therefore, the contrasting experience of the local governments may better be explained by agency problems rather than by political decentralization. In fact, the weakening of party discipline through the emergence of powerful local leaders may be contributing to growth of local industry as the strong arm of central planning is held at bay by these leaders.

e) *Interest group capture.* Opportunities for corruption increase due to a greater influence of interest groups at the local level (Prud'homme 1994). In this regard, Bardhan and Mookherjee (2001) argue that the probability of capture by local interest groups could be greater at the local level if, for example, interest group cohesiveness (fraction of the richest class that contribute to lobby) is higher, or the proportion of informed voters is lower at the local level. Lower levels of political awareness at the local level and less coverage of local elections by media may also impair local democracy and lead to higher capture. The notion of capture at the local levels due to weaknesses of the democratic system has also been raised by Shah (1998). Concerns about risks of local capture are also expressed in a recent World Bank Study (World Bank 2004). The study argues that decentralization may increase opportunities for corruption in some developing countries where interference in public administration is the norm, merit culture and management systems in the civil service are weak and institutions of participation and accountability are ineffective. The issue is significant, for example, in Pakistan and Philippines and also relevant to Guatemala and Tanzania where more limited decentralization has been carried out. Pakistan has recently carried out a strong program of devolution to the provinces (Shah 2012). Given systemic politicization of public services in Pakistan, decentralization to the provinces may intensify rather than reduce pressures for political/bureaucratic collusion, although this may be further mitigated by further administrative decentralization, giving elected local officials the power to, hire, fire and set terms of employment of civil servants in their jurisdiction. Note that administration decentralization in areas under feudal influence is likely to exacerbate the corruption concerns. Identical concerns are pertinent in Philippines, where legislation in 1991 devolved to regions and localities powers to provide services and raise revenues. In Philippines, there is a long tradition of elected local public offices rotating among family members. The World Bank study is concerned with the effect of decentralization on corruption when there is a local capture by political and bureaucratic elites. There is little disagreement in the literature that in such a situation, localization without fundamental electoral and land reforms, is likely to increase corruption. On the contrary, the perception of localization as a breeding ground for corruption in the presence of democratic participation and accountability, is neither grounded in theory nor in evidence.

f) *Lack of competition fosters collusive practices.* It has been argued that in environments with weak or less developed private sector, as found in many developing countries, lack of competition at the local level fosters corruption in public-private sector interface as third party oversight is missing in such an environment. A national database on benchmarking could limit such opportunities for corruption as local residents would be better informed about costs of comparable operations in other jurisdictions.

Table 6.3 attempts to capture the impact of the multitude of negative influences of decentralization on the incidence of corruption at various

Table 6.3 Perils of decentralized provision of infrastructure at various decision points

Decision point	*Impact of decentralization on the incidence of corruption*	*Impact by type of corruption*
At appraisal/planning stage		
Legislative framework	In rural areas where feudal or industrial elites may dominate local councils local government may serve the interests of elite to the neglect of its services to rural residents at large	Enhanced opportunities for grand corruption through state capture
Policymaking	Rural councils dominated by elites can impose policy framework to suit special interest groups and bribe payers	Enhanced executive capture, grand corruption
Regulation	Greater possibility of having zoning to favor developer interests in exchange for political finance and bribes and regulatory framework tailored to favor special interest groups	Enhanced executive capture, grand corruption
Planning and budgeting	Greater opportunities for rezoning and selection of projects based upon bribes and other benefits received	Enhanced executive capture, grand corruption
At project financing stage		
External financing	Higher costs of externally financed projects, Donors favor PPPs especially with foreign participation. Kickbacks in return for favorable terms	Enhanced executive capture, grand corruption, most developing countries
Bond financing	No impact	Negligible incidence of corruption
Grant financing	Some pork barrel grants as quid pro quo for political finance still possible	Some grand corruption by financing pork projects as bridge to nowhere in Alaska, most countries
Tax financing	Little impact	
At implementation stage		
Public-private partnerships	Collusion among public managers and private providers to give favorable terms to private participants in return for a bribe commonly practiced in energy and road projects, re-negotiation of contracts during and after execution	Grand corruption persists when transparency and competitive pressures are lacking
Program and project management	Little perverse impact	

(*continued*)

Table 6.3 (continued)

Decision point	*Impact of decentralization on the incidence of corruption*	*Impact by type of corruption*
Public procurement	Kickbacks, rigged bidding and tendering still possible. Mechanisms: intermediary collusion, consulting fees, false services, overpayment, payment to a front company, collusion among competitors Procurement cycle: registration, manipulating specifications, insider info, quality reduction, clearance from inspectors, expediting payments	Grand corruption could be enhanced in the short run
Construction	Use of low-quality materials, theft of materials, false prices	Mostly grand corruption, most developing countries
At operation stage		
Operations and maintenance	False reporting still possible	Mostly grand corruption, most developing countries
User charges	Theft and free ridership feasible	Petty corruption could go up in the short run
Public access	Isolated incidences of delays or denial of access still possible	Some petty corruption
At ex-post evaluation stage		
Evaluation	Biased favorable evaluation	Patronage—most countries

Source: Shah (2016)

decision points. These negative influences dominate in the absence of representative democracy and competitive market pressures typically found in rural feudal-dominated local governments. They are typically found also in urban areas when a few dominant developers build special patronage relationships with local council members.

Table 6.4 attempts to draw the implications of these negative influences for corruption in individual sectors. Patron-client relationships immune from public scrutiny are the major sources of various forms of corruption.

Table 6.4 Enhanced vulnerability to corruption introduced by decentralized provision of infrastructure in various sectors

Water and sanitation	Favoritism in selection of contractors, bid rigging, bribes for connections, meter tampering, conflict of interest with officials involved in private provision, collusion with companies offering bottled water or tanker provision
Roads, bridges and mass transit	Favoritism in selection of contractors, some false procurement and maintenance expenditures, and false certification of quality of construction still possible
Electricity	*Public utilities*: equipment purchase and repair mark ups, patronage appointments, defective meters, meter tampering, theft of electricity by tapping distribution lines with side payments, connections delays, false billing, response to non-payment of bills, false subsidy payments, public sector guarantees for assured demand for supply at above market rates *Private utilities*: selection, regulatory regime, price hikes, regulators turning blind eye to capital deterioration
Hospitals	False procurement and padding up of construction costs, bribes for admissions and drugs
Schools	False procurement and padding up of construction costs, false enrollments, bribes for admissions
Fitness, sports and recreation centers	Padding up cost of construction and purchase of equipment

Source: Shah (2016)

6.4 The Promise of Decentralized Provision of Infrastructure in Limiting Opportunities for Corruption

Decentralization's ability to curtail corruption opportunities has been commonly based on the potential for greater accountability when the decision-making is closer to the people. This line of thought is supported from the following perspectives:

a) *Competition among local governments* for mobile factors of production reinforces the accountability culture. Such enhanced accountability has the potential to reduce corruption (Weinsgast 1995; Arikan 2000).
b) *Exit and voice mechanisms at the local level.* There is a general agreement in the literature that localization can open up greater opportunities for voice and choice thereby making the public sector more

responsive and accountable to citizens-voters. Furthermore, due to regional heterogeneity of political preferences localization may reduce the range of potential capture by a unique nationally dominant party.

c) *Higher levels of information.* Seabright (1996) argues that accountability is always better at the local level, since local citizens who are better informed about government performance can vote these governments out of office. Under centralization people vote for parties or candidates partly on the basis of performance in other regions and partly on issues of national interest. As a result, accountability is defused and potential for corruption increases. Bardhan and Mookherjee (2001) also argue that decentralization in developing countries promotes cost-effectiveness and reduces corruption, owing to the superior access of local governments to information on local costs and needs.
d) *Lower expected gains from corruption but greater probability of detection and punishment.* Administrative decentralization causes a loss in control to higher levels, thus curbing their incentives to monitor and detect corrupt activities. However, it also lowers the expected gains from corruption as, following decentralization, the number of individuals who are in charge of a single decision is reduced. It is then more likely that corrupt agents are called to bear the consequences of their actions. This line of thought complements those put forward by Carbonara (1999); who concludes that decentralization although creating agency problems inside an organization can help in controlling corruption; and Wildasin (1995), who argues that local officials with limited powers have little scope to engage in grand corruption.
e) *Reduced corruption due to reduction in information asymmetry between politicians and bureaucrats.* Ahlin (2000) has argued that deconcentration has the potential to increase corruption, whereas political decentralization has the potential to contain it due to inter-jurisdictional competition. This may result from a reduction in the information asymmetry between bureaucrats and the politicians that appoint them vis-à-vis a politically centralized system. Crook and Manor (2000) examined the process of political decentralization in India (Karnataka state), Bangladesh, Côte d'Ivoire and Ghana and find that such decentralization leads to enhanced transparency. With this enhanced transparency, ordinary citizen become

better aware of government's successes and failures and they may perceive the government institutions more corrupt than the perception they had before. They observed that in Karnataka, India, political decentralization substantially reduced the amount of public funds diverted by powerful individuals. However, since citizens were not aware of these diversions, they concluded that corruption had increased. Crook and Manor, based up evidence from Karnataka, conclude that political decentralization reduces grand theft but increases petty corruption in the short run but in the long run both may go down. Olowu (1993) also finds political centralization as a root cause of endemic corruption in Africa. Fiszbein (1997) based upon a review of political decentralization in Colombia concludes that competition for political office opened the door for responsible and innovative leadership that in turn became the driving force behind capacity building, improved service delivery and reduced corruption at the local level.

f) *Improved local accountability with administrative decentralization reduces corruption.* A few studies show that administrative decentralization reduces corruption. Wade (1997) finds that over-centralized top-down management accompanied by weak communication and monitoring systems contributes to corruption and poor delivery performance for canal irrigation in India. Kuncoro (2000) finds that with administrative decentralization in Indonesia, firms relocated to areas with lower bribes.

g) *Local fiscal autonomy improves economic management and reduces corruption.* Huther and Shah (1998) using international cross-section and time series data find that fiscal decentralization is associated with enhanced quality of governance as measured by citizen participation, political and bureaucratic accountability, social justice, improved economic management and reduced corruption. Arikan (2004) reconfirms the same result. De Mello and Barenstein (2001) based upon cross-country data conclude that tax decentralization is positively associated with improved quality of governance. Fisman and Gatti (2002) find a negative relation between fiscal decentralization and corruption. Gurgur and Shah (2002) is the only study providing a comprehensive theoretical and empirical framework on the root causes of corruption. They identify major drivers of corruption in order to isolate the effect of decentralization. In a sample of industrial and non-industrial countries, lack of service orientation in the public sector, weak democratic institutions, economic isolation (closed economy), colonial past, internal bureaucratic controls and centralized decision-making are identified as the major causes of corruption. For a non-industrial countries sample, drivers for corruption are lack of service orientation in the public sector, weak democratic institutions and closed economy. Decentralization reduces corruption but has a greater negative impact on corruption in unitary countries than in federal countries. They conclude that decentralization is confirmed to support greater accountability in the public sector and reduced corruption.

h) *Lower transactions costs for citizens to hold the government to account.* Decentralization brings greater clarity in division of responsibilities and services that are delivered locally, citizens' transactions costs to hold the government to account are significantly reduced as they have better information on service delivery performance and costs as well as redress opportunities and mechanisms.
i) *Greater Transparency.* Local government operations are by their nature more transparent due to greater local knowledge. In the United States, this transparency is further enhanced by output-based budgeting and reporting adopted by most local governments voluntarily to build citizens' trust. In such an environment collusive practices are well recognized by citizens thereby curtailing corrupt practices.

Table 6.5 captures the combined impact of the confluence of factors mentioned above to limit opportunities for corruption while enhancing potential for detection and prosecution at various points in public decision-making. The table shows that decentralization will have some positive influence on curtailing corruption at almost all decision points. However, decentralization offers some promising entry points for having a major impact on reducing corruption. First major entry point is public hearings on zoning. This process offers residents an opportunity to learn reasons behind rezoning and interest groups involved. The second and probably the most important entry point in curtailing corruption is the public procurement process. The transparency and integrity of this process will significantly curtail the incidence of corruption. The incidence of corruption also depends upon the nature and source of infrastructure finance available to local governments. If financing is no concern as in oil rich countries, incidence of corruption may be higher as the local governments no longer

Table 6.5 Potential of decentralization in curtailing corruption at various decision points

Decision point	*Impact of decentralization on the Incidence of corruption*	*Impact by the type of corruption*
At appraisal/planning stage		
Legislative framework	In urban areas with greater citizens engagement, lobbying influences and perks and privileges in exchange for legislative favors are constrained	Opportunities for grand corruption are curtailed due to smaller projects and greater transparency. State capture rare in urban areas
Policymaking	Policy framework to suit special interest groups and bribe payers stunted due to adversarial citizen watch groups	Executive capture and grand corruption is reduced in most countries
Regulation	Extortion over licensing is eliminated	Executive capture and grand corruption is reduced in most countries
Planning and budgeting	Competitive providers limit rezoning and selection of projects based upon bribes received	Executive capture, grand corruption is reduced in most countries
At project financing stage		
External financing	No positive impact	Executive capture, grand corruption, most developing countries
Bond financing	Little opportunity for corruption in bond financing as it is only done for major metropolitan areas with central oversight	Incidence of corruption is minimal
Grant financing	Competitive interjurisdictional pressures typically result in transparent formula driven grant financing limiting funds for pork barrel grants as quid pro quo for political finance	Grand corruption opportunities are constrained
Tax financing	Greater transparency in local tax policy and administration limits elite capture	Grand corruption though tax expenditures and financing of projects preferred by elites is curtailed
At implementation stage		
Public-private partnerships	Little impact on public official and private managers collusive practices due to complex contractual relationship not easily understood by residents/voters	Little impact on opportunities for grand corruption in most countries

(*continued*)

Table 6.5 (continued)

Decision point	*Impact of decentralization on the Incidence of corruption*	*Impact by the type of corruption*
Program and project management	Greater transparency in decentralized provision largely eliminates potential for ghost projects, ghost employees, phantom expenditures	Opportunities for grand corruption are greatly constrained
Public procurement	Potential for kickbacks, rigged bidding and tendering is greatly reduced	Opportunities for grand corruption reduced in most countries
Construction	Benchmarking limits opportunities for padding costs	Grand corruption is curtailed
At operation stage		
Operations and maintenance	False reporting, ghost workers constrained due to citizen feedback loops	Opportunities for grand corruption curtailed in most developing countries
User charges	Little impact	Little impact on petty corruption
Public access	Some positive impact on delay or denial of access due to timely recourse and lower transactions costs for citizens to hold corrupt officials to account	Petty corruption reduced
At ex post evaluation stage		
Evaluation	Independent evaluations and citizen-based monitoring and evaluation lead to fair evaluations	Patronage curtailed

Source: Author's perspectives

have to seek approval of additional financing or justify such expenses to local electorate. The incidence of corruption is accentuated by having non-elected local governments as in the Middle East. Local governments that finance infrastructure projects from own sources are likely to have a greater integrity of the entire project cycle due to active involvement of electorate in ensuring that their tax dollars to put to best use. Thus citizen activism and openness of the democratic processes plays a critical role in curtailing the impact of corruption.

Table 6.6 embodies the influence of decentralized institutions on combating corruption to develop an aggregate view of these influences at the sector level. The table highlights potential positive influences of government closeness to the people on the integrity of provision of infrastructure at the local level. The table shows that while decentralization limits

Table 6.6 Promise of decentralization in reducing vulnerability to corruption observed in provision of infrastructure in various sectors

Water and sanitation	Diminished potential for land acquisition at above market rate due to wider local knowledge of land values, lower potential for compromising quality due to improved citizen feedback loops
Roads, bridges and mass transit	Diminished potential for land acquisition at above market prices, diminished opportunities for false procurement and maintenance expenditures, constrained opportunities for false certification of quality of construction
Electricity	*Public utilities*: diminished potential land acquisition at above market rates and acquiring the rights of way, and false subsidy payments and public sector guarantees for assured demand for supply at above market rates *Private utilities:* reduced potential for corruption in the regulatory regime due to greater citizen oversight
Hospitals	Eliminates opportunity for ghost hospitals
Schools	Eliminates opportunities for ghost schools
Fitness, sports and recreation centers	Little impact on padding up costs

Source: Shah (2016)

opportunities for corruption especially grand corruption, overall positive impact may be less observable for fitness, sports and recreation centers due to the non-standard nature of these projects benchmarking of costs may be more difficult as compared to standard infrastructure projects such as roads and bridges.

In all, a small yet growing body of theoretical and empirical literature confirms that localization offers significant potential in bringing greater accountability and responsiveness to the public sector at the local level and reducing the incidence of grand corruption. While most of this literature is focused on decentralized provision of all services yet their conclusion apply in equal force to infrastructure as infrastructure provision dominates local government expenditures.

6.5 The Evidence

While a growing number of empirical studies have examined the relationship between decentralization and corruption (see Ivanyna and Shah 2011a; Boadway and Shah 2009: chapter 16), only a handful of these studies have examined the specific impact of decentralized provision of infrastructure. Santos discovered that sectoral allocation of spending improved with participatory budgeting in Porto Alegre, Brazil. Isham and Kahkonen (1999) observed improvements in water services in Central Java, Indonesia with local community management. A World Bank study (2004) found improvement in a few local government areas in decentralized provision of water and sanitation services. A study of local government procurement in the Philippines revealed that (see Tapales 2001, p. 21) "*contractors admit to paying mayors of the towns where they have projects, because, they say, the officials can delay the work by withholding necessary permits or harassing the workers. Municipal mayors get seven percent while the barangay (village) captain is given three percent. The heads of implementing agencies – usually the district, municipal or city engineer – get about 10 percent.*" A study of canal irrigation in India attributed corruption to centralization of management (Wade 1997).

A World Bank study (World Development Report 1994) compared results under centralized versus decentralized maintenance of roads and found that countries with decentralized maintenance had better roads (see Fig. 6.1). This finding indirectly implies that with centralized provision

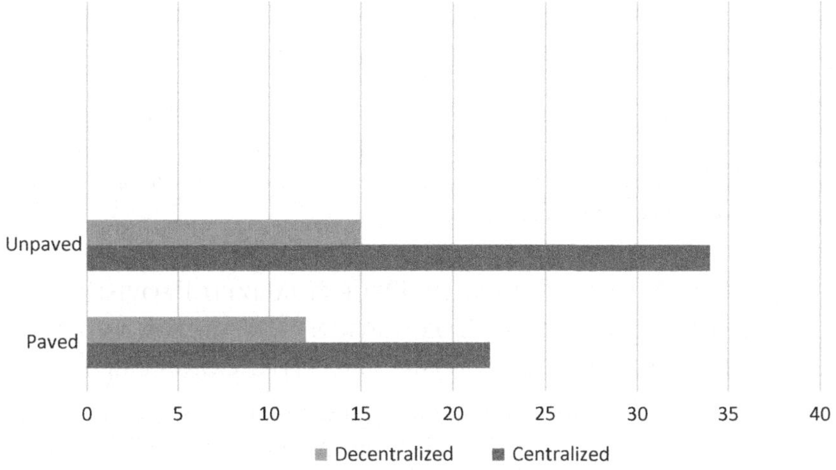

Fig. 6.1 Countries with decentralized road maintenance have better roads (percentage of roads in poor condition). (Source: World Development Report 1994, p. 75)

there were greater leakage of public funds through mismanagement, inefficiency, waste and corruption.

Empirical work on the impact of decentralization on the incidence of corruption is seriously hampered by a lack of reliable data especially on the incidence of corruption. The two most widely used sources are the Transparency International's Corruption Perception Indexes (CPIs) and Worldwide Governance Indicators (WGIs) published by the World Bank. Both measures are seriously flawed and indefensible as they make false comparisons across countries for any year and over time and for tracking any country overtime. Underlying data bases they use simply do not permit such rankings and comparisons as different sources of survey data and questions with weights that vary overtime for each country and across countries are used (see Arndt 2008a, b; Ivanyna and Shah 2011b for a critique and illustration of this point using data sources and weights used by both CPI and WGI indicators and for an illustration of an alternate methodology). Professor Joel Slemrod, from the University of Michigan, has aptly remarked in another context but his saying applies equally well here: "Whatever we have learned is false and whatever we know is half-truth. We really do not know what we do know or do not know." Moreover, these measures are simply not available at subnational levels. What is needed is a worldwide survey using uniform questionnaire and employing a stratified random sampling approach in each country to seek an aggregate view of local perceptions on the incidence of corruption. Ivanyna and Shah (2011a, b, 2014) take a first small step in this direction as well as developing subnational indicators. There is also need for rigorous case study work in this area. In recent years, the University of Gotenburg and the World Bank have taken small steps to improve our knowledge on quality of governance at subnational levels.

6.6 Overall Impact of Decentralized Provision of Infrastructure on Corruption—By Sector and by Type of Corruption: Some Tentative Conclusions

Earlier section demonstrated that empirical work on the impact of decentralized provision of infrastructure is scant. A handful of studies available indicate overall positive influence of decentralization on the integrity of public infrastructure provision. Given the paucity of evidence, one cannot, however, reach any conclusive view on this issue. Conceptual literature on the subject, is however, vast and yet equally inconclusive. While the dominant theme in this literature again is the positive influence of decentralization in curtailing corruption, yet it cannot serve as the basis for reaching any definitive conclusions. In fact, there is some wisdom in not reaching any conclusive view as the incidence is case dependent. Much depends upon the history, culture, organization and public and private sector environment of each case study. Recognizing this important proviso, Table 6.7 presents a stylized conjectural view of the overall impact of decentralized provision of infrastructure on the sector and type of corruption. Short-run (SR) impact of decentralization on petty corruption is conjectured to be positive in curtailing corruption for water and sanitation, transportation and electricity and sports and recreation centers but petty bribes for hospital and school admissions and drugs may continue and could be perceived to have increased in view of greater access to information and transparency with decentralization. In the long run, greater local accountability and oversight kicks in to reduce petty corruption in all sectors. Decentralization is also expected to reduce grant corruption in all sectors except sports and recreation centers in the short run. For sports and recreation centers in the short run, it may be difficult to hold local government to account due to a lack of adequate information in view of the non-standard nature of these infrastructures but in the long run grand

Table 6.7 Overall impact of decentralization on curtailing corruption in infrastructure in developing countries

Sector	*Type of corruption*							
	Petty		*Grand*		*State or regulatory capture*		*Clientelism*	
	SR	*LR*	*SR*	*LR*	*SR*	*LR*	*SR*	*LR*
Water and sanitation	+	+	+	+	–	–	–	–
Roads, bridges, mass transit	+	+	+	+	–	–	–	–
Electricity (public)	+	+	+	+	–	–	–	–
Electricity (private)	+	+	+	+	–	–	–	–
Hospitals	–	+	+	+	–	–	–	–
Schools	–	+	+	+	–	–	–	–
Fitness, sports and recreation centers	+	+	–	+	–	–	–	–
Overall	?	+	+	+	–	–	–	–

Source: Shah (2016)

corruption is expected to be reduced in all sectors due to better information and greater local accountability. State or regulatory captures or clientelism where it persists may not be overcome by decentralization either in the short run or in the long run as these phenomena are related to the nature of political and cultural institutions and may be hard to overcome without fundamental political finance and land reforms. And the latter reforms may be blocked by powerful local elites.

6.7 Ensuring Integrity of Decentralized Provision of Public Infrastructure: The Way Forward

The decentralized provision of infrastructure holds the promise of curtailing corruption provided there is no elite capture, strong institutions of accountability in governance, results-based governance culture and an educated and empowered citizenry. These ideal conditions are absent to varying degrees in most countries. In view of this, one has to tailor institutional design for integrity to individual country and locality conditions. In the following, we provide a stylized view of such policies based on the initial state of public governance in the country.

As a starting point, one has to consider unbundling infrastructure services for market competition. By isolating first the natural monopoly segments of the sector, one can examine range of market alternatives for unbundling rest of infrastructure provision. This includes regulatory framework that encourages: (a) competition for substitutes; (b) competition for infrastructure markets; (c) competition for the right to supply the entire market through leases and concessions; (d) privatization of some monopolies to reap efficiency gains; and (e) having national and regional data bases to provide benchmark on similar operations.

Beyond that one has to apply a "corruption opportunity test" (Khan 2008) to each case of government intervention by asking the following:

1. Is the culture of government organization and environment conducive to corruption?
2. What is the probability that applicable laws, rules, regulations, procedures, instructions or practices, could be misused or bypassed by corrupt intentions?
3. Are there controls in place that would forestall a corrupt person from indulging in corruption by abuse of authority or misuse of discretion or misinterpretation or disregard of rules?

Answers to these questions will help in developing location-specific safeguards in ensuring integrity of public financing or provision of infrastructure. In dealing with various forms of corruption in infrastructure provision, policy and institutional response will vary according to local circumstances. Table 6.8 provides a stylized view of such responses in two polar cases of countries and localities with good and poor governance. The table stresses the importance of more fundamental policy and institutional reforms in the case of poor governance and mostly direct focus on detection and punishment of corruption in case of good governance.

Table 6.8 Ensuring integrity of decentralized provision of public infrastructure: options

Type of corruption	*Existing state of governance in national and local jurisdictions*	
	Good	*Poor*
Legislative capture	Political finance reforms	Establish rule of law, strengthen institutions of accountability in governance, land reforms, citizen empowerment, media independence
Executive capture	Separation of legislative and executive powers, citizen empowerment	Transparency in governance, anti-monopoly and pro-competition legal framework, results-based accountability
Grand corruption at various decision points	Transparency requirements. Investigations and prosecution	Managing for results human resource framework. Transparency rules. Police, justice reforms. Output-based budgeting and activity-based accounting, benchmarking, results-based and competitive financing of all providers. Text messaging to a complaints bureau, prosecution, punitive sanctions on conviction
Grand corruption in public procurement	Investigations and prosecution	PFM reforms, corruption opportunity test framework for procurement, transparency, competitive open bidding, independent tender evaluation, simplification of tender document, smaller size contracts, benchmarking requirements, severe sanctions for non-compliance

(*continued*)

Table 6.8 (continued)

Type of corruption	*Existing state of governance in national and local jurisdictions*	
	Good	*Poor*
Grand corruption in public-private partnerships	Transparency provisions for contracts. Managerial accountability for safeguarding public interest. Prohibition on renegotiating contracts during or post implementation. Investigations and prosecution	Facilitating private sector development and enhancement of competition to provide public services. Transparent and open contracts subject to legislative ratification, public scrutiny and examination, benchmarking requirements, investigations and prosecution
Administrative corruption and theft in public distribution	Investigations and prosecution	Rights-based approach to public services. Greater voice and exit options. Transparency, open management information system, mopping operations
Conflict of interest by employees	Oversight and sanctions by peers	Citizen complaints bureaus, peer-based sanctions

Source: Shah (2016)

Table 6.9 presents options for improving governance of individual sectors to ensure incorruptible governance. The table emphasizes creating an incentive-cum-accountability regime to ensure that all stakeholders advance public interest. This is best done by introducing a bottom-line for government where no bottom-line exists, introducing competition to improve voice and exit options for citizens and strengthening citizens' oversight of all providers and sunshine provisions to ensure that government and private providers are subjected to continuous scrutiny. These practices are expected to improve management of infrastructure provisions and its responsiveness to citizens' needs and preferences as well accountability of providers to residents. Such incentives and accountability regime is expected to improve efficiency, equity and integrity of public provision of infrastructure.

Having a broader local public finance management framework that is focused on incorruptible, responsible and accountable governance at the local level can also help in safeguarding against malfeasance and corruption. This framework emphasizes fiscal transparency, a framework for fiscal

Table 6.9 Ensuring integrity of decentralized provision of public infrastructure: Options for sectoral reforms in developing countries

Sector	*Policies for incorruptible management*
Water and sanitation	Commercialized public authority, concessions and lease, local community, user group oversight, transparency requirements
Roads, bridges and mass transit	Commercialized public authority, concession or lease with tolls, rural roads by community self-help or user groups, user group oversight, transparency of financial and service delivery reports
Electricity (public utilities)	Commercialization of public utilities with explicit contractual mandates, and citizen oversight boards, transparency requirements
Electricity (private utilities)	Regulatory oversight on capital and maintenance, price regulation, citizens oversight board, transparency requirements
Hospitals	Competitive financing of public and private hospitals to foster competition commercialization of public hospitals with autonomous citizen management and oversight boards, transparency requirements
Schools	Competitive financing of public and private schools to foster competition, parents' committees oversight on all aspects of school operations, transparency requirements
Fitness, sports and recreation centers	Citizens' oversight boards, referenda provisions for approving new projects, transparency requirements

Source: Shah (2016)

discipline, output-based central-local financing, output-based budgeting and activity-based costing, people empowerment, competitive financing and provision with voice and exit options, contractual rather than life-long local service appointments, output-based performance contracts and external audits (see Shah and Shah 2006 for details on the institutional framework for FAIR [fair, accountable, incorruptible and responsive] governance).

In short, the success of decentralized provision of infrastructure with integrity strongly rests on having an open local government with citizen-based accountability framework that is reinforced by results-based higher-level financing. Once there is at least a fair level of institutional framework that supports such local governance, then there are some promising entry points such as open process of zoning or a framework for integrity in procurement and results-based management that have the significant potential to curtail corruption at the local level.

6.8 Concluding Remarks

During the past three decades, a large number of countries have introduced reforms to decentralize public decision-making. Such reforms have proved controversial. Critics of these reforms argue that decentralized provision of infrastructure enhances vulnerability to corruption. Proponents of these reforms counter that corruption arises from lack of people empowerment and decentralization by bringing decision-making closer to people shines sunlight on government operations and empowers people to hold government to account and thereby offers potential for combating corruption in the long run. They further state that decentralized provision of infrastructure holds a great promise in upgrading infrastructure to underserviced especially rural areas with local self-government. In theory, such decentralization is also expected to improve integrity of such operations especially in the event of local financing. These debates, nevertheless, remain unsettled as empirical evidence on the impact of decentralization on infrastructure provision is scant or non-existent. Empirical work is hampered by a lack of reliable data on the incidence of corruption. This chapter has presented conceptual underpinnings of the impact of decentralized provision of infrastructure on the incidence of corruption and synthesized scant available empirical evidence to make a case for further empirical research to document the real-world experiences to update our current state of knowledge on this subject. Much work lies ahead to limit our wide zone of ignorance in this area.

References

Abed, George T., and Hamid Davoodi. 2000. Corruption, Structural Reforms, and Economic Performance in the Transition Economies. International Monetary Fund Working Paper No. 00/132.

Acconcia, Antonio, Marcello D'Amato, and Riccardo Martina. 2003. Corruption and Tax Evasion With Competitive Bribes, 112. CSEF Working Papers. University of Salerno: Centre for Studies in Economics and Finance.

Advig, Jens Chr, and Karl O. Moene. 1990. How Corruption May Corrupt. *Journal of Economic Behavior and Organization* 13: 63–76.

Ahlin, Christian. 2000. *Corruption, Aggregate Economic Activity and Political Organization*. University of Chicago, processed.

———. 2001. Corruption: Political Determinants and Macroeconomic Effects. Working Paper. Vanderbilt University: Department of Economics No. 01-W26.

Andrews, Matthew, and Anwar Shah. 2005. Towards Citizen-Centered Local Budgets in Developing Countries. In *Public Expenditure Analysis*, ed. Anwar Shah. Washington, DC: World Bank.

Arikan, Gulsun. 2000. *Fiscal Decentralization: A Remedy for Corruption?* Department of Economics, University of Illinois at Urbana-Champaign, Processed.

———. 2004. Fiscal Decentralization: A Remedy for Corruption? *International Tax and Public Finance* 11: 175–1995.

Arndt, C. 2008a. The Politics of Governance Ratings. *International Public Management Journal* 11: 275–297.

———. 2008b. *What Is Happening to the Level of Corruption in ECA and the World, PowerPoint Presentation at the World Bank*. Washington, DC: Mimeo.

Bac, Mehmet, and Parimal K. Bag. 1998. *Corruption, Collusion and Implementation: A Hierarchial Design*. Mimeo: University of Liverpool.

Banfield, Edward. 1975. Corruption as Feature of Government Organization. *Journal of Law and Economics* 18: 587–695.

Bardhan, Pranab. 1997. Corruption and Development: A Review of Issues. *Journal of Economic Literature* 35: 1320–1346.

Bardhan, Pranab, and Dilip Mookherjee. 2001. Corruption and Decentralization of Infrastructure Delivery in Developing Countries. Working Paper, Berkeley: University of California.

Batley, R. 1999. *The Role of Government in Adjusting Economies: An Overview of Findings*. Birmingham: International Development Department, University of Birmingham.

Becker, Gary Stanley. 1968. Crime and Punishment: An Economic Approach. *Journal of Political Economy* 76 (2): 169–217.

———. 1983. A Theory of Competition Among Pressure Groups for Political Influence. *Quarterly Journal of Economics* XCVII (3): 371–400.

Becker, Gary Stanley, and George Stigler. 1974. Law Enforcement, Malfeasance and the Compensation of Enforcers. *The Journal of Legal Studies* 3: 1–19.

Blanchard, Olivier, and Andrei Shleifer. 2000. Federalism With and Without Political Centralization: China Versus Russia, 1–14. Working Paper. National Bureau of Economic Research No. 7616, March.

Boadway, Robin, and Anwar Shah. 2009. *Fiscal Federalism: Principles and Practice of Multiorder Governance*. New York/London: Cambridge University Press.

Carbonara, Emanuela. 1999. Bureaucracy, Corruption and Decentralization. University of Bologna, Department of Economics Working Paper No. 342/33.

Carillo, Juan D. 2000. *Corruption in Hierarchies*, vol. 59: 37–61. Annales D'economie Et De Statistique/Institut National De La Statistique Et Des Etudes Economiques.

Chand, Sheetal K., and Karl O. Moene. 1997. Controlling Fiscal Corruption. International Monetary Fund Working Paper WP/97/100.

Crook, Richard, and James Manor. 2000. Democratic Decentralization. OED Working Paper Series No. 11. Washington, DC: World Bank.

De Mello, Luis, and Matias Barenstein. 2001. Fiscal Decentralization and Governance – A Cross-Country Analysis. IMF Working Paper 01/71.

Ehlermann-Cache, Nicola. 2007. *Bribery in Public Procurement: Methods, Actors and Counter-Measures*. Paris: OECD.

Fan, C., Lin, C. and Treisman, D. 2009. Political Decentralizationand Corruption: Evidence from Around the World. *Journal of Public Economics* 93: 14–34.

Fisman, Raymond, and Roberta Gatti. 2002. Decentralization and Corruption: Evidence Across Countries. *Journal of Public Economics* 83: 325–345.

Fiszbein, Ariel. 1997. Emergence of Local Capacity: Lessons from Colombia. *World Development* 25 (7): 1029–1043.

Flatters, Frank, and W. Bentley Macleod. 1995. Administrative Corruption and Taxation. *International Tax and Public Finance* 2: 397–417.

Grossman, Gene M., and Elhanan Helpman. 1994. Protection for Sale. *American Economic Review* 84 (4): 833–850.

Gurgur, Tugrul, and Anwar Shah. 2002. Localization and Corruption: Panacea or Pandora's Box? In *Managing Fiscal Decentralization*, ed. Ehtisham Ahmad and Vito Tanzi, 46–67. London/New York: Routledge Press.

Guriev, Sergei. 1999. A Theory of Informative Red Tape with an Application to Top-Level Corruption. Working Paper 99/007. New Economic School, Moscow.

Huther, Jeff, and Anwar Shah. 1998. Applying a Simple Measure of Good Governance to the Debate on Fiscal Decentralization. Policy Research Working Paper 1894. Washington, DC: World Bank.

Isham, Jonathan, and Satu Kahkonen. 1999. What Determines the Effectiveness of Community-Based Water Projects? Evidence from Central Java, Indonesia on Demand Responsiveness, Service Roles and Social Capital. Social Capital Initiative Working Paper Series 14 (Washington, DC: World Bank).

Ivanyna, Maksym, and Anwar Shah. 2011a. Decentralization and Corruption: New Cross-Country Evidence. *Environment and Planning C: Government and Policy* 29 (2): 344–362.

———. 2011b. Citizen-Centric Governance Indicators: Measuring and Monitoring Governance by Listening to the People. *CESifo Forum* 1: 59–71.

———. 2014. How Close Is Your Government to Its People? Worldwide Indicators on Localization and Decentralization. *Economics: The Open-Access, Open-Assessment E-Journal* 8 (3): 1–61. https://doi.org/10.5018/economics-ejournal.ja.2014-3.

Khan, Akram. 2008. *Auditing for Combatting Corruption in Procurement*. Unpublished paper, World Bank Institute.

Klitgaard, Robert E. 1988. *Controlling Corruption*. Berkeley: University of California Press.

———. 1991. Gifts and Bribes. In *Strategy and Choice*, ed. Richard Zeckhauser. Cambridge, MA: MIT Press.

Kuncoro, Ari. 2000. *The Impact of Licensing Decentralization on Firm Location Choice: The Case of Indonesia*. Faculty of Economics, University of Indonesia, processed.

Olowu, Dele. 1993. Roots and Remedies of Government Corruption in Africa. *Corruption and Reform* 7 (3): 227–236.

Prud'homme, Remy. 1994. On the Dangers of Decentralization. World Bank Policy Research Working Paper 1252. Washington, DC: World Bank.

Rose-Ackerman, S. 1975. The Economics of Corruption. *Journal of Public Economics* 4: 187–203.

———. 1978. *Corruption a Study in Political Economy*. New York/San Francisco/London: Academic Press.

Scharpf, Fritz W. 1997. *Games Real Actors Play – Actor-Centered Institutionalism in Policy Research*. Boulder: Westview Print.

Seabright, Paul. 1996. Accountability and Decentralization in Government: An Incomplete Contracts Model. *European Economic Review* 40 (1): 61–89.

Shah, Anwar. 1998. Balance, Accountability, and Responsiveness: Lessons About Decentralization. World Bank Policy Research Working Paper Series 2021, December.

———. 1999. Governing for Results in a Globalized and Localized World. *The Pakistan Development Review* 38 (4): 385–431.

———. 2005. On Getting the Giant to Kneel: Approaches to a Change in the Bureaucratic Culture. In *Fiscal Management. Public Sector Governance and Accountability Series*, ed. Anwar Shah, 211–229. Washington, DC: World Bank.

———. 2006. Decentralized Governance and Corruption. In *Handbook of Fiscal Federalism*, ed. E. Ahmad and G. Brosio, 478–498. Cheltenham: Edward Elgar.

———. 2012. The 18th Constitutional Amendment: Glue or Solvent for Nation Building and Citizenship in Pakistan. *The Lahore Journal of Economics* 17: 387–424.

———. 2016. Decentralized Provision of Public Infrastructure and Corruption. In *Decentralization and Infrastructure in the Global Economy*, ed. Jonas Frank and Jorge Martinez-Vazquez, 418–454. New York: Routledge Press.

Shah, Anwar, and Mark Schacter (2004). Combating Corruption. Look Before You Leap. *Finance and Development* 41 (4): 40–43. Washington. DC: IMF.

Shah, Anwar, and Sana Shah. 2006. The New Vision of Local Governance and the Evolving Role of Local Governments. In *Local Governance in Developing Countries*, ed. Anwar Shah. Washington, DC: World Bank.

Shah, Anwar, Theresa Thompson, and Heng-fu Zou. 2004. The Impact of Decentralization on Service Delivery, Corruption, Fiscal Management and Growth in Developing and Emerging Market Economies: A Synthesis of Empirical Evidence. *CESifo Dice Report, A Quarterly Journal for Institutional Comparisons* 2: 10–14.

Shleifer, Andrei, and Roberth W. Vishny. 1993. Corruption. *Quarterly Journal of Economics* 108: 599–617.

Tanzi, Vito. 1995. Fiscal Federalism and Decentralization: A Review of Some Efficiency and Macroecoomic Aspects. In *Annual World Bank Conference on Development Economics*, 295–316. Washington, DC: World Bank.

Tanzi, Vito, and Hamid Davoodi. 1997. Corruption, Public Investment, and Growth. International Monetary Fund Working Paper 97/139.

Tapales, Prosperpina. 2001. An Evaluation of Anti-corruption Programs in Philippines. World Bank Operations Evaluation Department, Washington, DC.

Tirole, Jean. 1986. Hierarchies and Bureaucracies: On the Role of Collusion in Organizations. *Journal of Law Economics and Organization* 2: 181–214.

Tomaszewska, Ewa, and Anwar Shah. 2000. Phantom Hospitals, Ghost Schools and Roads to Nowhere: The Impact of Corruption on Public Service Delivery Performance in Developing Countries. Working Paper Operations Evaluation Department, World Bank.

Treisman, Daniel S. 1999. *After the Deluge: Regional Crises and Political Consolidation in Russia*. Ann Arbor: University of Michigan Press.

———. 2000. The Causes of Corruption: A Cross National Study. *Journal of Public Economics* 76 (3): 399–457.

Van Rijckeghem, Caroline, and Beatrice Weder. 2001. Bureaucratic Corruption and the Rate of Temptation: Do Low Wages in Civil Service Cause Corruption? *Journal of Development Economics* 65: 307–331.

Von Maravic, Patrick. 2003. *How to Analyse Corruption in the Context of Public Management Reform?* Paper presented at the first meeting of the Study Group on Ethics and Integrity of Governance EGPA Conference, September. Portugal.

Wade, Robert. 1997. How Infrastructure Agencies Motivate Staff: Canal Irrigation in India and the Republic of Korea. In *Infrastructure Strategies in East Asia*, ed. Ashoka Mody. Washington, DC: World Bank.

Waller, Christopher J., Thierry A. Verdier, and Roy Gardner. 2002. Corruption: Top–Down or Bottom–Up. *Economic Inquiry* 40 (4): 688–703.

Weinsgast, Barry. 1995. The Economic Role of Political Institutions: Market Preserving Federalism and Economic Growth. *Journal of Law, Economics, and Organization* 11: 1–31.

Wildasin, David. 1995. Comment on 'Fiscal Federalism and Decentralization'. In *Annual World Bank Conference on Development Economics*, 323–328. Washington, DC: World Bank.

World Bank. 1994. World Development Report, 1994. Washington, DC: World Bank.

———. 2004. *Mainstreaming Anti-Corruption Activities in World Bank Assistance—A Review of Progress Since 1997*. Washington, DC: World Bank.

CHAPTER 7

Measuring and Monitoring Local Government Performance

7.1 Introduction

Democratization through political decentralization spread like wildfire in developing and transition economies in the 1990s yet fruits of this democratic participation remain largely elusive. What went wrong? This chapter argues that these disappointing results may be attributable to a lack of progress in citizen empowerment to hold governments accountable in between elections as a median voter lacks the information to evaluate government performance and hold it to account. Such a situation can arise because it is in the interest of political and bureaucratic elites to ensure that the status quo prevails and the sun does not shine on government operations. Unraveling of this system requires fundamental institutional and legal reforms to ensure greater transparency and to empower citizens to demand accountability for performance from their governments. This chapter focuses on the role of local governments to bring about this change. Local governments around the world have made important innovations to strengthen local accountability to earn the trust of their residents. The practice in this area, however, has leapfrogged the conceptual perspectives. This chapter attempts to fill this void by developing a general framework for performance accountability of local governments and by relating real-world practices to aspects of this framework.

The rest of this chapter is organized as follows. Widely used mandatory and voluntary approaches to monitor local government performance are highlighted first. This is followed by a hybrid theory and practice approach

B. Dollery et al., *Local Public, Fiscal and Financial Governance*,
https://doi.org/10.1007/978-3-030-36725-1_7

on local government accountability and thoughts on its implementation methods and processes are presented. This is followed by highlighting real-world examples of better as well not-so-good practices in local government performance accountability. A concluding section draws general lessons from these experiences.

7.2 Approaches to Local Government Performance Monitoring

In outlining approaches to local government performance monitoring, we are primarily focused on practices followed in both industrial and developing countries. In recent years some of these practices are strongly influenced by theoretical literature. Our discussion on practices is organized by mandatory or voluntary nature of these practices.

7.2.1 Mandatory Approaches: Approaches Mandated by Higher-Order Governments

Mandatory approaches can be classified into three categories: (a) conformity with due processes; (b) conformity with higher-order mandates and (c) conformity with local fiscal discipline.

Conformity with Due Process Conformity with due process requires following applicable legislative, legal and other formal requirements, for example, following the principle of ultra vires. That is, local government can only engage in activities that are duly authorized by local government act in that they are required to follow legislative guidance regarding the generation and collection of revenues, process requirements in resource disbursement and the provision of services (Andrews and Shah 2005a, b). The laws typically limit both the kind of revenues that local governments can raise and the ways they can raise different revenue types. Local governments are typically subjected to legislated mandates regarding level of spending on and the provision of specific services. They may be subjected to specified minimum standards for quality, quantity and access of some services such as elementary education. Local governments are also required to establish and follow procedure bylaw. They are required to prepare and have legislative approval of local master plans and budgets and zonal bylaws and regulations. Local governments are subject to disclosure requirements especially regarding their finances. In industrial countries they are typically required to submit commercially audited financial statements on a quarterly or annual basis. Conformity with due processes is usually an important element of the evaluation framework carried out by higher-order government audit agencies/commissions.

Conformity with Higher-Order Government Mandates Local governments are expected to comply with funded and unfunded higher-order mandates. Unfunded mandates are spending or monitoring and enforcement of regularity compliance with higher-order government legislation that must be complied with using local funds. Funded mandates typically come in the form of conditions attached to higher-order financial assistance.

Conformity with Local Fiscal Discipline Local governments are typically not allowed to run a deficit on the operating budget and required to follow the golden rule for borrowing, that is, borrowing must be for capital projects. In a large number of developing countries access to capital market finance by local governments is outrightly prohibited. Still, it is possible for local governments to observe this prohibition on direct borrowing but instead borrow through public enterprises and other autonomous agencies as happened in China resulting in a large overhang of local public debt. Therefore, an evaluation of conformity with this legislation must take a closer and comprehensive look at all budgetary and off-budget operations of the local government to get a better view of its fiscal health. Beyond this, it is quite a common practice to enact ex ante fiscal rules that impose limits on expenditures and borrowing by local governments and contains sanctions for non-compliance. Some countries monitor fiscal health of local governments on a regular basis to detect early warning signs of fiscal distress (see Chap. 7, this volume, for details). Such analysis involves tax effort, fiscal prudence in local spending and borrowing. There are instances where local governments have defeated the intent of legislated fiscal rules on balanced budget and limits on borrowing and size of debt through creative accounting. Such practices must be discovered through evaluation and discouraged through appropriate sanctions and penalties. Niesner (1999, 32) argues that evaluators must "check compliance with accounting controls – whether rules had been followed, procedures had been established, proper accounting had been made, and controls (internal and external) were in place and functioning".

7.2.2 Voluntary Approaches: Approaches Used by Local Governments Voluntarily

Quite a large number of practices are followed by local governments especially in industrial countries to measure, monitor and disseminate their performance to build public trust in their operations. These include:

Results-Based Management Results-based management entails monitoring the results-based chain of local government operations: programs, activities, inputs, intermediate outputs, final outputs, outcomes, impact and reach of those operations to determine the consistency of the programs in achieving the desired results. Such results-based management is assisted by various management tools such as performance-based budgeting (see Chap. 6), benchmarking of performance against self over time and against competitive local governments. Activity-based costing helps monitor product or service costs and accrual accounting gives a better financial picture by capturing costs when commitments are made regardless of when expenditure is undertaken and a balanced score card helps a local government assess its overall performance against a composite evaluation criteria (see Table 7.1).

Benchmarking Analysis Benchmarking analysis is also a tool frequently used by local governments for self-evaluation and improvement of their performance (see Table 7.1 for a listing of principal tools for results-oriented management). Through benchmarking, a local government can have specific goals to judge their performance against itself as well as against comparators at a point in time and overtime. The indicators frequently used for this purpose, with examples for police protection and roadways, are:

- the cost of general administration (e.g., per capita general administration overhead costs);
- the cost of various public services (e.g., per capita expenditures);
- the workload of public services (e.g., average number of police calls, lane miles to be constructed and maintained);

Table 7.1 Tools for results-oriented management—external, citizen focus

Questions for results-oriented management	*Management tool*	*The entire process driven by a citizen focus*
Contract information—What is the final product we must produce and what do we receive to produce such product?	Performance-based budget	All these tools are connected to total quality management and such devices used to create a results and participation culture, and work effectively where roles emphasize results.
How do we know how we are doing in terms of the contract, and in terms of other producers from whom we can learn?	Benchmarking	
How much does it cost to produce such product (the total cost)? How can we produce the product better so we can be sure of meeting and exceeding our contract obligation and receiving rewards?	Activity-based costing (and others)	
How do we report our results?	Full reporting using accrual accounting	
How do we manage the new reporting, production, and contract obligation we have, as well as run a citizen friendly administration?	Balanced scorecard	

Source: Andrews and Shah (2005a, b)

- the efficiency of public services (e.g., average cost per incident, annual maintenance cost per lane mile);
- the equity of public service provision (e.g., crime prevention in poor neighborhoods, access to public transit by the poor and the needy);
- the quality and quantity of public services (e.g., percentage of cases cleared, percentage of lane miles in good repair); and
- the quality of life in the municipality (e.g., incident of violent crimes per 1000 people, citizens' satisfaction with services).

The above information can be highly useful to policymakers in improving performance and to citizens for performance accountability of their local governments.

Access to Information and Transparency Access to information by local residents is critical to their understanding and appreciation of local government performance. Fortunately, information revolution has expanded boundaries of access to information on local government operations.

Table 7.2 Key principles and indicators for assessing local government performance

Principles	*Indicators*
Conformity with the law and due process	Establishes procedure bylaw Local master plan and budgets Zoning laws and regulations
Aggregate fiscal discipline	Aggregate budget envelope established in advance of spending decisions and sustainable over the medium and long term Local revenue means consistent with local expenditure needs Fiscal gap minimized by exploring additional own source revenues Operating budget financed by current revenues and capital budget from borrowing and reserves Budgeting linked with planning through medium term expenditure framework Debt management framework formalized External and internal controls in place Ex ante fiscal rules regarding deficit and debt and sanctions for non-compliance
Allocative efficiency	Expenditure priorities based upon the most effective programs consistent with citizens' preferences for public services Businesses taxed for services to businesses, residents taxed for services to residents, and no cross-subsidization Spending limits established for various services, and departments encouraged to reallocate funds within this envelope depending upon evaluation findings of program effectiveness Departmental managers acquire and disseminate information on the resources used and results achieved
Operational efficiency	Local public services provided in a least-cost manner based upon best value for the tax payers' money Local managers held accountable for output targets and given flexibility in the use of resources and the modes of service delivery Local provisions subjected to competitive pressures from alternative service providers, and residents have voice and exit options Local government performance on individual services benchmarked against comparator local jurisdictions
Equity	Local governments strive to ensure fairness in service delivery and social inclusion Redistributive programs financed by higher-level governments so that local economic development objectives are not compromised
Accountability to residents and higher-level governments	Local governments accountable to local residents and higher-level governments Full disclosure of all information on local government operations to residents and higher-level governments Comprehensive, transparent, and output-based budgeting presented in user-friendly format and disseminated in timely fashion

Source: Shah (2014b)

Allocational Efficiency Allocative efficiency refers to sectoral allocation choices consistent with citizen preferences for various public services. An important rationale for having local self-rule is to ensure consistency of public decision-making at the local level with local preferences. This principle should guide the legislative and executive decisions on local public spending. Monitoring of local government performance against this criterion is typically done by external often academic evaluations (see also Table 7.2).

Operational Efficiency According to this criterion, local public services should be provided in a least cost manner based upon best value for the taxpayers' money. Recent literature suggests that operational efficiency is best achieved when local government acts as a catalyst for network provision of public services by strengthening collaborative as well competitive public service delivery through a variety of public and non-public providers—the so-called alternative public service delivery approach. Further local government acts as a purchaser but not necessarily a provider of public services. Such an environment fosters competition and innovation in public service provision creating substantial gains in operational efficiency. As measuring operational efficiency is a complex subject, only occasional monitoring of local government operational efficiency is available through periodic academic evaluations.

Equity Local government operations protect the needy and the poor and promote social inclusion. Such an evaluation is only available periodically through academic research.

7.3 Responsibility with Accountability: A FAIR Governance Framework for Performance Accountability of Local Governments[1]

The earlier section reported the approaches followed in practice to monitor local government performance. This section presents a hybrid theory and practice approach to measuring and monitoring local government

[1] This section is based upon: Shah, Anwar (2014). "Responsibility with accountability: A FAIR governance framework for performance accountability of local governments": Journal of Economics and Business, Croatia, December 2014 (Zbornik radova Ekonomskog

performance. This hybrid approach develops a rating framework, proposed below, that attempts to reinforce the desired role of the local government for the twenty-first century. In view of this, the rating framework would serve as a useful reference for assessing the institutional framework for local governance for a country as well as rating individual local governments. The framework is intended not just to guide the performance improvements that a local government may be able to undertake itself but also to facilitate reforms that empower local governments to play their due role to improve economic and social outcomes for local residents.

A FAIR governance framework lays down the following four principles for local government performance accountability:

- *Fair Governance*. Fair governance requires that the local government provides equal and fair access to essential public services with equitable sharing of local tax burdens. It also acts as an equal opportunity employer. For peace, order and good government, the local government mediates conflicting interests, is focused on consensus building and inclusiveness and ensures a sense of participation by all and protection of the poor, the minorities and the disadvantaged members of the society.
- *Accountable governance*. Accountable governance requires that citizens may be able to hold the government to account for all its actions while incurring minimum transactions costs. This requires that the local government lets sunshine in on its operations and works to strengthen voice and exit options for principals (Paul 1992). It also means that the government truly respects the role of countervailing formal and informal institutions of accountability in governance. A local government should be accountable to its electorate. It should adhere to appropriate safeguards to ensure that it serves the public interest with integrity. Legal and institutional reforms may be needed to enable local governments to deal with accountability between elections—reforms such as a citizen's charter and a provision for recall of public officials (Shah 2005, 2008).
- *Incorruptible governance*. Incorruptible governance requires that the local government does it right; that is, governmental authority is carried out following due process with integrity (absence of corruption), with fiscal prudence, with concern for providing the best value

fakulteta u Rijeci: časopis za ekonomsku teoriju i praksu/Proceedings of Rijeka Faculty of Economics)

for money and with a view to earning the trust of the people. The government should also do it right—that is, manage its fiscal resources prudently. It should earn the trust of residents by working better and costing less and by managing fiscal and social risks for the community. It should strive to improve the quality and quantity of and access to public services. To do so, it needs to benchmark its performance with the best-performing local government.
- *Responsive governance*. The fundamental task of governing is to promote and pursue collective interest while respecting formal (rule of law) and informal norms. This is done by local government creating an enabling environment to do the right things—that is, it promotes and delivers services consistent with citizen preferences. Further, the government carries out only the tasks that it is authorized to do, that is, it follows the compact authorized by citizens at large.

A rating framework based upon the above principles is embodied in Table 7.3. The table outlines specific criteria on which local governments can be rated for performance. Overall, the rating framework accentuates local government focus on citizen-centered governance. The distinguishing features of citizen-centered governance are:

- Citizen empowerment through a rights-based approach—direct democracy provisions, citizens' charter (see Shah 2008 for details of such an approach)
- Bottom-up accountability for results
- Evaluation of government performance as the facilitator of a network of providers by citizens as governors, taxpayers, and consumers of public services

The framework emphasizes principles that strengthen the role of citizens as the principals and create incentives for government agents to comply with their mandates. The commitment problem may be mitigated by creating citizen-centered local governance—by having direct democracy provisions, introducing governing for results in government operations, and reforming the structure of governance, thus shifting decision-making closer to the people. Direct democracy provisions require referenda on major issues and large projects and require that citizens have the right to veto any legislation or government program. The FAIR governance framework requires government accountability to citizens for service delivery

Table 7.3 A fair governance framework for rating performance accountability of local governments

Fair Governance	*Accountable governance*	*Incorruptible governance*	*Responsive Governance*
Is inclusive	Lets the sunshine in:	Follows due process:	Is citizen focused and customer driven
Protects the poor and the disadvantaged members of the society	Local government bylaw on citizens' right to know	The principle of ultra vires or general competence or community governance	Bylaw on taxpayer rights
Equal and fair access to essential local public services	Budgetary proposals and annual performance reports posted on the internet	The procedure bylaw	Has subsidiarity and home rule
Equal opportunity employer	All decisions, including the costs of concessions, posted on the internet	Local master plans and budgets	Has direct democracy provisions
Equitable sharing of local tax burdens	Value for money performance audits by independent think tanks	Zoning bylaws and regulations	Has budget priorities consistent with citizens' preferences
	Open information and public assessment	Funded mandates	Specifies and meets standards for access to local services
	Works to strengthen citizen voice and exit:	Is fiscally prudent:	Improves social outcomes
	Citizens' charter	Operating budget in balance	Offers security of life and property
	Service standards	Golden rule for borrowing	Offers shelter and food for all
	Requirements for citizens' voice and choice	New capital projects that specify upkeep costs and how debt is to be repaid	Has clean air, safe water, and sanitation
	Sunshine rights	Conservative fiscal rules to ensure sustainable debt levels	Has a noise-free and preserved environment
	Sunset clauses on government programs	Major capital projects that are subject to referenda	Offers ease of commute and pothole-free roads
	Has access to equity- and output-based intergovernmental finance	Maintenance of positive net worth	Has primary school at a walking distance
		Commercially audited financial statements	Has acceptable fire and ambulance response times
		Earns trust:	Has libraries and internet access
		Professionalism and integrity of staff	Has park and recreation programs and facilities
		Safeguards against malfeasance	
		Streamlined processes and e-governance	
		Complaints and feedback acted on	
		Honest and fair tax administration	
		Strict compliance with service standards	

Citizen-oriented performance (output) budgeting	Citizen-friendly output budgets and service delivery performance reports
Service delivery outputs and costs	Participatory budgeting and planning
Citizens' report card on service delivery performance	Works better and costs less:
Budget, contracts, and performance reports defended at open town hall meetings	All tasks subjected to alternative service delivery test—that is, competitive provision involving government providers and entities beyond government
All documents subjected to citizen-friendly requirements	Financing that creates incentives for competition and innovation
Open processes for contract bids	Comparative evaluation of service providers
Mandatory referenda on large projects	Public sector as a purchaser through performance contracts but not necessarily a provider of services
Steps taken so that at least 50% of eligible voters vote	Managerial flexibility, but accountability for results
Citizens' boards to provide scorecard and feedback on service delivery performance	No lifelong or rotating appointments
Provisions for popular initiatives and recall of public officials	Task specialization
	Budgetary allocation and output-based performance contracts
	Activity-based costing
	Charges for capital use
	Accrual accounting
	Benchmarking with the best
	General administration costs subjected to public scrutiny
	Boundaries that balance benefits and costs of scale and scope economies, externalities, and decision-making
	Boundaries consistent with fiscal sustainability

Source: Shah (2006)

performance. Hence, citizens have a charter defining their basic rights as well as their rights of access to specific standards of public services. Output-based intergovernmental transfers strengthen compliance with such standards and strengthen accountability and citizen empowerment (Shah 2010).

The local government performance accountability framework described above has important implications for reforming the structure of government. Top-down mandates on local governance will need to be replaced by bottom-up compacts. Furthermore, the role of local government must be expanded to serve as a catalyst for the formulation, development, and operation of a network of both government providers and entities beyond government. Local government's traditionally acknowledged technical capacity becomes less relevant in this framework. More important are its institutional strengths as a purchaser of services and as a facilitator of alliances, partnerships, associations, clubs, and networks for developing social capital and improving social outcomes.

Table 7.3 provides a comprehensive rating framework to evaluate local governments on the four aspects of FAIR governance. This evaluation would require both inspections and audits for conformity with the law and reporting and requirements on fiscal and financial management and service delivery performance of local governments. It will also require citizens' opinion surveys conducted by independent researchers, think-tanks or non-governmental organizations to assess citizens' evaluations of local government services. These issues are taken up in the next section.

7.3.1 *Implementation of the FAIR Governance Performance Accountability Framework: Process and Methods*

Local government monitoring and oversight requires (a) verifying their conformity with law in following due processes; (b) ensuring that they follow prudent and transparent fiscal and financial management practices (*fiscal discipline*); (c) expenditure priorities are consistent with local preferences (*allocative efficiency*); (d) deliver services in the most cost effective manner (*operational efficiency*); (d) strive to ensure fairness in service delivery and social inclusion and protecting the poor and the needy (*equity*); and (e) are accountable to local residents *(local accountability*). The former two criteria require voluntary compliance and verification through occasional inspections and audits. Table 7.4 presents indicators that are useful for both self-assessment as well as external assessment relating to these concerns.

Table 7.4 Key service delivery performance indicators for local governments

No.	*Function*	*Key performance indicators*
0	General administration	Total full-time equivalent employees Total costs (wages, benefits, pension etc.)
1.	Roads, walkways, and sidewalks (footpaths)	Length: Roads (KM), Walkways and footpaths (KM) Total roads in KM resurfaced each year Physical conditions (rate each): % good, fair or poor condition:
2.	Public electricity	No. of connections Average no. of hours of uninterrupted service per month. No. of billing complaints
3.	Drainage	Length of total wastewater main Length of storm water system Physical condition of drainage infrastructure: % good, fair or poor % of network not completed—wastewater and storm water No. of business and households served No. of incidents of wastewater main backups
4.	Water supply	Total length of water main Physical condition of water infrastructure: % good, fair or poor Percentage of homes with access to safe drinking water 24/7 No. of water main breakup incidents No. of contamination incidents
5.	Child and youth development	Number of children and youth participating in LG-sponsored events
6.	Sports promotion	Number participating in local government sponsored classes or events No. of playgrounds maintained to fair or good condition Square meters of outdoor sports and recreation local government-owned facility space per thousand person
7.	Promotion of elderly	No. of elderly provided with home care (general or nursing visits)
8.	Supporting disadvantaged groups	Total number of disadvantaged clients served

(*continued*)

Table 7.4 (continued)

No.	*Function*	*Key performance indicators*
9.	Public health	Total no. of clinics Number of visitors Number of vaccinations Number of clinics staffed with a qualified GP Number of clinics staffed with a nurse Number with adequate medicines
10.	Promotion of women	Total number of women participating in locally sponsored programs
11.	Promotion of careers	Hours of training/skill-building offered Total participants
12.	Disaster prevention and mitigation	Description of work performed
13.	Promotion of religion, arts, and culture	Total number of participants in local government sponsored events
14.	Promotion of tourism	Total number of tourists Total revenue from tourism
15.	Management of Natural Resources	Description of work
16.	Public education	School-age population Total enrollments Total teachers Completion rates Achievement scores on standardized tests

Source: Shah (2014a)

Several criteria in Tables 7.3 and 7.4 nevertheless require formal periodic reporting requirements. Higher-level government should provide legislative backing for such reporting. All local governments should be required on a quarterly basis to submit reports on their revenues and expenditures. They may also be required to submit annual commercially audited financial balance sheet detailing the previous year revenues and expenditures—both operating and capital, and assets and liabilities within three months after the end of the fiscal year. This should also be accompanied by annual report detailing service delivery performance using a standard format prescribed for all local governments of the same type and size class. Table 7.4 provides a format for reporting service delivery performance. This format can be amended to include additional services performed by local governments or to exclude services listed here but not performed. It is important to publish on the web annually both the financial balance sheet as well as the service delivery performance of local governments so that independent researchers and citizens can vouch for the authenticity of the data being reported as well as develop benchmarking analysis (see also Roberts 2005 for issues associated with government-wide performance monitoring).

The Council of Australian Government specifies a useful set of considerations in deciding upon the performance indicators to be used. These considerations include:

- Meaningful and understandable
- Timely
- Comparable
- Administratively simple/cost effective
- Accurate
- Hierarchical
- Avoid perverse incentives
- Measurable
- Documentable

7.4 Practices in Local Government Performance Accountability

Local governments in industrial countries are subject to stringent higher-level regulations and fiscal rules to ensure fiscal discipline and fiscal sustainability. These typically include compliance with the laws and reporting requirements for financial flows, assets and liabilities. Occasionally, as done by Ontario, Canada, higher-level governments impose reporting requirements for service delivery performance. Beyond this, local governments do more in fiscal and operations transparency to strive to earn the trust of their local residents. In the following paragraphs we highlight useful examples from a select group of countries.

7.4.1 Mandatory Higher-Level Oversight of Local Government Fiscal Health

This is typically done through the requirements of submission of commercially audited financial statements on a quarterly or on an annual basis. These statements are used to develop an early warning system of fiscal stress. For example, in Russia an oblast or a rayon is rated "in fiscal distress" if its debt-to-revenue ratio exceeds 30% and 15% respectively. Debt services to revenue ratio exceeding specified limits is seen in Italy and Spain (25%), Japan (20%) and Russia (15%) indicating fiscal stress. Colombia has developed a traffic light system to rate local government fiscal health (see Crivelli and Shah 2009 and Chap. 5, this volume). A local government is considered to be in good fiscal health (green light) if its interest payments to revenue surplus (excess of current operating revenues over current operating expenditures) ratio is less than 40% and its debt to current income is less than 80%. It is considered in fiscal distress (red light) and subject to central oversight if its ratio of interest payments to revenue surplus exceeds 60% and its ratio of debt to current income exceeds 80%. A ratio of interest payments to revenue surplus in the range of 40–60% qualifies for a close surveillance status (yellow light). The *state of Michigan, United States*, has developed a 10-point fiscal stress indicator for local governments. These points include: population growth (2 years), real taxable value growth (2 years) large decreases in real taxable value, general fund expenditures as percentage of taxable value, general fund operating deficit, prior general fund operating deficits, general fund finances as a percentage of general fund revenues, current and previous year deficit in a major fund, general long-term debt as a percentage of real taxable value. The *state of Ohio, United States*, has a fiscal watch program for its local governments. A local government is placed under fiscal watch if deficit exceeds 8.3% of revenues and the state auditor suggests a workout. A local government is placed under fiscal emergency if it incurs more than 30 days default on debt obligations and/or payment of salaries or deficit or overdue amounts payable exceed one-sixth of the previous year revenues. Such a local government is then placed under a state-appointed control board or planning and supervisory commission (see Chap. 5, Table 5.3). In Philippines, the Central Ministry of Finance has a comprehensive program monitoring fiscal health of local governments.

7.4.2 *Mandatory Local Government Service Delivery Performance Reporting Requirements*

The Province of Ontario, Canada, initiated Municipal Performance Measurement Program (MPMP) in 2000. This was followed in 2000 by the Provinces of Nova Scotia Municipal Indicators Program (MIP) and the Province of Quebec in 2003 initiating Municipal Performance

Measurement System (MPMS). The Ontario program is concerned with measuring the cost efficiency and effectiveness of municipal services and benchmarking inter-local performance in the delivery of services. For each service a minimum set of standardized indicators have been developed (see Table 7.5).

This contrasts with an exhaustive set of indicators used by the UK Audit Commission discussed below. Two examples of benchmarking analysis used by MPMP are presented in Figs. 7.1 and 7.2.

An Update Mandatory nature of MPMP program was discontinued in 2015, and currently the province has a fewer set of indicators than MPMP which municipalities report voluntarily as part of their annual financial return. These indicators pertain to the following services and the province act as a web-based repository and disseminator of these indicators:

- fire departments
- police
- roadways
- transit
- wastewater
- storm water
- drinking water
- solid waste management
- parks and recreation
- library services
- land-use planning
- building services

The indicators are available for individual municipalities but the province no longer provides benchmarking analysis for the province as a whole (see Ontario 2019).

7.4.3 Self-Imposed Transparency and Responsiveness in Local Governance

This is an area where many local governments in the United States excel. They do this by presenting the following information in their annual budgets for each service category. Fairfax County, Virginia, and Cities of Conrad and Cary, North Carolina, represent outstanding examples of full

Table 7.5 Annual list of measures in the Ontario municipal performance measurement program (MPMP) for selected services

Service area	*Objective*	*Types of measure*	*Measures*
Local government:			
Governance and corporate management	Efficient municipal government	Efficiency	Operating costs for governance and corporate management as a percentage of total municipal operating costs
Fire:			
Fire services	Efficient fire services	Efficiency	Operating cost for fire services per $1000 of assessment
Police:			
Police services	Efficient police services	Efficiency	Operating costs for police services per household
Violent crime rate	Safe communities	Effectiveness	Violent crime rate per 1000 persons
Propoerty crime rate	Safe communities	Effectiveness	Property crime rate per 1000 persons
Total crime rate	Safe communities	Effectiveness	Total crime rate per 1000 persons (Criminal Code offences excluding traffic)
Youth crime rate	Safe communities	Effectiveness	Youth crime rate per 1000 youths
Roadways:			
Paved roads	Efficient maintenance	Efficiency	Operating costs for paved (hard top) roads per land kilometer
Unpaved roads	Efficient maintenance	Efficiency	Operating costs for unpaved (loose top) roads per lane kilometer
Winter maintenance of roadways	Efficient maintenance	Efficiency	Operating costs for winter maintenance of roadways per lane kilometer maintained in winter
Pavement condition	Pavement condition meets municipal objectives	Effectiveness	Percentage of paved lane kilometers where the condition is rated as good to very good
Response to winter storm events	Appropriate repose to winter storm events	Effectiveness	Percentage of winter events where the response met or exceeded locally determined road maintenance standards

(*continued*)

Table 7.5 (continued)

Service area	*Objective*	*Types of measure*	*Measures*
Transit:			
Conventional transit Conventional transit ridership	Efficient conventional transit Maximum utilization of conventional transit services	Efficiency Effectiveness	Operating costs for conventional transit per regular service passenger trip Number of conventional transit passenger trips per person in the service area in a year
Drinking water:			
Water treatment Water distribution Water treatment and distribution (integrated system) Boil water advisories Water main breaks	Efficient municipal water treatment services Efficient distribution Efficient system Water is safe and meets local needs Improve system reliability	Efficiency Efficiency Efficiency Effectiveness Effectiveness	Operating costs for the treatment of drinking water per megaliter Operating costs for the distribution of drinking water per kilometer of water distribution pipe Operating costs for the treatment and distribution of drinking water per megaliter Weighted number of days when a boil water advisory issued by the Medical Officer of Health, applicable to a municipal water supply was in effect Number of water main breaks per 100 kilometers of water distribution pipe in a year

Source: Government of Ontario (2019)

Notes: The above is a partial list as the MPMP also provides indicators for wastewater, storm water, solid waste management, parks and recreation, library services and land use planning. See Government of Ontario (2019)

disclosure of their operations through performance budgeting on their website. A performance budget presents details on the entire results-based chain and in the process provides information that is relevant for policy-makers as well as citizens-based local government accountability. Furthermore, such an approach to budgeting reinforces results-based accountability of local governments (see Shah and Shen 2007). City of Sunnyvale, California, presents an annual report card of municipal

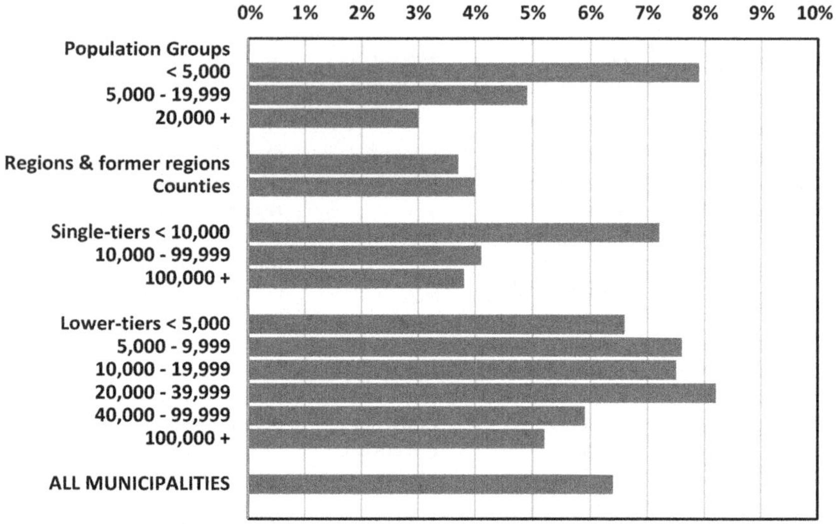

Fig. 7.1 Operating costs for governance and corporate management as a percentage of total municipal operating costs, 2007 (Median). (Source: Government of Ontario website)

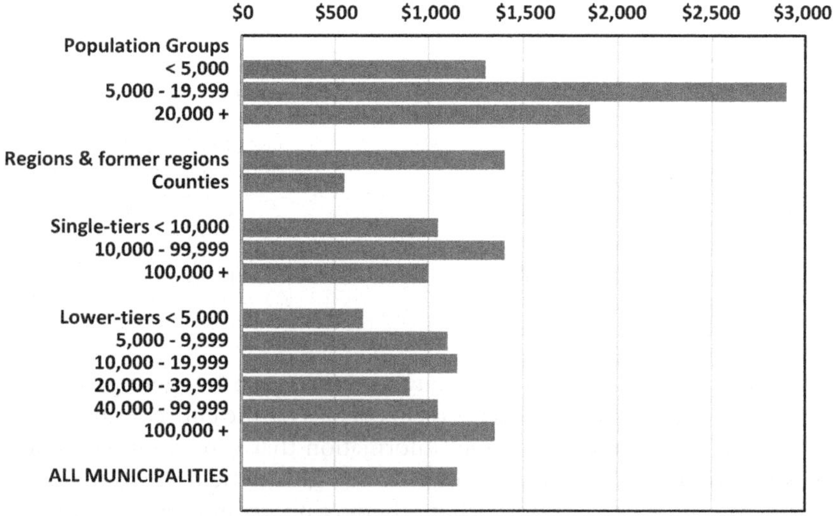

Fig. 7.2 Operating costs for paved (hard top) roads per lane kilometer, 2007 (Median). (Source: Government of Ontario website)

performance. Municipal Benchmarking Network established in 2019 reports municipal performance measures for 16 participating municipalities across Canada. Naga City in Philippines championed the Naga city charter that established services standards for city services and provides an annual performance report in meeting these standards. Hong Kong disseminates comprehensive information on its operations. In Bangalore, information on municipal operations is disseminated through NGOs by so-called Bangalore Report Cards (Paul 1996, 2007). Jenkins and Goetz (1999, 605) note that such dissemination "reinforces democratic notions regarding the obligations of elected representatives as public servants" and leads to performance in service delivery. Porto Alegre, Brazil, represents an important example of municipal initiative to improve people participation in local public decision-making while improving transparency and responsiveness of its budgetary allocation processes. It has established formal processes to seek community participation and translate those inputs into budgetary plans to influence sectoral allocations consistent with community's preferences—the so-called practice of participatory budgeting (see Wampler 2007 and Goldfrank 2007 for details).

7.5 Case Studies in Failure

Two examples from United Kingdom (UK) and Indonesia, of poorly designed and heavy-handed central government oversight of local governments are reviewed in the following paragraphs to draw lessons of interest to other countries.

7.5.1 *The Curious Case of Higher-Level Local Government Intrusive Oversight: UK Audit Commission*

United Kingdom represents the most ambitious yet a curious case of higher-level oversight of local governments. Through the Local Government Act, 1999, it introduced the Best Value Framework (BVF) as a statutory requirement for all local governments to deliver services to specified standards in the most efficient and effective manner possible. The BVF required every local government to report pre-specified set of cost and quality Best Value Performance Indicators (BVPIs) for each service and also expectations and needs of their clients for various services. The UK Audit Commission served as the custodian of this program to ensure the integrity of data. The Commission subjected local governments to rigorous inspections and audits. In 2002, BVPIs were replaced by a Comprehensive Performance Assessment (CPA; see Audit Commission 2002). The CPA represented one of the most ambitious system to provide oversight on local governments. The new system augmented individual service indicators by developing aggregate indicators of overall efficiency and effectiveness of individual authorities. These aggregate indicators showed how each local government performed for each service and overall and in comparisons with other local governments. The CPA system led to significant improvements in service delivery performance. The system proved controversial though as local governments became wary of the Audit Commission's intervention in their day-to-day management and also complained about the heavy burden of reporting and inspections and audits. In response, Comprehensive Area Assessment (CAA) replaced comprehensive performance assessment (CPA) in April 2009. CAA seeks to assess how well communities are being served by their local public services, including councils, police, health, and fire and rescue services. It emphasizes the quality of life of residents, and how well these bodies, working together, are achieving improvement and progressing towards long-term goals. It will also highlight best practices and innovation, and identify any barriers to improvement. The intention is also for CAA to provide information to local people about their local services. This will increase their awareness of the services available to them, empowering them to make better decisions and get value for money (Audit Commission 2010).

To do this, CAA included two elements:

1. Area Assessment

An area assessment is a combined inspectorate judgment, which assesses the extent to which councils and their partners are delivering improvements on the issues that matter to people within the local area. It considers whether the priorities set in the area reflect those of the people who live there. Area assessments also look at how effectively improvements are delivered now and in the future. The starting point for the area assessment is the sustainable community strategy (SCS) and local area agreement (LAA). The SCS sets out the vision and aspirations for an area and the LAA sets out how it shall be measured. The area assessment is not scored or 'star rated'. It is a narrative report providing an overview of key priorities for the area, overall success and challenges, and a summary of prospects for improvement.

Area assessments may award green or red 'flags':

- *Green flags* highlight exceptional performance or outstanding improvement from which others can learn.
- *Red flags* represent significant concerns about outcomes or future prospects where more or different actions are required.

2. Organizational Assessment

This focuses on the individual public bodies within an area to make sure they are accountable for quality and impact. It involves two assessments:

- managing performance
- use of resources, which consists of three themes: managing finances, governing the business, and managing resources.

The organizational assessment is scored from 1 to 4, with a rating from 'performs poorly' to 'performs excellently'.

The new system, outlined above, proved to be too costly and too controversial. According to independent analysis, the reporting requirements cost each local government about 1.8 million pounds and about 20 million pounds for the audit commission expenses for the system. Responding to local government complaints about too intrusive oversight and his departments' view about the cost-effectiveness of the program, Communities and Local Government Secretary Eric Pickles on August 13, 2010, announced plans to discontinue the CAA and disband the Audit Commission. He argued that replacing the audit commission by a strengthened system of local democratic accountability will save the central government about 50 million pounds a year in addition to enormous cost savings for local governments. He announced plans to encourage local governments to have full and complete reporting to their residents and strengthen citizens' rights to have greater recourse against local government failures. In addition, the auditing standards will be strengthened. This is precisely the approach followed in United States and Canada for the past half a century.

7.5.2 *The Tragic Case of Central Government Oversight of Local Governments in Indonesia*

Indonesia represents a tragic case of a costly local government performance-monitoring system implemented with external technical assistance that have yielded little useful performance information while imposing a huge cost for the Indonesian local governments. The system comprises three distinct subsystems: (a) indicators required at inception (62 indicators): general indicators on each local government detailing boundaries, organization, functions and finances and assets; (b) annual performance indicators mandatory for all (79 indicators): demographic, process and service delivery, and general indicators, for example, "book titles as proportion of number of books"(?); and (c) indicators to discover problem local governments (115 indicators) a mixture of macro, demographic, service, area, investment climate, arts and culture and human resource indicators. Four major issues identified with these indicators are (a) lack of any useful information on fiscal health; (b) inadequate focus on service delivery and an overwhelming focus on macro indicators beyond the control of local governments; (c) local governments are required to undertake sophisticated statistical analysis to report inequality (Gini coefficients) and human development indicators; and (d) indicators to discover problem local governments are mostly not relevant for any judgment on fiscal sustainability or service delivery performance. In addition, while an enormous amount of data is collected, these are never tabulated and analyzed for benchmarking or absolute analysis and no feedback is provided either to local governments or citizens at large. Overall the system represents a significant waste of public resources.

The two examples cited above illustrate adverse impact of well intentioned but poorly designed central government oversight of local governments. In both the examples, central government oversight was overbearing and placed high demands on scarce local government resources for compliance. The framework for oversight was not focused on critical issues of local fiscal health and public service delivery performance especially as observed by local residents and providing timely feedback for corrective action. Instead, in both cases the reporting framework was too demanding and in the Indonesian case the approach was also leaning toward academic research not relevant for local government operations. As a result, in both the examples, local governments were hindered rather than helped by central government oversight. The United Kingdom had the good sense to roll back this failed approach while Indonesia following advice by external donors seems to pile on existing requirements thereby leading to a significant diversion of scarce local resources simply to satisfy central bureaucratic demands.

7.6 Concluding Remarks

Local government performance accountability requires four types of assessments: (a) their compliance with due process and law; (b) monitoring of fiscal health for sustainability; (c) monitoring of service delivery; and (d) citizens' satisfaction with local services. This chapter reviewed examples of better practices and not-so-good practices. Several important lessons emerge from this review:

1. No formal higher-order government managed information system is necessary to monitor compliance with due process and laws. Such non-compliance could be discovered by stratified random sampling audits/inspections.
2. Fiscal health is best monitored through requirement of periodic submission of commercially audited financial statements.
3. Output-based higher-order government fiscal transfers to finance merit goods to local governments preserve local autonomy and flexibility while strengthening local accountability to own residents. This is because such transfers create incentives for competition and innovation by strengthening voice and exit options for local residents. Such transfers also facilitate better monitoring of local service delivery and its consistency with required standards by local residents and donor governments.
4. Service delivery performance is best monitored by having local government performance budgeting and occasional external agency or academic research surveys. To the extent a higher-level monitoring system is required, it must focus only on a few relevant fiscal health and service delivery indicators and must allow open access to such information and must provide timely feedback through analytical reports especially benchmarking analysis.
5. Citizens' satisfaction is best measured by having recourse to independent sources such as an Ombudsman's office, surveys by academic researchers and think tanks and an open website to register citizens' complaints.

We noted at the outset that "disappointing" results of decentralization efforts are attributable to lack of citizen empowerment. While this chapter did not directly address strategies to enhance citizen empowerment per se but monitoring how well local residents are served and strengthening citizen-based local government performance accountability is an essential ingredient of a broader system of people empowerment. The politics of transforming citizen-based local government performance accountability to people empowerment is not addressed here but this subject is receiving some early attention in recent literature in politics and administration (see Shah 2008 and Jong and Rizvi 2008). Hopefully such literature will contribute to a paradigm shift of treating citizens as governors and masters as opposed to subjects and clients.

References

Andrews, Matthew, and Anwar Shah. 2005a. Assessing Local Government Performance in Developing Countries. In *Public Services Delivery*, Chapter 3, ed. Anwar Shah, 63–80. Washington, DC: World Bank.

———. 2005b. Citizen-Centered Governance: A New Approach to Public Sector Reform. In *Public Expenditure Analysis*, ed. Anwar Shah, 153–182. Washington, DC: World Bank.

Audit Commission. 2002. *Comprehensive Performance Assessment: Scores and Analysis of Performance*. London: Audit Commission.

Audit Commisssion. 2010. *Comprehensive Area Assessment*. London: Audit Commission.https://webarchive.nationalarchives.gov.uk/20100806160008/http://www.audit-commission.gov.uk/localgov/audit/caa/pages/default.aspx.

Crivelli, Ernesto, and Anwar Shah. 2009. *Fiscal Rules at the Local Level*. Washington, DC: World Bank Institute.

Goldfrank, Benjamin. 2007. Lessons from Latin America's Experience with Participatory Budgeting. In *Participatory Budgeting*, Chapter 3, ed. Anwar Shah, 91–126. Washington, DC: World Bank.

Government of the Province of Ontario. 2019. Municipal Performance Measurement Program. https://www.ontario.ca/data/municipal-performance-measurement-program

de Jong, Jorrit, and Gowher Rizvi, eds. 2008. *The State of Access. Success and Failure of Democracies to Create Equal Opportunities*. Washington, DC: Brookings Institution.

Jenkins, Rob, and Goetz, Anne Marie. 1999. Accounts and Accountability: Theoretical Implications of the Right-to-Information Movement in India. *Third World Quarterly* 20 (3): 603–622.

Niesner, Helen. 1999. Local Government Auditing -Improving the Performance of Government in the Next Century. *Government Accountants Journal* 68: 32–38.

Paul, Samuel. 1992. Accountability in Public Services: Exit, Voice and Control. *World Development* 20: 1047–1060.

———. 1996. Strengthening Public Accountability Through Participation. In *Participation in Practice*, World Bank Discussion Paper 333, ed. Jennifer Rietbergen-McCracken. Washington, DC: World Bank.

———. 2007. India: Civic Participation in Subnational Budgeting. In *Participatory Budgeting*. On CD ROM, ed. Anwar Shah. Washington, DC: World Bank.

Roberts, Alasdair. 2005. Issues Associated with the Implementation of Governmentwide Performance Monitoring. In *Public Services Delivery*, Chapter1, ed. Anwar Shah, 1–38. Washington, DC: World Bank.

Shah, Anwar. 2005. On Getting the Giant to Kneel. Approaches to a Change in the Bureaucratic Culture. In *Fiscal Management*, Chapter 9, ed. Anwar Shah, 211–228. Washington, DC: World Bank.

———, ed. 2006. *Local Governance in Developing Countries*. Washington, DC: World Bank.

———. 2008. Demanding to Be Served. Holding Governments to Account for Improved Access. In *The State of Access. Success and Failure of Democracies to Create Equal Opportunities*, Chapter 10, ed. Jorrit de Jong and Gowher Rizvi, 207–228. Washington, DC: Brookings Institution.

———. 2010. Sponsoring a Race to the Top: The Case for Output-Based Grants for Merit Goods. In *Financing Local Governments*, ed. Junghun Kim and Jurgen Lotz. Ministry of Finance: Copenhagen.

———. 2014a. Responsibility with Accountability: A FAIR Governance Framework for Performance Accountability of Local Governments. *Journal of Economics and Business*, Croatia, December 2014 (Zbornik radova Ekonomskog fakulteta u Rijeci: časopis za ekonomsku teoriju i praksu/Proceedings of Rijeka Faculty of Economics).

———. 2014b. Local Public Finance and Debt Management in the Peoples Republic of China. Report to the Ministry of Finance, PRC, April 2014.

Shah, Anwar, and Chunli Shen. 2007. Citizen-Centric Performance Budgeting at the Local Level. In *Local Budgeting*, Chapter 6, ed. Anwar Shah, 151–178. Washington, DC: World Bank.

Wampler, Brian. 2007. A Guide to Participatory Budgeting. In *Participatory Budgeting*, Chapter 1, ed. Anwar Shah, 21–54. Washington, DC: World Bank.

PART IV

Local Government Reform Imperatives

CHAPTER 8

Structural Reform: Municipal Mergers

8.1 Introduction

The genesis of modern local government is complicated (Sancton 2011). One consequence is that contemporary municipal systems exhibit an astonishingly wide range of local institutions and functions. Scholars of local government have nonetheless sought to identify various patterns in local government and they have constructed numerous taxonomic systems (Dollery et al. 2012). For example, in one of the most comprehensive typologies, Shah (2006a) proposed ten distinctive models: the Australian, British, Chinese, French, German, Indian, Japanese, Nordic, North American and Swiss municipal groupings, which he differentiated in terms of specific characteristics, such as autonomy, decentralization of functions, finance and service delivery. Despite multifarious limitations, these taxonomies have served to reduce the complexities of local government systems and render them more amenable to detailed scholarly analysis.

Over the past several decades, numerous local government systems across the world have undergone significant reform (see, e.g., Denters and Rose 2005; Shah 2006b; Dollery and Robotti 2008; Kuhlmann and Bouckaert 2016). A useful way of conceptualizing local government reform is to invoke the taxonomy proposed by Garcea and LeSage (2005). They distinguished between five different kinds of local government reform: financial reform, functional reform, jurisdictional reform, "internal governance and management reform" and structural reform.

B. Dollery et al., *Local Public, Fiscal and Financial Governance*,
https://doi.org/10.1007/978-3-030-36725-1_8

In this chapter, we focus on structural reform aimed at increasing the size of local government entities. Following Garcea and LeSage (2005), we define structural reform as changes to the boundaries, numbers and types of local authorities in a given local government system. Three main instruments exist which can be employed in the pursuit of structural reform: municipal mergers, annexation and municipal incorporations (Carr and Feiock 2016; Leon-Moreta 2015). In this chapter we concentrate on council consolidation since it is by far the most widely used of these structural reform policy instruments.

The chapter is divided into four main parts. Section 8.2 provides a synoptic account of the frequency and magnitude of municipal mergers in the post–World War II era. Section 8.3 considers the voluminous theoretical literature on council consolidation in terms of the impact of mergers on scale and scope economies, externalities and jurisdictional spillovers, local economic development and growth, administrative and strategic capacity, as well as local democracy. Section 8.4 briefly examines available empirical evidence of the effects of council amalgamation on these various dimensions of local government. The chapter ends with some concluding remarks in Sect. 8.5.

8.2 Magnitude of Municipal Mergers

While municipal mergers can be traced back to antiquity (Guarini et al. 2018), structural reform through council consolidation gained currency in the post–World War II era and served to transform local government in much of the developed world (Blom-Hansen et al. 2016). In his comprehensive survey of the scholarly literature on amalgamation, Tavaris (2018, p. 5) observed that "this trend could be seen across the globe, including such diverse places as Canada, Japan, Australia, New Zealand, Israel, and multiple countries in Western Europe", adding that "in Western Europe, following an initial set of amalgamation reforms in the post-war period, the first two decades of the 21st century have seen a resurgence of this tendency".

In the aftermath of World War II, a majority of developed countries established welfare states in which the role of the public sector, including local government, was steadily expanded. In this process municipal structures created in earlier periods of more limited government were frequently assumed to be too small by population size not only to reap the full benefits of scale economies (Baldersheim and Lawrence 2010; Callanan et al. 2012; Keating 1995), but also to acquire the requisite capacity in terms of administrative and technical skills.

In its *Subnational Governments Around the World: Structure and Finance*, the OECD/UCLG (2016, p. 10) noted that the "average size of municipalities is 56,000 inhabitants", with municipal size by population "larger in Africa and Asia-Pacific than in Europe, Eurasia and North America". Furthermore, it observed that in multi-level governmental countries, local authorities are "smaller on average in three-tiered countries than in two- or single-tiered systems". Moreover, "where municipalities are large, there is often a structured network of sub-municipal entities, such as villages, civil parishes, communities and wards, which support local governments in service delivery and other functions".

Structural reform through municipal mergers has spanned the globe. Blom-Hansen et al. (2016, p. 813) offered a synoptic review of council consolidation and they argued that "municipal merger mania has swept the developed world", differentiated mainly by degree. Thus, whereas in Britain the local government system has been "comprehensively restructured", in other countries, like France, reform has been much more limited. In addition, significant variation exists in the size of local authorities by population. Thus, whereas in Australia, Denmark, Ireland, Japan, the Netherlands and New Zealand, the average population size exceeds 40,000 residents, by contrast in Austria, France and Switzerland population remains below 5000 inhabitants. Moreover, Blom-Hansen et al. (2016, p. 813) observed that "among many developing and post-communist countries, democratization has often prompted the division of administrative units into ever smaller pieces", especially among African nations and in Brazil, but also elsewhere, particularly in Indonesia and Vietnam (Grossman and Lewis 2014, p. 196).

Table 8.1 briefly summarizes changes in the absolute number of local authorities in selected developed countries, as well as fluctuations in the average population size of municipalities, over the ten-year period 2007–2017.

It is clear from Table 8.1 that among the OECD countries included, almost all experienced increases in the size of local authorities by population. Indeed, in some cases, like Denmark, New Zealand and the United States, these increases have been substantial.

Table 8.1 Average size of local authorities, 2007 and 2017

OECD country	*Number of local authorities, 2007*	*Number of local authorities, 2017*	*Average population size of local authorities, 2007*	*Average population size of local authorities, 2017*
Australia	559	562	38,000	43,568
Austria	2357	2098	3500	4166
Belgium	589	589	18,000	19,177
Britain	415	380	143,000	167,858
Canada	3752	3959	9000	9166
Denmark	271	98	20,000	58,459
Finland	416	311	12,500	17,670
France	36,783	35,357	1500	1885
Germany	12,340	11,054	6500	7449
Netherlands	441	380	37,000	44,816
New Zealand	85	67	49,500	70,448
Northern Ireland	26	11	65,500	169,282
Poland	2793	2478	13,500	15,507
Portugal	308	308	34,500	33,524
Sweden	290	290	31,500	34,218
Switzerland	2758	2222	2500	3768
United States	71,343	35,879	4000	8969

Source: OECD (2019), Callanan et al. (2012)

8.3 Conceptual Perspectives on Municipal Mergers

A voluminous conceptual literature exists on the optimal size of local government entities (see, e.g., Ostrom, Tiebout and Warren (1961), Hirschman (1970), Oates (1972, 1999), Corness and Sandler (1986), Wildasin (1986), Breton (1996), Boyne (1998), Bailey (1999), Oakerson (1999), Sancton (2000), Dollery, Crase and Johnson (2006), Dollery and Robotti (2008), Boadway and Shah (2009), Holzer et al. (2009), Lago-Penas and Martinez-Vazquez (2013), Denters et al. (2014) and Tavaris (2018)). In his pioneering book *Fiscal Federalism*, Oates (1972) framed the theoretical debate in economics over the question of optimal size in local government in terms of a trade-off between scale economies and interjurisdictional externalities versus efficiency losses from heterogeneous preferences. Put differently, optimal scale in local government rests on a trade-off between various advantages that purportedly flow from large local authorities, like economies of scale and the ability to "internalize" interjurisdictional spillovers, and countervailing benefits that favor smaller councils, such as the capacity to better match local preferences for municipal services (Blom-Hansen et al. 2016, p. 813). For instance, if economies of scale exist in local public administration, then these may accrue through council consolidation and average costs will fall. However, notwithstanding the realization of scale economies, larger local authorities could generate efficiency losses due to preference heterogeneity among their residents since heterogeneous preferences imply that a larger number of small municipalities would be more likely to provide a mix of local public services more closely aligned with the preferences of local residents.

Within the public choice literature, theoretical discussion has concentrated on the inefficiencies that can flow from a centralized local government structure. Following Tiebout (1956), it is commonly contended that competition among local governments in a decentralized governmental structure will not only provide a wider choice of local public services, but also improve efficiency by inter alia constraining the impact of a budget-maximising bureaucracy. This "decentralization theorem" holds that there is a positive relationship between the size of the public sector and its degree of centralization (Brennan and Buchanan 1980). Policies employing municipal mergers to increase the size of local government entities may thus increase aggregate expenditure growth.

All municipal merger programs rest implicitly on the proposition that industrial structure has predictable and systematic effects on industry behavior and industry performance in any given industry. This concept originated in the industrial organization literature in the form of the structure-conduct-performance (SCP) paradigm developed by Mason (1949), Bain (1951) and other economists. The SCP paradigm holds that a stable causal relationship exists between the structure of an industry, its organizational conduct and its subsequent organizational performance. In a private sector context, the SCP model suggests that increased industrial concentration tends to foster collusion between large corporations that leads invariably to anti-competitive practices, most notably higher prices (Baumol et al. 1982).

Notwithstanding the numerous differences between private and public sector entities, not least an absence of the profit motive in the latter category, many participants in the debate over the impact of structural reform through municipal mergers explicitly or implicitly invoke the logic of SCP in their argumentation. Thus, for instance, proponents of council consolidation contend that "bigger is better", "bigger is cheaper" and sometimes even "bigger is smarter" on grounds that larger local councils will inexorably generate economies of scale and scope economies, cost savings, efficiency gains, enhanced administrative and technical capacity, greater "strategic capacity", and other desirable outcomes contingent upon size. Accordingly, policymakers should use council consolidation to reduce the number of local authorities in order to increase their size by population. By contrast, opponents of forced amalgamation typically contest these claims by disputing the imputed consequences of municipal mergers (Bish 2000; Sancton 2000).

Fortunately, a voluminous positive and normative theoretical literature has developed on the nature and functions of the public sector in market economies, largely in the economics discipline, which can inform the theoretical debate over municipal mergers, including the thorny question of the optimum size of local government. We now consider the main theoretical arguments over the optimal size of local governmental units.

8.3.1 Economies of Scale in Municipal Service Provision

It is often argued in the conceptual literature on the structural reform of local government through municipal mergers that larger local authorities can provide local public services at lower average costs as a result of scale economies, economies of scope and size economies (Dollery and Fleming 2006; Bikker and van der Linde 2016). However, the scale economies claim has been attacked on three main fronts (Boyne 1992, 1996; Tavaris 2018). In the first place, local authorities almost always provide a wide range of local goods and services using different production techniques embodying varying capital/labor ratios. There is thus no a priori rationale for simply assuming that scale economies are uniform across all these services. For instance, for labor-intensive services, frequently characterized by fixed labor/output ratios, higher levels of output require correspondingly greater levels of employment since scale economies are absent. By contrast, in capital-intensive services, as well as in much local infrastructure, especially in water services, high fixed costs imply substantial scale economies attendant upon serving a larger population. Given that the composition of local services can vary substantially, not only between different local government systems, but also between different local authorities within a given municipal system, there are no *ex ante* reasons for presuming larger local councils will necessarily exhibit scale economies in aggregate.

Secondly, defining municipal size in terms of population and then using it to calculate scale economies in local government is problematic. Empirical studies of scale economies in local government typically employ population as a proxy measure for the output of municipal services, notwithstanding broad recognition that "population size is an inappropriate measure of the scale of service production" and that "economies of scale is concerned with the impact of service output on unit costs, not the impact of the number of local inhabitants" (Boyne 1995, p. 217). In practice, population size is still used largely on pragmatic grounds, due to the fact that "even if measures of the separate outputs of all services were available, it is far from obvious that they could be weighted and combined into a single index" (Andrews and Boyne 2009, p. 747). These difficulties are echoed by Holcombe and Williams (2009, p. 419), who observed that "government output is multidimensional, so even if one could define a unit of police services, or a unit of sewer services, if some communities produce more police services and others produce more sewerage services they cannot be added up to create a homogeneous measure of government output". Moreover, numerous factors influence the costs of service provision in addition to operational scale, including demographic factors, like the age composition of the local population, socioeconomic characteristics, such as employment and income levels, the quality of local services, topography and seasonal fluctuations in population attendant upon tourism, agriculture, and the like. Many of these factors are "non-discretionary" in the sense that they fall outside the control of municipal managers. In the context of Australian local government, Drew and Dollery (2014) have shown that the number of households and businesses in a given local council provides more accurate estimates of scale economies than population *per se*.

Thirdly, strong grounds exist to assume that after some threshold population level has been reached, diseconomies of scale will inevitably result. For example, in large local authorities, effective and timely communication flows become more difficult between departments, divisions and central management, coordination is often more onerous, and multi-layered municipal structures tend to breed more acute principal/agent problems (Holmstrom and Roberts 1998; Holzer et al. 2009). The net effect of these factors is to increase managerial marginal costs, thereby inducing scale diseconomies.

Finally, it has been argued that given the fact that different municipal functions and services exhibit different scale characteristics, council consolidation is a clumsy and inept method of attempting to secure the cost reductions that can flow from economies of scale (Dollery et al. 2006). A much more efficacious approach is to deliver local services characterized by scale economies through intermunicipal cooperation by means of shared services, resource sharing and other forms of regional collaboration between local authorities (Tomkinson 2007; Dollery et al. 2013). Exponents of this view have pointed to extensive supportive empirical evidence for this approach. However, as we shall see, recent empirical work embodying a "whole-of-government" approach to the assessment of the impact of shared services on municipal costs has cast some doubt on this claim (Bel and Warner 2015). Moreover, efforts to outsource the provision of services to private sector entities have been shown to have had mixed outcomes (Bel and Gradus 2018).

8.3.2 Economies of Scope in Municipal Service Provision

Production processes that allow for the simultaneous joint production of two or more outputs generate returns to scope. In common with returns to scale, returns to scope can take one of three forms: increasing, constant and decreasing returns to scope. Thus, for example, under increasing returns to scope, joint production by a single local authority will spawn more output than separate production processes undertaken by two different municipalities using an identical quantum of inputs. In addition, returns to scope and economies of scope echo the relationship between returns to scale and economies of scale. In both cases we have a physical measure and an equivalent monetary measure of the same phenomenon. Thus, for instance, in pecuniary terms, increasing returns to scope is mirrored in increasing economies of scope (i.e., a falling average cost of output) (Ferguson 1969; Panzar and Willig 1981; Dollery and Fleming 2006; Dollery et al. 2012; Dafflon 2015).

While in principle scope economies can occur where the output in question consists of goods or services or some combination of goods and services, in the local government realm they typically cover local service provision and local municipal functions. Within the institutional environment of local government, it is possible to identify four possible causes of economies and diseconomies of scope: (a) diminishing returns to inputs; (b) jointness in inputs; (c) jointness in outputs; and (d) interactions between the processes of service provision or production.

In the first place, diminishing returns to inputs in a given production process generating two local services indicates that increasing quantities of service X have to be foregone as a given local council specializes in the production of the other service Y. By way of a practical example, this could occur where two functions previously undertaken by two separate departments are transferred to a single division within the council, such as a single front office simultaneously dealing with both public inquiries on council fees and property taxes as well as tourist information.

Secondly, jointness in inputs arises where one input can be employed in the production of more than one output. In the municipal sphere, this is often the case with administrative functions. For instance, under a shared service arrangement, given administrative input factors can service a range of different activities, thus saving costs that would otherwise be incurred by participating councils each generating the same outputs using their own separate administrative resources.

Economies and diseconomies of scope can also flow from jointness in outputs. This occurs when more than one output is produced from the same set of inputs. In production systems of this kind, one output has secondary importance (often termed a "by-product"). In this regard, a distinction is customarily drawn between pure and impure by-products. For example, a sewerage processing plant may not only store sewage, but also convert it into recycled water for non-potable commercial purposes. Under these circumstances, the combined costs of sewage storage and sewage water recycling would be lower than performing sewerage processing separately from recycled water provision.

Finally, interactions between production processes occur when production processes generate independent outputs: they thus vary in kind not only from jointness in outputs (where outputs are interdependent), but also from jointness in inputs (because there is no common input usage). However, a connection exists between these independent processes since outputs from one process are inputs into the second process. For example, the application of municipal bylaws to control noxious plants often simultaneously yields valuable information to municipal weed-spraying units. Similarly, annual municipal satisfaction surveys of local residents not only generate useful information in their own right, but the information collected can also be used to improve local services.

8.3.3 *Externalities and Interjurisdictional Spillovers*

In the context of local government in a multi-tiered state, externalities may be defined as uncompensated third-party effects resulting from the production and/or consumption of local services, where the externality derives from any difference between the private cost or benefit of a local service and the social cost or benefit of that local service (Dollery and Robotti 2008). An interjurisdictional spillover consists of a positive or negative externality that overlaps into areas beyond the authority of the local authority in which the externality is generated. For instance, a flood control weir across a river in a given municipal area may offer flood protection to downstream communities in other local government areas thereby imposing a positive externality upon them. By contrast, air pollution in a specific municipal area may negatively affect residents in surrounding municipalities (King 1984). Similarly, large urban centers often provide property tax–funded services that are used by residents of small adjacent municipalities without payment.

Municipal interjurisdictional externalities can be tackled by higher tiers of government with broader jurisdictional authority in order to correct or at least alleviate these interjurisdictional externalities since central and/or state governments enjoy jurisdiction over where the externality originates and where its effects are felt (Boadway and Shah 2009). Moreover, state and national governments also often not only control policy instruments that can address interjurisdictional externalities, but they may also possess greater expertise in dealing with these externalities. For interjurisdictional externalities at the local government level, several policy remedies exist (Bailey 1999).

In the present context, policymakers at the responsible higher tier of government can intervene to internalize the interjurisdictional externality in question by simply merging all affected municipal areas to form a single larger local government completely encompassing the spatial impact area of the externality (Miyazaki 2018). In this regard, it is also sometimes argued that free-riding arising from interjurisdictional spillovers will occur less in large merged municipalities since the council consolidation will generate better synchronicity between local jurisdictional boundaries and the areas covered by local authorities (see, for instance, Swianiewicz 2010, 2018). However, this would represent a "second-best" form of policy intervention since consolidation would induce efficiency losses in municipal service provision from heterogeneous preferences (Oates 1972).

A second possibility would be for the level of government with constitutional responsibility for local government to intervene legislatively to prescribe uniform standards for municipal service provision. For example, if the interjurisdictional externality in question derives from local industrial activity that creates air pollution, then the state government can impose air pollution emission standards that diminish the problem, with no need for municipal mergers. By contrast, if the externality is positive—as in regional flood mitigation—then state government intervention can take the form of intergovernmental subsidies or grants (King 1984).

A preponderance of conceptual work on the internalization of interjurisdictional externalities has concentrated on the trade-off between the benefits of scale economies in service provision with the welfare losses derived from heterogeneous preferences across the new large jurisdictional area (see, e.g., Ellingsen (1998) and Dur and Staal (2008)). Some more recent work has considered the impact of interjurisdictional spillover effects on council consolidation decisions (Miyazaki 2018).

8.3.4 Economic Growth

An additional argument sometimes marshalled in favor of larger merged municipalities centers on their presumed ability to more effectively stimulate local economic growth (Denters et al. 2014). For example, it is often claimed that due to comparatively lower interest rates available to bigger local authorities on grounds of lower risk, they can more easily afford superior local infrastructure that serves to boost local growth. It is also sometimes claimed that "consolidation may reduce uncertainty for private investors through structures that lower transaction costs, such as unified regulatory processes" (Carr and Feiock 1999, p. 478). Moreover, "metropolitan development may provide an antidote to inefficient zero-sum competition for development among local jurisdictions". In a similar vein, exponents of the "bigger means faster growth" view frequently contend that large municipalities have greater administrative and technical capacity and thus enjoy the capacity to provide a more efficacious development planning and approval system. It is held that improved planning of this kind will promote local economic development and thereby increase local economic growth (Lago-Penas and Martinez-Vazquez 2013).

8.3.5 *Administrative and Strategic Capacity*

A further closely aligned claim on the question of municipal size has focused on the administrative and strategic advantages purportedly flowing from larger local government entities. For example, in the recent New South Wales local government structural reform program, the state-appointed Independent Local Government Review Panel (ILGRP) (2013, p. 32) proposed sweeping municipal mergers based *inter alia* on the urgent need for improved "strategic capacity", observing that there is a "need for councils to shift their focus towards a more strategic view of their operations; to have the ability to respond to the diverse and changing needs of different communities; and to take on new functions or deliver improved services in order to meet those needs". The Panel argued that "this implies a move to larger, more robust organisations that can generate increased resources through economies of scale and scope, and then plough back efficiency gains into infrastructure, services and other benefits for their communities". Furthermore, the Panel argued that "adequate scale and capacity" should be the chief criterion for determining which local councils would be forcibly amalgamated (Dollery 2017).

These sentiments echo earlier arguments frequently voiced in American debates over city-county consolidations and the achievement of metropolitan and regional government (see, e.g., Durning (1989) and Blodgett (1996)). Carr and Feiock (1999, p. 477) have noted that in principle this approach holds that "city-county consolidations are a comprehensive restructuring of local government, resulting in a single government organization in which there were previously several". The fruits of this form of regional local government include "reduced costs of service delivery; clearer lines of governmental authority and, with it, improved accountability of elected officials; and increased regional coordination with respect to economic development". Other writers have argued that municipal mergers improve capacity and this results in improvements in local service quality and the breadth of local service offerings.

A substantial conceptual literature has focused on governance capacity as well as policymaking capacity in local government (Dollery et al. 2015). For instance, Polidano (2000, p. 810) has distinguished between "policy capacity", defined as "the ability to structure the decision-making process, coordinate it throughout government, and feed analysis into it", "implementation authority", described as "the ability to carry out decisions and enforce rules, within the public sector itself and the wider society" and "operational efficiency", designated as "the ability to deliver services … efficiently and at a reasonable level of quality". Grindle (1996) has posited a more comprehensive quadrilateral taxonomy of local government capacity divided into "policy-making capacity", comprising institutional capacity, technical capacity and administrative capacity and "political capacity".

8.3.6 *Local Democracy*

In democratic countries, it is often argued that local government plays a dual role by simultaneously embodying a mechanism for the expression of local democracy as well as a means of providing local services. For example, in the context of Anglo-Westminster systems of government, like Australia, Britain, Canada and New Zealand, Aulich (2005, p. 198) has observed that local government "gives voice to local aspirations for decentralized governance" while concurrently acting as an entity "for the efficient delivery of services to local communities". Furthermore, Aulich (2005, p. 198) has argued that these two roles have "given rise to two polar approaches to local government reform – one which focuses on local democracy and stresses democratic and local values over efficiency values; the other primarily concerned with structural efficiency and emphasising the importance of efficient distribution of services to local communities". Aulich (2005) contends that there is thus an inevitable tension between effective local democracy and efficient local service provision. This tension is exacerbated when structural reform programs pursue efficiency through compulsory council consolidation aimed at increasing the population size of local authorities (Dollery and Grant 2011).

In general, two schools of thought exist on the question of municipal size (by population) and local democracy (Andrews et al. 2018). McDonnell (2019, p. 2) has argued that a "small-is-beautiful school posits that citizens of small municipalities will feel a higher level of political efficacy and will consequently participate to a greater degree in local politics", whereas a "large-is-lively school argues that participation should increase in line with population size, on the basis that the greater importance and scope of political matters will incite increased party-political mobilisation". Between these conflicting perspectives an agnostic middle ground holds that "municipality size has no effect on participatory attitudes and behaviours, and that any perceived effect is rather the result of indirect factors, such as socio-economic status".

8.4 Empirical Perspectives on Municipal Mergers

In common with theoretical inquiry dealing with council consolidation, a substantial and rapidly growing empirical literature has investigated municipal mergers (see, e.g., Blom-Hansen et al. 2016; Callanan et al. 2012; Dollery et al. 2012; Lago-Penas and Martinez-Vazquez 2013; Narbón-Perpiñá and De Witte 2018a, b). This body of work has examined the effects of municipal mergers on numerous dimensions of local government performance. In Sect. 8.4, we consider some of the findings of the empirical literature on the different aspects of local government discussed in Sect. 8.3.

8.4.1 Economies of Scale in Municipal Service Provision

The empirical literature on scale economies in local government falls into two main strands (Narbón-Perpiñá and De Witte 2018a, b). In the first place, one strand has concentrated on the investigation of scale and efficiency of single municipal services, especially waste (Pérez-López et al. 2016), water (Marques and De Witte 2011; Guerrini et al. 2015) and public transport (Daraio et al. 2016). While the empirical evidence is mixed, in general, scale economies are more common in large capital-intensive local services, especially water, than in labor-intensive services. Local circumstances also affect scale economies. For instance, municipalities may specialize in particular aspects of service provision as a consequence of local factors, like the age composition of the local population. As a result, they may secure efficiencies in these specific services (Kalb et al. 2012).

A second strand in the empirical literature on economies of scale has focused on overall or global efficiency in local government. An obvious complication with this approach derives from the fact that cost functions for each type of municipal service will have different characteristics. Thus no given local government size will generate all its services at minimum cost. The net result will be scale economies in some services and diseconomies of scale in other services (Drew and Dollery 2014; Drew et al. 2014).

From the perspective of the ongoing debate over the impact of municipal mergers, the empirical literature on scale has thus far not provided robust support for employing council consolidation in order to secure scale economies. Indeed, the weight of evidence suggests that there is no optimal size for all local authorities in a given local system. Available empirical evidence has demonstrated that scale economies varied widely between different municipal functions (Byrnes and Dollery 2002; Drew et al. 2014; Narbón-Perpiñá and De Witte 2018a, b). The question of whether amalgamation improves global municipal efficiency through its scale effects has thus been answered in the negative.

8.4.2 Economies of Scope in Municipal Service Provision

As we have already noted, a substantial empirical literature exists on scale economies in local government (see, for instance, Byrnes and Dollery 2002; Holcombe and Williams 2009; Bikker and van der Linde 2016) and much is known about the scale characteristics of different municipal functions (Dafflon 2015; Fahey et al. 2016). By contrast, comparatively little empirical work has been undertaken on economies of scope in local government despite its potential impact on municipal efficiency (Dollery and Fleming 2006).

Caldas et al. (2018, Table 1) provide a useful contemporary survey of empirical work on economics of scope in local government. Only six studies are identified dealing specifically with local government, including an analysis of Californian local government by Grosskopf and Yaisawarng (1990), as well as three papers on Belgian local government, De Borger, Kerstens, Moesen, and Vanneste (1994) and De Borger and Kerstens (1996a, b).

With respect to this slim body of empirical work, Caldas et al. (2018, p. 5) concluded that "extant empirical work on scope economies suggests that economic and political attributes, as well as the use of both discretionary variables (which can be controlled by local management) and non-discretionary variables (which cannot be controlled by councils), are important determinants of local performance". Moreover, only "a small proportion of the empirical literature on efficiency of local government is devoted to the assessment of economies (or efficiencies) of scope in local governments using benchmarking tools". As a consequence, significant gaps are evident in the empirical literature on scope economies.

In their Portuguese study, Caldas et al. (2018, p. 13) found that "economies of scope exist independently of council size", with "very small and very large councils deriving scope economies from service provision" and "diseconomies of scope more likely to occur in councils with population range from 150,000 to 250,000 local residents".

8.4.3 *Externalities and Interjurisdictional Spillovers*

As we have seen, externalities and jurisdictional spillovers take a myriad of forms and this is mirrored in the empirical literature in which different strands of the literature examine different types of spillover. For example, numerous studies have investigated fiscal spillovers in which the fiscal decisions of one municipal jurisdiction influence fiscal decisions in neighboring local councils in an effort to determine the extent and magnitude of these spillovers (see, for instance, Bordignon et al. 2003). In general, "the empirical literature has tended to find large positive spillovers across jurisdictions" (Isen 2014, p. 57).

A second strand of the empirical literature has examined predictions in the theoretical literature stemming from the hypothesized trade-off between benefits from the internalization of externalities and costs associated with unitary provision. It has been argued that this purported trade-off represents a pivotal factor in decisions on regional integration through municipal mergers since the larger the magnitude of public good spillovers, the greater will be the efficiency gains from council consolidation (Brueckner 2003). In his study of municipal mergers in Japanese local government, Miyazaki (2018, p. 1084) found that "residents of the municipalities that can internalize large interregional spillovers of public goods provision through consolidation tend to increase their preferences for consolidation", with "the size of spillovers among potential consolidation partners a key determinant of merger preferences".

A third strand has investigated yardstick competition in local government. Yardstick competition models evaluate how local residents use neighboring municipalities' service provision range and quality and tax regimes to assess their own local council's performance. In general, the results of this body of work have been mixed (Costa et al. 2015).

8.4.4 *Economic Growth*

In contrast to many other dimensions of municipal size, almost no research effort has been expended on the impact of municipal mergers on local economic growth, with some exceptions, like Carr and Feiock (1999) and more recently Wei Tang and Hewings (2017). Carr and Feiock (1999) used time series data to analyze economic growth in nine consolidated American municipalities over the period 1950–1993. They found "no evidence of a link between consolidation and economic development", with "neither manufacturing nor retail and service sector growth significantly different in consolidated counties than for other counties in the state". Moreover, Carr and Feiock (1999, p. 481) found "county population size and the extent of consolidation did not make a difference in the outcome". By contrast, in their study of the effect of local government amalgamation on local growth in China, Wei and Hewings (2017, p. 463) established a "positive impact of city–county mergers in China on local economic development" and concluded that these results "are robust to a series of different model specifications". Moreover, they provide empirical evidence that "improved transport infrastructure and urban agglomeration economies are important channels for positive merger effects".

8.4.5 *Administrative and Strategic Capacity*

In comparison with the other dimensions of local government affected by municipal mergers, much less empirical effort has been directed at the impact of consolidation on administrative capacity in local government (Bhatti and Hansen 2011; Mussari and Ruggiero 2017). Despite this paucity of work, some noteworthy findings can be identified. For example, in his study of five Canadian mergers, Vojnovic (1997, p. 114) found scant evidence of cost savings due in part to "higher wages resulting from a more specialized and professionalized bureaucracy", thereby suggesting an improvement in administrative capacity. Similarly, in their Canadian study, Kushiner and Siegel (2008) found administrative capacity improved in cases where very small municipalities amalgamated. In their analysis of the impact of municipal mergers on administrative efficiency in Ibaraki prefecture in Japan, Haneda, Hashimoto and Tsuneyoshi (2012) found that while post-merger improvements were not substantial, they nevertheless exceeded gains in non-merged municipalities in the same prefecture. In an analogous vein, in their comparative study of the impact of council consolidation in Australia and Japan, Dollery and Yamazaki (2018) found minimal gains in administrative capacity from amalgamation.

8.4.6 *Local Democracy*

As we have seen, two opposing camps exist in the theoretical literature on the impact of local government size on local democracy: a "small-is-beautiful" school and a "large-is-lively" school. However, both sides rely on contrasting behavioral assumptions whose validity can ultimately only be assessed on the basis of empirical evidence. A significant empirical literature has examined the relationship between municipal size and local democracy (see, e.g., Andrews et al. 2018; Tavaris 2018; McDonnell 2019).

Van Houwelingen (2017, p. 411) conducted a meta-study of empirical work on the relationship between municipal size and a "behavioural indicator of political participation such as election turnout, contacting a politician or attending a political activity" in Dutch local government. Fifteen studies were included. Van Houwelingen (2017, p. 424) found that "the population size of a municipality appears, at least as far as political participation is concerned, to be quite an important 'system variable'". In essence, "the larger the population size of a municipality, the more difficult it becomes for the population to remain informed and interested about all issues of importance in their municipality, the less likely they are to initiate contact with a civil servant or politician and the less likely it will be that one's effort to influence municipal politics will make a difference".

Van Houwelingen (2017, p. 425) considered the public policy implications of his meta-study for structural reform in the Netherlands which had relied heavily on compulsory council consolidation. He argued that while "we have not tried to find an 'optimal scale' for local democracy" in Holland "the studies and data we collected seem to suggest, very roughly speaking, that an optimal scale for a (local) democracy, as far as political participation is concerned, is a population of somewhere between 10,000 and 100,000 persons". The Dutch government's "policy goal of creating 100,000+ municipalities … therefore appears to be overly ambitious".

McDonnell (2019) conducted a comprehensive survey of available empirical evidence on the relationship between local government size, political efficacy and political participation. With respect to political efficacy—defined as the perception that political action by individual persons can affect political processes—McDonnell (2019, p. 10) examined nine empirical studies. The great majority of these studies found that residents of smaller municipalities felt "a greater sense of political efficacy", with the "size-effect greater among smaller municipalities, with participation declining in an exponential rather than linear manner" as size increased.

With regard to the impact of municipal size on political participation, defined as "electoral participation" and not "civic participation" or "administrative participation", McDonnell (2019, p. 12) considered 22 studies on this question "reporting on 65 separate tests of the municipality size–political (electoral) participation relationship". The net result was strongly in "favour of small-is-beautiful: forty-eight out of the 65 tests show a negative relationship between municipality size and participation".

Following his survey of the empirical literature on political efficacy, McDonnell (2019, p. 15) concluded that given "recent scholarly concern with political alienation", his finding that "municipality size can have a negative effect on political efficacy and participation deserves greater attention". While political alienation is a complex "multi-factorial phenomenon", in the local government sphere "municipal mergers should perhaps be taken more seriously as one of the explanations" and "smaller local government as one of the cures".

8.5 Conclusion

This chapter has sought to provide a synoptic review of the theoretical and empirical literature on the impact of structural change through municipal mergers. Given the heated controversy surrounding local government reform of this kind, especially in the form of compulsory council consolidation, as well as its frequency and ubiquity worldwide, it is hardly surprising that a voluminous literature has arisen on the question. As we have seen, both the conceptual literature and its empirical counterpart are far from unanimous on the effects of municipal mergers. In general, while fairly strong *a priori* grounds exist for anticipating that larger local government entities will generate various economic benefits, especially in terms of cost savings through scale economies and economies of scope, these expectations have not been confirmed by the weight of empirical evidence. By contrast, convincing *ex ante* reasons have been advanced that local democracy would flourish best in smaller local polities and the comparatively limited available empirical evidence seems to bear this out.

References

Andrews, R., and G. Boyne. 2009. Size, Structure and Administrative Overheads: An Empirical Analysis of English Local Authorities. *Urban Studies* 46 (4): 739–759.

Andrews, R., T. Entwistle, and V. Guarneros-Meza. 2018. Local Government Size and Political Efficacy: Do Citizen Panels Make a Difference? *International Journal of Public Administration* 42 (8): 664–676.

Aulich, C. 2005. Australia: Still a Tale of Cinderella? In *Comparing Local Governance: Trends and Developments*, ed. B. Denters and L.E. Rose. Basingstoke: Palgrave Macmillan.

Bailey, S. 1999. *Local Government Economics: Principles and Practice*. Basingstoke: Macmillan.

Bain, J.S. 1951. Relation of Profit Rate to Industry Concentration: American Manufacturing 1936–1940. *Quarterly Journal of Economics* 65 (2): 293–324.
Baldersheim, H., and E.R. Lawrence. 2010. Territorial Choice: Rescaling Governance in European States. In *Territorial Choice*, ed. H. Baldersheim and L.E. Rose, 1–20. Houndmills: Palgrave Macmillan.
Baumol, W.J., J.C. Panzar, and R.D. Willig. 1982. *Contestable Markets and the Theory of Industry Structure*. San Diego: Harcourt Brace Jovanovich.
Bel, G., and R. Gradus. 2018. Privatisation, Contracting-Out and Inter-Municipal Cooperation: New Developments in Local Public Service Delivery. *Local Government Studies* 44 (1): 11–21.
Bel, G., and M.E. Warner. 2015. Inter-Municipal Cooperation and Costs: Expectations and Evidence. *Public Administration* 93 (1): 52–67.
Bhatti, Y., and K.M. Hansen. 2011. Who "Marries" Whom? The Influence of Societal Connectedness, Economic and Political Homogeneity, and Population Size on Jurisdictional Consolidations. *European Journal of Political Research* 50 (2): 212–238.
Bikker, J., and D. van der Linde. 2016. Scale Economies in Local Production. *Local Government Studies* 42 (3): 441–463.
Bish, R. 2000. *Local Government Amalgamations: 19th Century Ideas for the 21st Century*. Toronto: Howe Institute.
Blodgett, T. 1996. *Current City-County Consolidation Attempts*. Washington, DC: National Association of Counties.
Blom-Hansen, J., K. Houlberg, S. Serritzlew, and D. Treisman. 2016. Jurisdiction Size and Local Government Policy Expenditure: Assessing the Effect of Municipal Amalgamation. *American Political Science Review* 110 (4): 812–831.
Boadway, R., and A. Shah. 2009. *Fiscal Federalism: Principles and Practice of Multi-Order Governance*. Cambridge, MA: Cambridge University Press.
Bordignon, M., F. Cerniglia, and F. Revelli. 2003. In Search of Yardstick Competition: A Spatial Analysis of Italian Municipality Property Tax Setting. *Journal of Urban Economics* 54 (2): 199–217.
Boyne, G.A. 1992. Local Government Structure and Performance: Lessons from America? *Public Administration* 70 (3): 333–357.
Boyne, G. 1995. Population Size and Economies of Scale in Local Government. *Policy and Politics* 23 (3): 213–222.
Boyne, G.A. 1996. Scale, Performance and the New Public Management: An Empirical Analysis of Local Authority Services. *Journal of Management Studies* 33 (6): 809–826.
———. 1998. *Public Choice Theory and Local Government*. Basingstoke: Macmillan.
Brennan, G., and J. Buchanan. 1980. *The Power to Tax: Analytical Foundations of a Fiscal Constitution*. Cambridge, MA: Cambridge University Press.

Breton, A. 1996. *Competitive Government. An Economic Theory of Politics and Public Finance*. New York: Cambridge University Press.

Brueckner, J.K. 2003. Strategic Interaction Among Governments: An Overview of Empirical Studies. *International Regional Science Review* 26 (2): 175–188.

Byrnes, J., and B.E. Dollery. 2002. Do Economies of Scale Exist in Australian Local Government? A Review of the Research Evidence. *Urban Policy and Research* 20 (4): 319–414.

Caldas, P., D. Ferreira, B.E. Dollery, and R. Marques. 2018. Economies of Scope in Portuguese Local Government Using an Augmented Hicks-Moorsteen Approach. *Regional Studies*. https://doi.org/10.1080/00343404.2018.1508872.

Callanan, M., R. Murphy, and A. Quinlivan. 2012. Myths and Realities of Economies of Scale in Local Government. In *Regional Studies Association – Irish Branch. Local Government Reform: Myth or Reality*. Symposium, NUI Maynooth, 8 March.

Carr, J.B., and R.C. Feiock. 1999. Metropolitan Government and Economic Development. *Urban Affairs Review* 34 (3): 476–488.

———. 2016. *City-County Consolidation and Its Alternatives: Reshaping the Local Government Landscape: Reshaping the Local Government Landscape*. London: Routledge.

Corness, R., and T. Sandler. 1986. *Theory of Externalities, Public Goods and Club Goods*. Cambridge, MA: Cambridge University Press.

Costa, H., L.G. Veiga, and M. Portelo. 2015. "Interactions in Local Governments" Spending Decisions: Evidence from Portugal. *Regional Studies* 49 (9): 1441–1456.

Dafflon, B. 2015. The Assignment of Functions to Decentralized Government: From Theory to Practice. In *Handbook of Multilevel Finance*, 163–199. Cheltenham: Edward Elgar.

Daraio, C., M. Diana, F. Di Costa, C. Leporelli, G. Matteucci, and A. Nastasi. 2016. Efficiency and Effectiveness in the Urban Public Transport Sector: A Critical Review With Directions for Future Research. *European Journal of Operational Research* 248 (1): 1–20.

De Borger, B., and K. Kerstens. 1996a. Cost Efficiency of Belgian Local Governments: A Comparative Analysis of FDH, DEA, and Econometric Approaches. *Regional Science and Urban Economics* 26 (2): 145–170.

———. 1996b. Radial and Non-radial Measures of Technical Efficiency: An Empirical Illustration for Belgian Local Governments Using an FDH Reference Technology. *Journal of Productivity Analysis* 7 (1): 41–62.

De Borger, B., K. Kerstens, W. Moesen, and J. Vanneste. 1994. Explaining Differences in Productive Efficiency: An Application to Belgian Municipalities. *Public Choice* 80 (3): 339–358.

Denters, B., and L. Rose, eds. 2005. *Comparing Local Governance: Trends and Developments*. Basingstoke: Palgrave Macmillan.

Denters, B., M. Goldsmith, A. Ladner, P.E. Mouritzen, and L. Rose. 2014. *Size and Local Democracy*. Cheltenham: Edward Elgar.

Dollery, B.E. 2017. *When Push Comes to Shove: Forced Amalgamation in New South Wales Local Government*. Paper presented to Local Politics Specialist Group, *67th Political Science Association Annual International Conference*, University of Strathclyde, Glasgow, 10 April.

Dollery, B.E., and E. Fleming. 2006. A Conceptual Note on Scale Economies, Size Economies and Scope Economies in Australian Local Government. *Urban Policy and Research* 24 (2): 271–282.

Dollery, B.E., and B. Grant. 2011. Economic Efficiency Versus Local Democracy? An Evaluation of Structural Change and Local Democracy in Australian Local Government. *Journal of Interdisciplinary Economics* 23 (1): 1–20.

Dollery, B., and L. Robotti, eds. 2008. *Theory and Practice of Local Government Reform*. Cheltenham: Edward Elgar.

Dollery, B.E., and K. Yamazaki. 2018. Is Bigger Really Better? A Comparative Analysis of Municipal Mergers in Australian and Japanese Local Government. *International Journal of Public Administration* 41 (9): 725–734.

Dollery, B.E., L. Crase, and A. Johnson. 2006. *Australian Local Government Economics*. Sydney: University of New South Wales Press.

Dollery, B.E., B. Grant, and M. Kortt. 2012. *Councils in Cooperation: Shared Services and Australian Local Government*. Sydney: Federation Press.

Dollery, B.E., M. Kortt, and B. Grant. 2013. *Funding the Future: Financial Sustainabilityand Infrastructure Finance in Australian Local Government*. Sydney: Federation Press.

Dollery, B.E., M.A. Kortt, and S. De Souza. 2015. Policy Analysis Capacity and Australian Local Government. In *Policy Analysis in Australia*, ed. B. Head and K. Crowley, 105–120. Bristol: Policy Press.

Drew, J., and B.E. Dollery. 2014. Keeping It In-House: Households Versus Population as Alternative Proxies for Local Government Output. *Australian Journal of Public Administration* 73 (2): 235–246.

Drew, J., M. Kortt, and B. Dollery. 2014. Economies of Scale and Local Government Expenditure: Evidence from Australia. *Administration & Society* 46 (6): 632–653.

Dur, R., and K. Staal. 2008. Local Public Good Provision, Municipal Consolidation, and National Transfers. *Regional Science and Urban Economics* 38 (1): 160–173.

Durning, D. 1989. *The Impacts of City County Government Consolidation*. Athens: Carl Vinson Institute of Government.

Ellingsen, T. 1998. Externalities vs. Internalities: A Model of Political Integration. *Journal of Public Economics* 68 (2): 251–268.

Fahey, G., J. Drew, and B.E. Dollery. 2016. Merger Myths: A Functional Analysis of Scale Economies in New South Wales Local Government. *Public Finance and Management* 16 (4): 362–382.

Ferguson, C.E. 1969. *The Neoclassical Theory of Production and Distribution.* London: Cambridge University Press.

Garcea, J., and E.C.J. LeSage, eds. 2005. *Municipal Reform in Canada: Reconfiguration, Re-Empowerment and Rebalancing.* Toronto: Oxford University Press.

Grindle, M. 1996. *Challenging the State.* Cambridge, MA: Cambridge University Press.

Grosskopf, S., and S. Yaisawarng. 1990. Economies of Scope in the Provision of Local Public Services. *National Tax Journal* 43: 61–74.

Grossman, G., and Janet I. Lewis. 2014. Administrative Unit Proliferation. *American Political Science Review* 108 (1): 196–217.

Guarini, E., F. Magli, and F. Nobolo. 2018. Accounting for Community Building: The Municipal Amalgamation of Milan in 1873–1876. *Accounting History Review* 28 (1/2): 5–30.

Guerrini, A., G. Romano, C. Leardini, and M. Martini. 2015. The Effects of Operational and Environmental Variables on Efficiency of Danish Water and Wastewater Utilities. *Water* 7 (7): 3263–3282.

Haneda, S., A. Hashimoto, and T. Tsuneyoshi. 2012. Evaluating Administrative Efficiency Change in the Post-Merger Period: A Study on Ibaraki Prefecture (1979–2004). *International Regional Science Review* 35 (2): 237–262.

Hirschman, A.O. 1970. *Exit, Voice and Loyalty.* Cambridge, MA: Cambridge University Press.

Holcombe, R., and D. Williams. 2009. Are There Economies of Scale in Municipal Government Expenditures? *Public Finance and Management* 9 (3): 416–438.

Holmstrom, B., and J. Roberts. 1998. The Boundaries of the Firm Revisited. *Journal of Economic Perspectives* 12 (4): 73–94.

Holzer, M., J. Fry, E. Charbonneau, G. Van Ryzin, T. Wang, and E. Burnash. 2009. *Literature Review and Analysis Related to Optimal Municipal Size and Efficiency.* School of Public Affairs and Administration, Rutgers University, Newark. Available at www.nj.gov/dca/affiliates/luarcc/pdf/final_optimal_municipal_size_ & _efficiency.pdf

Isen, A. 2014. Do Local Government Fiscal Spillovers Exist? Evidence from Counties, Municipalities, and School Districts. *Journal of Public Economics* 110 (1): 57–73.

Kalb, A., B. Geys, and F. Heinemann. 2012. Value for Money? German Local Government Efficiency in a Comparative Perspective. *Applied Economics* 44: 201–218.

Keating, M. 1995. Size, Efficiency and Democracy: Consolidation, Fragmentation and Public Choice. In *Theories of Urban Politics*, ed. D. Judge, G. Stoker, and H. Wolman, 117–135. London: Sage.

King, D. 1984. *Fiscal Tiers: The Economics of Multilevel Government.* London: George Allen and Unwin.

Kuhlmann, S., and G. Bouckaert. 2016. *Local Public Sector Reforms in Times of Crisis.* London: Palgrave Macmillan.

Kushiner, J., and D. Siegel. 2008. Are Services Delivered More Efficiently After Municipal Amalgamations? *Canadian Public Administration* 48 (2): 251–267.

Lago-Penas, S., and J. Martinez-Vazquez, eds. 2013. *Challenge of Local Government Size.* Cheltenham: Edward Elgar Press.

Leon-Moreta, A. 2015. Municipal Incorporation in the United States. *Urban Studies* 52 (16): 3160–3180.

Marques, R., and De Witte, K. (2011). "Is Big Better? On Scale and Scope Economies in the Portuguese Water Sector," *Economic Modelling*, 28: 1009–1016.

Mason, E.S. 1949. The Current State of the Monopoly Problem in the United States. *Harvard Law Review* 62 (4): 1265–1285.

McDonnell, J. 2019. Municipality Size, Political Efficacy and Political Participation: A Systematic Review. *Local Government Studies* https://doi.org/10.1080/03003930.2019.1600510.

Miyazaki, T. 2018. Internalization of Externalities and Local Government Consolidation: Empirical Evidence from Japan. *Empirical Economics* 54 (3): 1061–1086.

Mussari, R., and P. Ruggiero. 2017. Merging for Capacity and a Capacity for Merging: Politicians, Citizens, and Discourses in Public Administrations. *Financial Accountability and Management* 33 (1): 27–47.

Narbón-Perpiñá, I., and K. De Witte. 2018a. "Local Governments" Efficiency: A Systematic Literature Review—Part I. *International Transactions in Operational Research* 25 (2): 431–468.

———. 2018b. "Local Governments" Efficiency: A Systematic Literature Review—Part II. *International Transactions in Operational Research* 25 (4): 1107–1136.

Oakerson, R. 1999. *Governing Local Public Economies: Creating the Civic Metropolis.* Oakland: ICS Press.

Oates, W.E. 1972. *Fiscal Federalism.* New York: Harcourt Brace Jovanovich.

———. 1999. An Essay on Fiscal Federalism. *Journal of Economic Literature* 37: 1120–1149.

OECD. 2019. *Subnational Governments in OECD Countries: Key Data 2018 Edition.* http://www.oecd.org/regional/Subnational-governments-in-OECD-Countries-Key-Data-2018.pdf. Accessed 11 Apr 2019.

Organization for Economic Co-operation and Development/United Cities and Local Governments (OECD/UCLG). 2016. *Subnational Governments Around the World: Structure and Finance*. Paris: OECD.

Ostrom, V., C. Tiebout, and R. Warren. 1961. The Organization of Government in Metropolitan Areas: A Theoretical Inquiry. *American Political Science Review* 55 (4): 831–842.

Panzar, J.C., and R.D. Willig. 1981. Economies of Scope. *American Economic Review* 71 (2): 268–272.

Pérez-López, G., D. Prior, J.L. Zafra-Gómez, and A.M. Plata-Díaz. 2016. Cost Efficiency in Municipal Solid Waste Service Delivery. Alternative Management Forms in Relation to Local Population Size. *European Journal of Operational Research* 255 (2): 583–592.

Polidano, C. 2000. Measuring Public Sector Capacity. *World Development* 28 (5): 805–822.

Sancton, A. 2000. *Merger Mania*. Montreal: McGill-Queen's University Press.

———. 2011. *Canadian Local Government: An Urban Perspective*. Toronto: Oxford University Press.

Shah, A., ed. 2006a. *Local Governance in Industrial Countries*. Washington, DC: World Bank.

———. 2006b. Chapter 1: The New Vision of Local Governance and the Evolving Roles of Local Governments. In *Local Governance in Industrial Countries*, ed. A. Shah, 1–46. Washington, DC: World Bank.

Swianiewicz, P. 2010. If Territorial Fragmentation Is a Problem, Is Amalgamation a Solution? An East European Perspective. *Local Government Studies* 36 (2): 183–203.

———. 2018. If Territorial Fragmentation Is a Problem, Is Amalgamation a Solution? – Ten Years Later. *Local Government Studies* 44 (1): 1–10.

Tang, Wei, and G.J.D. Hewings. 2017. Do City–County Mergers in China Promote Local Economic Development? *The Economics of Transition* 25 (3): 439–469.

Tavaris, A.F. 2018. Municipal Amalgamations and Their Effects: A Literature Review. *Miscellanea Geographica – Regional Studies in Development* 22 (1): 5–15.

Tiebout, C. 1956. A Pure Theory of Local Public Expenditures. *Journal of Political Economy* 64 (2): 416–424.

Tomkinson, R. 2007. *Shared Services in Local Government*. Aldershot: Gower Publications.

Van Houwelingen, P. 2017. Political Participation and Municipal Population Size: A Meta-Study. *Local Government Studies* 43 (3): 408–428.

Vojnovic, I. 1997. *Municipal Consolidation the 1990s: An Analysis of Five Canadian Municipalities*. Toronto: ICURR Press.

Wildasin, D.E. 1986. *Urban Public Finance*. Chur: Harwood.

CHAPTER 9

Intermunicipal Cooperation

9.1 Introduction

In Chap. 8 we examined the conceptual and empirical debate surrounding the claim that municipal mergers aimed at the creation of larger local government entities offer significant economic and other benefits. The bulk of empirical literature obliged us to conclude that—on balance—available evidence indicated that council consolidation often failed to meet these expectations. However, it is important to bear in mind that other methods apart from draconian municipal mergers exist which can offer many of the benefits attendant upon size without the costs of consolidation. These include privatization and outsourcing as well as public sector collaboration through intermunicipal cooperation, intergovernmental contracting and other approaches (see, e.g., Steiner 2003; Hulst and van Montfort 2007; Bel and Mur 2009; Dollery and Akimov 2009; Tavares and Camões 2010; Wollmann 2011; Bel et al. 2013; Homsy and Warner 2014; Tavares and Feiock 2014; Bel and Warner 2016; Teles 2016; Silvestre et al. 2018). In Chap. 9 we focus on intermunicipal cooperation.

Following Agranoff and McGuire (2003), Bel and Warner (2016, p. 91) have defined intermunicipal cooperation by local councils as involving "contracts or joint production with other local governments as a means to gain economies of scale, improve service quality, and promote regional service coordination across fragmented local government regions". Growing disenchantment with privatization, outsourcing, competitive tendering and other market-based methods (Domberger and

B. Dollery et al., *Local Public, Fiscal and Financial Governance*,
https://doi.org/10.1007/978-3-030-36725-1_9

Jensen 1997; Domberger and Rimmer 1994; Bel and Fageda 2007), stimulated largely by the New Public Management (NPM) doctrine in the 1980s (Hefetz and Warner 2007; Pérez-López et al. 2015), has spawned extensive "in-sourcing" of local service provision through public production, often in the form of intermunicipal cooperation in the local government realm (Holzer and Fry 2011; Henderson 2015; Voorn et al. 2017).

Intermunicipal cooperation in its various forms is a global phenomenon. In terms of the developed world, it is common in Australasia (Dollery et al. 2012), in Europe (Hulst and van Montfort 2012), North America (Warner 2006) as well as parts of North Asia, notably Japan and South Korea (Hoon and Hyun 2014). Intermunicipal cooperation is also expanding rapidly in some developing countries, such as Brazil (Silvestre et al. 2019). As we shall see, intermunicipal cooperation has taken a myriad of institutional forms across different countries with different governmental structures and legal systems (Tavares and Feiock 2014).

Chapter 9 is divided into four main parts. Section 9.2 considers the varied nature of intermunicipal cooperation and the different forms which it has taken. Section 9.3 discusses the major theoretical foundations of intermunicipal cooperation whereas Sect. 9.4 examines the empirical literature on intermunicipal cooperation. Chapter 9 ends with some brief concluding remarks in Sect. 9.5.

9.2 Nature of Intermunicipal Cooperation

Intermunicipal cooperation varies widely by both degree and type, ranging from informal resource-sharing between adjacent rural councils to large municipal corporations jointly owned by member municipalities. Hulst and van Montfort (2007) have observed that in post-war Europe municipal cooperation has been manifest in numerous different forms extending from single to multipurpose cooperation and from informal consultation to formal joint operations of councils, involving both small and large numbers of municipalities, at different spatial scales.

Various scholars have proposed taxonomies of intermunicipal cooperation (Dollery et al. 2012), which are typically fashioned in line with the institutional circumstances of specific national or subnational local government systems. For instance, writing in the context of British local government, Tomkinson (2007) laid out a quadrilateral typology of intermunicipal cooperation in his *Shared Services in Local Government* containing an "intra-service model" covering limited shared service options, like "regional procurement models", a "service model" embodying a degree of formality enabling participating councils to cede control to a "lead council" in terms of budgeting, service specification, statutory service responsibilities, and the like, a "corporatist model" representing a joint arrangement to deliver services with the costs borne by partner councils involving a "joint governing body", and a "supra-corporate model" centered on a separate "special purpose vehicle"—such as a joint venture company, a limited liability company, a not-for-profit organization or a limited liability partnership—to deliver services on behalf of member councils.

Similarly, with respect to shared services in Australian local government, Dollery et al. (2010) advanced a tripartite typology comprising "horizontal shared services", "vertical shared services" and "intergovernmental contracting shared service" models. In this schema, the "horizontal shared service model" involves partnership arrangements between local authorities ranging from simple *ad hoc* resource sharing to fully-fledged area integration models. While these arrangements exhibit numerous different forms, all horizontal shared service models are wholly operated and owned by local councils. Vertical shared service models encompass cooperation between all or some local councils in a given state local government system and the peak state local government association. They often cover service procurement, such as insurance, where bulk purchases offer significant cost savings. Whereas vertical shared service models exist in all Australian state and territory local government jurisdictions, they are the most developed in Queensland (Dollery et al. 2008). Finally, under intergovernmental contracting, local councils *voluntarily* carry out various functions on behalf of public agencies from state and federal government.

Thirdly, after an examination of intermunicipal cooperation in eight European countries, Hulst and van Montfort (2012, p. 127) developed a quadrilateral typology comprising "quasi-regional governments", "planning forums", "service delivery organizations" and "service delivery agreements". Quasi-regional governments are "standing organizations governed by municipalities that engage in the co-ordination of local government policies and/or in supra-municipal planning in one or more sectors". They enjoy "formal decision-making power" and are typically run by a council and an executive board drawn from participating councils. Quasi-regional governments cover numerous policy areas, notably spatial planning and regional development, and occasionally offer service delivery. Planning forums consist of "loosely coupled networks of municipalities and other public or private actors that engage in [the] coordination and planning".

They have no standing entity empowered with formal decision-making authority and usually deal with economic development, planning and public housing. Service delivery organizations represent standing organizations which focus on public service delivery. They possess independent decision-making power given to them by participating councils. In addition, they often function as agents to specific local authorities. Finally, service delivery agreements facilitate formal agreements between participating councils without the need for formal joint standing organizations. These agreements can cover a multitude of different arrangements between participants, ranging from larger municipalities providing services to smaller member councils to joint purchasing agreements.

Other commentators have focused on common organizational structures employed in intermunicipal cooperation. For example, Voorn et al. (2017, p. 820) focused on “municipally owned corporations (MOCs)” defined as “autonomous organisations owned by municipalities, used to produce or deliver local public services outside the local bureaucracy” which are frequently used in European local government systems. In terms of their characterization, a MOC must possess “independent corporate status (with legal autonomy)”, it must be managed by “an executive board appointed primarily by local government officials (with managerial autonomy)” and it should have “majority public ownership” (Voorn et al. 2017, p. 823). Table 9.1 summarizes the chief characteristics of MOCs, compared to local authorities

Voorn et al. (2017, p. 822) note that in Europe MOCs are quintessentially “corporations constituted by municipalities to provide typically a single service, most often bus services, water and sewerage services, and refuse collection”, which “differ from bureaucracy in that they are governed by appointed executive boards and have independent corporate

Table 9.1 Municipally owned corporations and local authorities

Characteristic	*Municipally owned corporations*	*Local authorities*
Legal status	Corporation	Public body
Governance	Multiple options	Municipal legislation
Governed by	Executive board	Elected politicians
Organisational form	Single-purpose	Multiple purpose
Funding	User payments	Taxes, fees and charges
Cooperative flexibility	High	Medium

Source: Adapted from Voorn et al. (2017, Table 1, p. 823)

status". In addition, in terms of revenue, systematic differences exist between MOCs and local authorities, with MOCs reliant on user pays income compared with local councils and special districts funded by means of taxation. While MOCs are typically "single-purpose organisations operating under private law" in a majority of European countries, they can be multipurpose and function under public law in some countries, notably Holland and Norway. Finally, "since ownership can be transferred, MOCs can facilitate cooperation between localities and between municipalities and the private sector".

In many respects the characteristics of MOCs in the European context are mirrored in the United States by "public authorities" (Lidstrom 2017). In an innovative empirical study, Savitch and Adhikari (2017) explored the phenomenon of "fragmented regionalism" in American metropolitan areas beset by a "regional paradox" in which "centrifugal forces" from "autonomous, competitive local governments" resisted "metropolitan integration" whereas "centripetal pressures" pushed for greater "regional policy coherence". In this context, Savitch and Adhikari (2017, p. 385) argue that "localities have sought to reconcile this paradox by bundling some services that fit within their territorial boundaries and unbundling other functions whose delivery necessitates a larger geographic scale", where "unbundling requires that burdens be shifted to 'third parties', like public authorities, whose territorial scope crosses multiple jurisdictions". In contrast to formal regional governments, "public authorities are flexible and fungible" since "they can be used in different ways, they are able to operate at different scales, and they have the capacity to shape missions that, more or less, correspond to variegated situations".

Savitch and Adhikari (2017, pp. 385/386) have defined public authorities as corporate entities "chartered by one or more governments, administered by an appointed board, and responsible for various functions that are conducted in metropolitan regions". Public authorities are able to finance their activities by levying user charges, securing finance from money markets, as well as receiving grants from state and federal governments. While on the one hand, public authorities have been "enormously 'messy,' 'disorganized' and not always democratic", on the other they are "efficient and custom-made to fit political exigencies" (Savitch and Adhikari 2017, p. 395).

Since fragmented regionalism is a global phenomenon, Savitch and Adhikari (2017, p. 396) contend that "in the generic sense of the term, public authorities are increasing in other advanced economies" and they have become "indispensable". Public authorities have thus materialized in Britain as quasi-autonomous nongovernmental organizations (QUANGOs), in France as *établissements publiques d'aménagements* (EPADs), in Chinese and Japanese metropolitan areas, as well as in other metropolises worldwide, such as Buenos Aires and Santiago.

Different kinds of intermunicipal cooperation possess different characteristics (Tomkinson 2007; Dollery et al. 2012;Tavares and Feiock 2014). Bel and Warner (2015, p. 54) have identified several critical dimensions that differentiate different forms of municipal cooperation. Thus, with respect to the "degree of institutionalization", cooperative arrangements range from "formal" to "informal". Formal cooperative arrangements can be divided into either "standing bureaucratic organizations" or "contractual agreements". In addition, with respect to the kinds of functions performed, Bel and Warner (2015, p. 54) contend they fall into two groupings, which are either "operational in nature (directly engaging in service delivery)" or "coordinative in nature (such as regional alliances of council)". With respect to the nature of the services generated, cooperative arrangements are either "single-purpose" or "multi-purpose". Furthermore, cooperative arrangements can be delineated on the basis of their governance structure, which can be either "single entity or multi-governmental". The final demarcation set out by Bel and Warner (2015, p. 55) is that the "governing boards" of cooperative arrangements "can be formed from elected representatives or from appointed managers".

Further useful insights on the nature of intergovernmental cooperation can be garnered from a typology of the forms of collaboration developed by Warner (2011). Warner (2011, p. 423) argued that intermunicipal cooperation can be conceived as a "continuum from informal to formal", ranging from "informal" kinds of cooperation, as, for instance, "mutual aid agreements to share services", such as road maintenance equipment, through "intermediate" approaches involving single service intermunicipal contracting, to fully-fledged regional integration models that provide a range of local services to member councils. Table 9.2 summarizes this taxonomy.

Additional insights into the nature of intermunicipal cooperation can be found in the governance literature, including multi-level governance (Baker et al. 2005), polycentric governance (McGinnis 1999), functional, overlapping, and competing jurisdictions (FOCJ) (Frey and Eichenberger 1999), fragmegration (Rosenau 2003) and especially multi-perspectival governance (Hooghe and Marks 2003). These approaches all rest on the

Table 9.2 Continuum of intermunicipal cooperation

Degree of formality in cooperation	*Examples of local services*
Informal	Agreements to share resources, like road maintenance equipment, or agreements to promote regional economic development
Intermediate	Intermunicipal contracting, such as single service joint production of waste collection, water provision and bus services
Formal	Regional integration models involving the joint production of a large number of services for member councils

Source: Adapted from Warner (2011, Table 1)

assumption that a dispersion of governance across multiple jurisdictions results in efficiency and equity gains compared with a single centralized government. Furthermore, they hold that governance must occur on multiple scales to be able to deal with externalities and interjurisdictional spillovers, with the scale of governance varying in order to internalize these externalities.

The multi-perspectival governance approach pioneered by Hooghe and Marks (2001, 2003, 2009) is especially important in terms of its insights into municipal cooperation. It is thus worth considering in more detail. Hooghe and Marks (2003, p. 236) identified four main questions that should be addressed in the design of a multi-tiered governance system: (a) Should governmental jurisdictions be designed around specific communities or should they center on specific policy areas? (b) Should jurisdictions "bundle competencies or should they rather be functionally specific?" (c) Should the number of jurisdictions be limited or should they be allowed to increase? (d) Should jurisdictions be "designed for posterity" or should they be "temporary and/or flexible"?

Hooghe and Marks (2003) have identified two diametrically opposed conceptual approaches to tackling these problems. In the first place, Hooghe and Marks (2003, p. 236) contend that "Type I governance" prescribes that formal authority should be dispersed to "a limited number of non-overlapping jurisdictions at a limited number of levels", with jurisdictions bundling authority into "quite large packages; they are usually non-overlapping; and they are relatively stable". By contrast, Type II governance specifies that "complex, fluid, patchwork of innumerable, overlapping jurisdictions" should be established with "extremely fungible competencies" and capable of being "spliced apart into functionally specific jurisdictions". These jurisdictions are frequently "overlapping", with a propensity to be "lean and flexible". Moreover, these jurisdictions can "come and go as demands for governance change". Table 9.3 outlines the main characteristics of Type I and Type II governance.

Hooghe and Marks (2003, p. 236) argue that Type I governance derives from the theoretical prescriptions of fiscal federalism which favor "power sharing among a limited number of governments operating at just a few levels". This multi-tiered governmental structure rests on "the relationship between central government and a tier of non-intersecting sub-national governments", with individual governments its primary "unit of analysis" and not individual policies (Oates 1999). In line with Type I governance, the prescribed governmental "framework is system-wide, the functions are bundled, and the levels of government are multiple but limited in number".

Hooghe and Marks (2003, p. 237) have argued that general-purpose jurisdictions embodying the characteristics of Type I combine numerous governmental functions into specific governmental entities, like general-purpose local authorities, which offer a wide range of services. The chief rationale for this method of structuring government rests on the twin assumptions that (a) there are costs to decomposing functional authority and (b) these costs can be minimized by limiting the number of governmental institutions.

It is evident from Table 9.3 that Type I governance design establishes governmental jurisdictions in a limited number of hierarchical levels in multi-tiered governmental systems. In both federal and unitary state structures this typically consists of three levels of government; central, intermediate and local government. In addition, Hooghe and Marks (2003, p. 236) contend that Type I governmental entities have "non-intersecting memberships" with membership territorially based as in most real-world

Table 9.3 Type I and Type II governance in multi-level governance

Type I governance	*Type II governance*
General-purpose jurisdictions	Task-specific jurisdictions
Non-intersecting memberships	Intersecting memberships
Jurisdictions at a limited number of levels	No limit to the number of jurisdictional levels
System-wide architecture	Flexible design

Source: Hooghe and Marks (2003, p. 235, Table 2)

multi-tiered systems of government, such as American central, state and local governments as well as the national, prefectural and local governments in Japan. In terms of the Type I approach, jurisdictions have durable spatial boundaries that are non-intersecting at any given level of government. However, under constitutional arrangements in many countries, these boundaries can be modified periodically through various public policies aimed at structural change, like municipal mergers, annexation and municipal incorporations in local government systems.

Finally, Hooghe and Marks (2003, p. 236) contend that Type I governance jurisdictions characteristically exhibit a "system-wide durable architecture". In real-world governance structures this normally arises as a consequence of deliberate constitutional design, as in the American, Australian and Canadian constitutions. As a result, jurisdictions are "durable" in the sense that "creating, abolishing, or radically adjusting new jurisdictions is costly and unusual".

As we have seen, Type II governance entities contrast sharply with Type I jurisdictions. In line with its conceptual foundations in neoclassical and public choice economics (see, for instance, Frey and Eichenberger (1999) and Ostrom and Ostrom (1999)), Type II governance entities are functionally task-specific instead of general-purpose, there is a limited number of jurisdictions, given jurisdictions engage in multi-level governmental alignments, thereby operating at varying territorial scales, and entities are innately flexible rather than durable.

As evident in Table 9.3, Type II governance comprises task-specific jurisdictions instead of multi-purpose entities. In most governmental systems, task-specific public agencies are common. For example, under Australian federalism, Sydney households purchase water from metropolitan-wide Sydney Water, they enjoy police protection provided by the state-wide police force, and they secure subsidized healthcare through the national Medicare health system, with each of these Type II governance entities delivering a well-defined service over a given spatial area. Type II jurisdictions normally have intersecting memberships in polycentric relationships since jurisdictions overlap each other and jurisdictional boundaries can be traversed.

In contrast to Type I entities, Type II jurisdictions can operate on numerous jurisdictional levels thereby embodying the economic logic that each public service should be provided by the jurisdiction that can most effectively internalize its benefits and costs. For instance, intermunicipal cooperation can yield specific services to member councils at a regional rather than a local or state level.

Type II jurisdictions are inherently flexible. They can thus react swiftly, rapidly and efficiently to new unforeseen circumstances. Furthermore, Type II may be transitory insofar as they are function-specific. They may thus simply disband when a given task is completed or when a specific function is no longer required. Examples of this attribute abound, such as taskforces established to tackle emergencies as in earthquakes, floods and fires.

In the context of local service provision, Type I and Type II each enjoy distinctive comparative institutional advantages. Hooghe and Marks (2003, p. 239) have argued that all multi-level systems of government present "coordination dilemma". This arises from the fact that whereas multi-level governance is flexible in terms of its operational scale this comes at the cost of coordinating multiple jurisdictions. The resultant coordination dilemma stems from the negative or positive externalities of given policies for other jurisdictions. Coordination is thus critical to minimize perverse unintended outcomes. As the number of jurisdictions increases, coordination costs will rise exponentially due to concomitant increasing and ultimately prohibitive transaction costs.

Hooghe and Marks (2003, p. 240) have argued that the coordination dilemma is conceptually analogous to an iterated prisoners' dilemma game since as jurisdictional numbers increase, it becomes progressively more difficult to effectively sanction offending entities. Type I and Type II jurisdictions offer different solutions to the coordination dilemma. Type I governmental structures minimize the need for interjurisdictional coordination by limiting the number of jurisdictions. In contrast, Type II governance systems restrict interaction between jurisdictions by "splicing competencies into functionally distinct units" to diminish externalities through the formation of "decomposable" institutional structures. This is done by fashioning independent special-purpose entities to "internalize" benefits and costs. Thus "Type II governance is designed with respect to particular policy problems – not particular communities or constituencies" in which "the scope of a jurisdiction, its mode of decision making, adjudication, and implementation can … be adapted to particular policy problems" (Hooghe and Marks 2003, p. 240).

Given their distinctive comparative institutional advantages, Type I and Type II governance systems are complementary approaches that should coexist in all multi-level governance systems. Indeed, this is apparent in almost all real-world multi-tiered governance systems which exhibit both Type I and Type II governance. Put differently, Hooghe and Marks (2003, p. 240) observe that actual existing governance structures comprise a "fluctuating number of relatively self-contained, functionally differentiated Type II jurisdictions alongside a more stable population of general-purpose, nested Type I jurisdictions".

Notwithstanding the coexistence of Type I and Type II entities in real-world governmental systems, Hooghe and Marks (2003, pp. 240/241) note that "they embody contrasting conceptions of community". Thus, whilst Type I entities are characteristically "encompassing communities", largely territorial in nature, often containing specific kinds of population, with "self-sufficient" policies, by contrast Type II jurisdictions are designed "to solve particular policy problems, such as managing a common pool resource, setting a technical standard, managing an urban service, or shipping hazardous waste".

Different approaches to problem resolution are apparent in Type I and Type II governmental entities. If we invoke Albert Hirschman's (1970) distinction between "exit" and "voice", Type I decision-making takes place mostly by means of formal democratic "voice" mechanisms, like elections and referenda, as well as more informal feedback mechanisms, because exit is normally impractical. By contrast, given that the nature of Type II jurisdictions enables relatively costless entry and exodus, dispute "exit" mechanisms can be employed. For instance, a discontented local council can simply exit from an intermunicipal arrangements it deems unsatisfactory.

While the Hooghe and Marks (2003) analysis offers useful insights into the nature of intermunicipal cooperation, it unfortunately neglects the democratic "legitimating" characteristics of Type I and Type II local government entities. This is unfortunate since they play a critical role in democratic countries.

9.3 Conceptual Considerations

9.3.1 Separation of Service Production and Service Provision

In conceptual terms, municipal cooperative arrangements rest on two central propositions. Firstly, powerful efficiency and equity grounds exist for the principle of "subsidiarity" in multi-tiered governmental systems which holds that "government powers should be exercised at the lowest level of government possible" (Bailey 1999, p. 18). In the local government sphere, this translates into decentralized democratic decision-making through political autonomy for local authorities.

Various efficiency arguments have been advanced for subsidiarity in local government. For example, in the theory of fiscal federalism the decentralization theorem holds that spatial variations in community preferences are best accommodated through decentralized decision-making which enhances social welfare (Oates 1972). Moreover, municipalities typically enjoy access to more accurate information on local demand and supply conditions than higher tiers of government. In addition, public choice scholars, such as Boyne (1998), as well as Tiebout (1956), Breton (1995) and other writers in the competitive federalism tradition, have advanced persuasive efficiency arguments in favor of the principle of subsidiarity. These arguments centre on the advantages stemming from competition between numerous local authorities in terms of both local service provision as well as property taxes, fees and charges.

In equity terms, it is argued that since local councils embody democratic decision-making at the local level, they can more effectively represent political aspirations of local communities on local questions than higher levels of government. Local government is thus the most legitimate seat of local fiscal, planning and other powers at the local level.

The second major conceptual foundations of municipal cooperation flows from Ronald Oakerson's (1999) *Governing Local Public Economies*. In his book, Oakerson (1999, p. 7) distinguished between local service "provision" and local service "production". The provision of local services encompasses deciding whether to deliver a given service, the regulation of local services, the quantity and quality of local services provided, associated revenue-raising and how these services should be produced. In comparison, local service production incorporates the creation of a local service rather than simply its fiscal provision. In contrast to most services delivered by higher tiers of government, Oakerson (1999, p. 15) maintained that the great majority of local public services hinge on the "availability of specific time-and-place information, such as neighbourhood conditions, to support effective production choices". As a consequence, the "scale and organization of the production process should allow producers to make locally informed judgments". If provision is separated from production, then municipal size and production scale are not intrinsically related.

Given these two pillars of intermunicipal cooperation, Oakerson (1999, pp. 15/16) identified three defining characteristics of local services. Firstly, in contrast to other goods and services, local "co-production" is vital. Used in this sense, co-production embraces the "productive efforts of citizen-consumers as an integral part of the production process". Co-production differs sharply from the "citizen-voter" role of local residents in local service provision. Under co-production local residents serve as the "eyes-and-ears" of local authorities in providing vital information on service reliability, quality and the like. In sum, the enthusiastic participation of local people is thus critical to efficient and effective local service delivery.

Secondly, Oakerson (1999) distinguished between "local public goods" and "local public services". Local public services, which range from health inspections to public toilet maintenance, are archetypally labor-intensive with limited economies of scale. By contrast, local public goods, such as waste processing, are largely capital-intensive and hence often display scale economies, as perhaps best exemplified by domestic waste processing. In general, economies of scale thus differ widely between different municipal activities. In common with substantial variation in scale economies between different local goods and services, Oakerson (1999, p. 16) demonstrated that "different economies may also be involved in increasing the level of production per capita as opposed to extending the same level of production per capita to a larger population". These factors have significant consequences for the organization of local production and provision.

Thirdly, Oakerson (1999) argued that coordination costs pivotal in determining the nature of production also play a crucial role in the way in which production should be tackled. Oakerson (1999, p. 16) characterized this aspect of municipal goods and services as follows:

> The production and delivery of goods and services can be broken down into a large number of components, distinguishing direct service components delivered to citizens from various support-service components to direct service producers. Each component may be associated with a different economy of scale (although services typically exhibit constant returns over a broad range). Yet different components of service production require coordination to varying degrees. Coordination is costly, mainly in terms of time and effort devoted to transactions.

The net result of the transaction costs associated with coordination is twofold: (a) These transaction costs limit the number of separate production units in a given local authority; and (b) they limit the number of separate services. In essence, determining the optimal number of production divisions rests on a trade-off between scale economies and coordination economies.

From the perspective of intermunicipal cooperation, Oakerson's (1999, pp. 17/18) pivotal separation of provision and production gives local government choice between different methods of producing given local services. In his taxonomy, Oakerson (1999, pp. 17/18) identified seven generic options that relate service provision and service production, which range from production and provision by councils themselves to the provision of service by giving local residents vouchers that can be used to purchase services from private firms.

In the first place, "in-house production" occurs where a municipality undertakes its own production to meet its service provision needs. Secondly, "coordinated production" transpires where cooperating councils coordinate their production activities. For example, the development appraisal departments of two adjacent councils may cooperate on activities that affect both local government areas. "Joint production" occurs where cooperating councils employ a single department to produce the service in question. Fourthly, "intergovernmental contracting" arises when one council produces a given service and provides it to other councils under contract. "Private contracting" occurs where a private firm undertakes production for a local authority, whereas "franchising" transpires when a municipality gives a private firm the exclusive right to produce a given service which residents can purchase. Finally, "vouchering" takes place when a local authority prescribes service standards and the level of provision, but permits local residents to secure services from any provider using a voucher.

Given the definition of intermunicipal cooperation by Bel and Warner (2016) cited earlier, which stipulated that it was restricted to cooperative arrangements between local councils, under Oakerson's (1999) typology, only "coordinated production", "joint production" and "intergovernmental contracting" constitute "*bona fide* intermunicipal cooperation". "Private contracting", "franchising" and "vouchering" do not meet this definition on grounds that they all comprise contractual arrangements outside of local government. They possess added economic and political attributes. For example, in stark contrast to local authorities, private-for-profit firms have strong incentives to reduce costs. In practice, this may manifest itself in lower quality. Given the problems involved in monitoring multifaceted municipal services, in practice this may lead to a loss of control over service provision on the part of contracting councils.

9.3.2 *Characteristics of Local Services Suitable for Cooperative Provision*

In addition to the theoretical basis for the municipal cooperation in service provision, scholars have also considered the characteristics of local services that lend themselves to cooperative provision (Dollery et al. 2012). In particular, Percy Allan (2001, 2003) postulated that six distinctive characteristics of local services rendered them suitable for cooperative provision: "low core capability" of local authorities; "high supplier availability"; "low task complexity"; substantial-scale economies; "specialized technology"; and "low asset specificity".

In terms of his categorization, Allan (2001, p. 39) used the term "core capability" to refer to the "steering" and not "rowing" capabilities of local councils. In this sense, core capability embraces "community consultation, policy planning, general governance, service monitoring, regulating private activity and funding public purposes", as opposed to the "production and delivery of services" *per se*. Allan (2001, 2003) argues that widespread consensus exists that local authorities without core capability cannot adequately discharge their functions. Moreover, when core capability is ceded to an intermunicipal service arrangement, this entails the risk that in the event of the unsatisfactory performance, or even collapse, of the intermunicipal cooperative arrangement, the municipality may be unable to accurately assess the problem, disengage itself and continue functioning smoothly. Allan (2003) thus contends that core council capabilities should only be relinquished with care. Accordingly, focus should fall on municipal cooperation arrangements involving low core capabilities.

Secondly, Allan (2001, p. 40) argued that "supplier availability" represented a key criterion for determining to secure a specific local council function from an intermunicipal cooperative entity or from another council by contract. The "competitiveness of the tender" was thus an important consideration. In Allan's (2001) categorization, tender competitiveness hinges on whether "there are a large number of potential contractors with the experience, skills and equipment to meet the specific needs of the council". This also has force when different intermunicipal arrangements within the local public sector are evaluated. If these attributes are not present, which Allan (2001) argues is often the case for regional and rural councils, then caution should be exercised.

"Task complexity" is an important consideration in determining whether to enter into intermunicipal cooperative arrangements. Allan (2001, p. 40) contends that high levels of task complexity mean that "complex tasks are difficult to monitor, hard to measure for inputs and require unique expertise to monitor". In principle, this renders these functions unsuitable for cooperative provision. However, given that task complexity makes complex tasks relatively expensive to execute, "task complexity" requires balancing potential risks against cost savings.

Fourthly, Allan (2001, p. 40) has argued that economies of scale are common in "specialized products and services that are mass produced and highly standardized". While we have seen in Chap. 8 that the presence of substantial-scale economies is hard to ascertain in practice, Allan (2006) has argued that a number of "back office" and "front office" functions offer substantial economies of scale. This makes them attractive for fruitful intermunicipal cooperation.

Allan (2001) argues that "specialized technology" involved in some local government functions often engenders specific cost characteristics to these functions. In particular, computer information systems represent a common form of specialized applied technology in local government. The costs involved in acquiring the requisite hardware and software, as well as subsequently maintaining, upgrading and operating this equipment are significant. As a consequence, computer systems represent a local function especially suitable for intermunicipal cooperative ventures.

Finally, Allan (2001) contends that "low asset specificity" is an important consideration. In this regard, Allan (2001, p. 40) has observed that "where a task requires an expensive and specific asset it may be more cost effective for the council to provide the asset" compared to contracting out the task to a private provider. However, by the same token, intermunicipal cooperative provision is attractive, especially in terms of cost savings.

9.3.3 *Benefits and Costs of Intermunicipal Cooperation*

A significant theoretical literature has considered factors which both motivate local authorities to engage in intermunicipal cooperation and which act as barriers to cooperation (Hawkins 2009; Warner 2011). A particularly insightful framework for considering the rationale for participating in intermunicipal cooperation was advanced by Hawkins (2009). Adopting the conceptual prism provided by transactions cost theory, Hawkins (2009) identified three main barriers to participation in local government cooperation; "coordination problems", "division problems" and "defection problems". Hawkins (2009, pp. 110/111) argued that cooperative agreements between local authorities often present difficulties centered on when "there are no joint gains", when the assignment of "roles and responsibilities for implementation" is challenging, and when there is uncertainty over "participant preferences and behaviour", including possible "future opportunistic behaviour", and there is an absence of "knowledge of the costs and benefits of an agreement".

Transactions cost analysis has been invoked by numerous scholars, including Hefetz and Warner (2012), Bel et al. (2013) and many others in order to "explain local production decisions in general and interlocal cooperation and shared service delivery more specifically" (Carr and Hawkins 2013, p. 225). This literature has focused on the three primary kinds of transaction risks associated with participating in intermunicipal cooperative agreements identified by Hawkins (2009): potential costs involving coordination, division and defection (see, e.g., Hawkins 2009; Hefetz and Warner 2012; Carr and Hawkins 2013; Drew et al. 2019).

Coordination involves the process of bringing together local authorities to create an intermunicipal cooperative agreement. Various kinds of coordination costs have been identified, each linked to different aspects of the coordination problem. For instance, the costs derived from negotiating an agreement can be high thereby discouraging efforts to establish an agreement. Other factors that can increase coordination costs include the complexity of intermunicipal agreements, as well as an absence of mutually agreed goals.

Division risks arise when local authorities "agree on the general goals for the collaboration, but encounter difficulty in dividing and distributing the expected benefits among the group" (Carr and Hawkins 2013, p. 227). The magnitude of division costs depends largely on the same factors driving coordination costs. In this regard, Steinacker (2004, 2010) has argued that asymmetries in political power and resource levels, as well as differences in policy preferences and demographic and socioeconomic composition, are vital factors in determining the level of division risk. In a similar vein, in his empirical study of the establishment of joint ventures in local government Hawkins (2009) found that dissimilarities in socioeconomic profiles and resource capacity of member municipalities heightened division problems.

Defection risks arise when one or more councils party to an intermunicipal agreement do not comply with the terms of the agreement. This may occur where initial commitment is weak and where there are strong incentives to abandon an agreement and free ride on its outcomes (Hawkins 2009). Two characteristics of local public services have been identified in the literature as especially important in the context of defection risks (Carr and Hawkins 2013, p. 228). Firstly, "asset specificity", which relates to the need for specialized equipment to produce a local service, is argued to increase defection risk. In essence, asset specificity means that a given asset cannot be used to produce other local services thereby reducing the number of potential service suppliers. Secondly, "measurement difficulties" mean that it is not easy to monitor local services in order to ascertain whether suppliers are meeting their service obligations. This means that effective performance monitoring is costly thus reducing any cost savings contingent on external service provision.

In addition to these three kinds of costs associated with intermunicipal agreements, Kwon and Feiock (2010) have argued that agency costs must also be considered. Agency costs occur when an agent fails to faithfully represent the interests of the principal. In the context of intermunicipal agreements, this problem arises, for instance, when a shared service entity's board does not accurately implement the objectives of constituent municipalities and the output of the entity accordingly does not meet the expectations of its council principals.

In the literature on intermunicipal cooperation, agency costs, coordination costs, division costs and defection costs have hitherto been associated with a given service provision through intermunicipal agreements. They have thus been calibrated in terms of the costs of the particular local service in question (Bel and Warner 2015). However, Drew et al. (2019) have recently argued that if the costs attached to service provision through intermunicipal agreements are computed at the level of the organization—rather than the level of the local service per se—then additional costs are evident. Drew et al. (2019, p. 6) articulated this argument as follows:

> [W]e consider the pecuniary outcomes of shared services at the level of the individual local government rather than just the local service in question. Because of the different lens through which we view shared services, many costs that reside outside of the specific service being shared become visible. We refer to these expenses as "exogenous costs" because they are not directly

> related to the service being shared and would generally fall outside of decision-making and empirical analyses conducted at the service level. Major exogenous costs include erosion of economies of scope, additional staff and resource burdens on municipalities as a result of reticence to meaningfully redeploy, as well as the need to continue to conduct residual elements of functions that have been shared (such as handling of complaints).

On the other side of the ledger, intermunicipal agreements also generate benefits to participating local authorities. In common with the debate surrounding the benefits associated with municipal mergers, which we considered in Chap. 10, the literature on intermunicipal cooperation has similarly examined the benefits that can flow from engaging in cooperative ventures (see, e.g., Tomkinson 2007; Dollery et al. 2012).

In the first place, scale economies are frequently advanced as a significant source of pecuniary benefit. Apart from cost savings spawned by lower unit production costs, additional advantages can flow from greater specialization associated with higher output and enhanced purchasing power. Secondly, greater spatial scale attendant upon cooperation often facilitates the internalization of both positive and negative externalities. From the perspective of individual councils this means that the benefits and costs of externalities can be shared across all member municipalities. Thirdly, municipal agreements can offer significant advantages in terms of the administrative and technical capacity to more efficaciously provide local services. For instance, the employment of highly skilled staff, the pooling of production knowledge, and other advantages of joint production can improve the efficiency and quality of local service provision (Brown and Potoski 2005; Bel and Warner 2015).

A useful synopsis of the pecuniary benefits and costs of moving from individual to joint production through municipal cooperation has been offered by Drew et al. (2019) and is summarized in Table 9.4. The pecuniary benefits and costs listed in Table 9.4 include benefits and costs at the level of the organization as well as at the level of specific services.

Drew et al. (2019, p. 8) offer a caveat on intermunicipal agreements stemming from their analysis. They argue that their "net pecuniary schema is also useful to scholars because it makes the calculus explicit for the case where services previously produced separately are moved to collaborative production". In addition, it specifies clearly "the different costs which only become apparent when a local government-level analysis is carried out". They argue that "given the preponderance of costs and the relative

Table 9.4 Pecuniary benefits/costs of shifting from separate to shared production

Pecuniary benefits	*Pecuniary costs*
Benefits of harmonising demand heterogeneity (at lower standard) and supply (with inputs more efficiently used)	Pecuniary costs of harmonising demand heterogeneity (at higher standard) and supply (with inputs less efficiently used)
Economies of scale	Upfront costs of finding partner councils, negotiating, contracting, consulting, etc., as well as accounting and regulatory costs of new process
Adjoining municipalities internalise externalities	Transaction costs arising from division, information, coordination, free-riding and defection, as well as agency costs
Dynamic efficiency gains from additional administrative and technical capacity from ability to recruit more skilled staff, learning by doing factors and the like	Exogenous costs from scope economies loss, capital and labour redundancies, and retention of residual functions

Source: Adapted from Drew, McQuestin and Dollery (2019, Table 1, p. 7)

uncertainty of some benefits occurring (such as economies of scale), it would seem likely that a move from separate to shared production may well result in an increase to unit expenditure" if aggregate costs are computed. This argument will be examined further when we consider the empirical evidence on intermunicipal cooperation in Sect. 9.4.

9.3.4 Social Capital and Intermunicipal Cooperation

While the theoretical dimensions of the putative benefits and costs of intermunicipal cooperation shed a good deal of light on intermunicipal agreements, they represent only a partial account of the motivating factors and barriers involved. A holistic understanding of intermunicipal cooperation should embrace a broader human dimension not captured by the "felicific calculus" of standard economic analysis. Indeed, Carr and Hawkins (2013, p. 236) are far from alone in their observation that social capital is a critical "precursor to cooperation" in the local government realm. We now thus briefly consider this line of inquiry that extends beyond the "situational determinism" of the more narrow "economistic" approach (Latsis 1972) that occasionally rests uncomfortably in the politicized environment of local government.

Although numerous approaches have considered the sociological and psychological bases of cooperative endeavors, in the municipal sphere the social capital perspective has proved especially insightful. In essence, social capital approaches to cooperative municipal action hinge on the presumption that social relationships represent a pivotal element in the success of intermunicipal cooperation. Drawing on the work of Coleman (1990), Fukuyama (1995), Putnam (1995) and other scholars working in this tradition, social capital theorists have argued that robust social networks underpin ongoing cooperation and trust essential for productive intermunicipal agreements. In this regard, following Nahapiet and Ghoshal (1998), it is useful to decompose social capital into three constituent elements; namely the structural, relational and cognitive dimensions of social capital. Under this tripartite classification, the structural dimension of social capital embraces social network links between actors, as well as their spatial location in the social structure of interactions. By contrast, the relational dimension of social capital rests on interpersonal trust and focuses on the quality of interrelationships between actors that enable them to agree upon mutually binding rules and actions in cooperation. Finally, the cognitive dimension comprises the "shared understandings" between cooperating actors. Drawing on this conception of social capital, Weber and Weber (2010) have argued that the greater the magnitude of structural, relational and cognitive social capital, the more likely the success of the cooperative venture.

Dollery et al. (2011) have applied this conceptual prism to intermunicipal cooperation in general and shared services in particular. Dollery et al. (2011, p. 161) have argued that in the municipal sphere the "social networks derived from structural social capital, as well as the relational attributes of shared norms and mutual trust that are likely to be especially significant, given the uncertainties which attend the desired outcomes of shared service models and the difficulties in deciding *ex ante* on the specific characteristics of how models will work in future and how their costs and benefits should be apportioned among member councils". Moreover, they contend that "these problems are intensified where shared service arrangements are designed for activities that are inherently difficult to measure, such as regional groups of local council forming representative bodies to lobby higher tiers of government and participate more broadly in the political process".

9.4 Empirical Evidence

As we have seen, intermunicipal cooperation represents an important alternative policy avenue to municipal mergers and privatization as a means of improving both efficiency and effectiveness in local service provision. It is thus vital from the perspective of public policymakers and local government managers alike that the comparative efficiency of intermunicipal agreements be established (Bel and Warner 2015). However, since the theoretical literature on intermunicipal cooperation has not been able to offer unequivocal direction on this question, it is critical to consider available empirical evidence (Allers and De Greef 2018). It is thus disappointing that in general the "systematic evidence on the relationship between inter-municipal cooperation and costs is scant and contradictory, and evidence on its role in promoting regional coordination is equally limited" (Bel and Warner 2015 p. 53).

In addition to its paucity (Dollery et al. 2016), the extant empirical literature on intermunicipal cooperation is beset by other problems. For instance, Drew et al. (2019, p. 2) have noted that "most of the evidence in both the scholarly and grey literature is survey based and frequently lacking in rigour". Furthermore, "much of the 'grey literature' is clouded by moral hazard", such as KPMG (2015). Similarly, as Bel and Warner (2015) have pointed out, most rigorous empirical analysis has been restricted to the evaluation of the cost impact on single local services, largely waste collection and processing.

In general terms, the empirical analysis of intermunicipal cooperation may be divided into two main strands (Allers and van Ommeren 2016). One line of inquiry has concentrated on the determinants of cooperation, such as Feiock et al. (2009), Hefetz and Warner (2011), Rodrigues et al. (2012) and Bel and Warner (2016). A second strand considered the impact of intermunicipal cooperation, largely by means of case studies (see, e.g., Henderson 2015).

In their book *Councils in Cooperation* Dollery et al. (2012) examined all available empirical evidence on intermunicipal arrangements in Australian and English local government. Dollery et al. (2012, p. 49) found that most studies were outside of peer-reviewed scholarly journals. They observed that "from existing 'soft-core' evidence it seems that shared service arrangements can be beneficial for councils both in terms of cost savings and enhanced service quality". However, the "success of particular arrangements seems to vary depending on the specific local circumstances". Moreover, the most popular local services in intermunicipal agreements were procurement, human resources, "governance", "compliance and audit services", IT and waste management. However, they cautioned that "there is little theoretical argument and no empirical evidence that shared service arrangements can solve all the service provision problems of local governments".

In their survey of the literature, Bel and Warner (2015) examined eight multivariate empirical papers on the impact of cooperation on costs, seven of which examined solid waste collection, one of the most common areas of municipal cooperation. Notwithstanding the limited number of papers, Bel and Warner (2015, p. 59) contended that the literature nonetheless "allows us to identify the main characteristics of cost structure and service delivery governance that should be taken into account under cooperation" and it "facilitates a better understanding of the importance of differing national structures of local government systems on the scope of cooperation reforms" given that "four different countries are covered". In essence, Bel and Warner (2015) find that cost savings depend on (a) the cost structure of public services, especially with respect to scale and density economies as well as externalities, (b) the structure of local government systems in terms of municipal size, "metropolitan location" and the powers granted to local authorities and (c) local/regional level governance framework. In general, empirical work in the European context concentrated on the effects of cooperation on costs whereas North American studies focused on the problems surrounding coordination.

As we noted earlier in Sect. 9.3.3, until recently empirical work on the pecuniary consequences of intermunicipal agreements has exclusively examined their impact on single or at most a few allied local services. However, this limitation was addressed by Drew et al. (2019) in their study involving a five-year panel of South Australian local government expenditure data. In essence, Drew et al. (2019, p. 13) "broadened the perspective taken on shared services from the level of the specific service to be shared to the level of the individual local government". They showed that—in addition to the benefits and costs traditionally computed at the service level—exogenous benefits and costs arise if the overall organization is considered. Their analysis thus sought to estimate "net pecuniary outcomes" at the level of individual local municipalities "associated with shared services by geographically adjacent municipalities under the assumption that services had previously been produced separately". They found that in South Australian local government the net effect of shared services had been to increase aggregate expenditure by around 8%. Drew et al. (2019, p. 14) concluded that their "empirical results challenge many previous service-level analyses and thus help to establish a case for local government-level analysis that may better capture all of the costs associated with the decision to shift from separate to shared production". They further observed that their findings "should give practitioners and scholars good reason to pause and rethink some of the pervasive assumptions regarding the pecuniary implications arising from shared service production that are commonly encountered in the grey and scholarly literatures".

While it remains to be seen whether empirical researchers of intermunicipal cooperation will adopt the approach developed by Drew et al. (2019) and whether they replicate its findings, it should be stressed that the empirical evidence on the pecuniary impact of intermunicipal agreements is mixed. Moreover, it is important to bear in mind that cost savings is only one of several reasons for engaging in intermunicipal cooperation. Numerous other motives have been identified, including enhancing administrative and technical expertise, improving service quality, negotiating with higher tiers of government, promoting "regional service coordination" and stimulating regional growth and development (Agranoff and McGuire 2003).

9.5 Conclusion

This chapter has sought to provide a synoptic account of the theoretical and empirical literature on intermunicipal cooperation in local government. We have considered the multifarious nature of intermunicipal cooperation and the many different forms which it has taken, as well as its major theoretical foundations and empirical attempts to estimate its impact.

As we have seen, intermunicipal cooperation can employ numerous different institutional vehicles, ranging from informal collaboration to fully-fledged regional integration models that provide a full range of services to member councils. Significant differences occur in the nature of municipal cooperation between different countries as a consequence of different constitutional and legal regimes and this is manifest in the structures that are used.

The theoretical foundations of intermunicipal cooperation rest on the firm ground prepared by Tiebout (1956), Oakerson (1999), Oates (1972) and other scholars. However, it unfortunately provides little *a priori* guidance on the likely benefits and costs that will flow from intermunicipal cooperation. Thus, much rests on the empirical analysis of intermunicipal agreements in terms of their real-world impact.

In contrast to other kinds of structural change in local government, the empirical analysis of intermunicipal cooperation has been comparatively limited. Moreover, it has tended to focus on a few well-defined services, especially waste collection and water. Studies have focused mostly on the pecuniary impact of municipal cooperation, particularly its effects on the costs of service provision, rather than on service quality, largely due to data constraints. The emphasis has fallen on benefits and costs at the level of the service in question. In general, the weight of empirical evidence indicated that cost savings often eventuated. However, as we noted, a recent paper by Drew et al. (2019) developed a methodology for investigating the impact of intermunicipal cooperation at the level of the organization. In its application to the South Australian local government system, Drew et al. (2019) found no pecuniary net benefits. However, given the number and persistence of intermunicipal cooperative agreements this finding is surprising. Future work along these lines will determine if this result holds in other institutional contexts.

References

Agranoff, R., and M. McGuire. 2003. *Collaborative Public Management: New Strategies for Local Governments*. Washington, DC: Georgetown University Press.

Allan, P. 2001. *Secession: A Manifesto for an Independent Balmain*. Balmain: Balmain Secession Movement.

———. 2003. Why Smaller Councils Make Sense. *Australian Journal of Public Administration* 62 (3): 74–81.

———. 2006. "What Drives Councils" Efficiency: Population Size or Density. In *Independent Inquiry into Local Government*. Sydney: NSW Local Government and Shires Association.

Allers, M.A., and J.A. de Greef. 2018. Intermunicipal Cooperation, Public Spending and Service Levels. *Local Government Studies* 44 (1): 127–150.

Allers, M.A., and B. van Ommeren. 2016. Intermunicipal Cooperation, Municipal Amalgamation and the Price of Credit. *Local Government Studies* 42 (5): 717–738.

Bailey, S.J. 1999. *Local Government Economics*. Basingstoke: Macmillian.

Baker, A., D. Hudson, and R. Woodward. 2005. *Governing Financial Globalization: International Political Economy and Multi-Level Governance*. London: Routledge.

Bel, G., and X. Fageda. 2007. Why Do Local Governments Privatise Local Services? A Survey of Empirical Studies. *Local Government Studies* 33 (4): 517–534.

Bel, G., and M. Mur. 2009. Intermunicipal Cooperation, Privatization and Waste Management Costs: Evidence from Rural Municipalities. *Waste Management* 29 (10): 2772–2778.

Bel, G., and M.E. Warner. 2015. Inter-Municipal Cooperation and Costs: Expectations and Evidence. *Public Administration* 93 (1): 52–67.

———. 2016. Factors Explaining Inter-Municipal Cooperation in Service Delivery: AMeta-Regression Analysis. *Journal of Economic Policy Reform* 19 (2): 91–115.

Bel, G., X. Fageda, and M. Mur. 2013. Why Do Municipalities Cooperate to Provide Local Public Services? An Empirical Analysis. *Local Government Studies* 39 (3): 435–454.

Boyne, G.A. 1998. *Public Choice Theory and Local Government*. Basingstoke: Macmillan.

Breton, A. 1995. *Competitive Governments*. Cambridge: Cambridge University Press.

Brown, T.L., and M. Potoski. 2005. Transaction Costs and Contracting: The Practitioner Perspective. *Public Performance & Management Review* 28: 326–351.

Carr, J., and C. Hawkins. 2013. The Costs of Cooperation: What the Research Tells Us About Managing the Risks of 2013 Service Collaborations in the U.S. *State and Local Government Review* 45 (4): 224–239.

Coleman, J.S. 1990. *Foundations of Social Theory*. Cambridge: Harvard University Press.

Dollery, B.E., and A. Akimov. 2009. Are Shared Services a Panacea for Australian Local Government: A Critical Note on Australian and International Empirical Evidence. *International Review of Public Administration* 12 (2): 1–11.

Dollery, B.E., G. Hallam, and J.L. Wallis. 2008. Shared Services in Australian Local Government: A Case Study of the Queensland Local Government Association Model. *Economic Papers* 27 (4): 343–354.

Dollery, B.E., B. Grant, and A. Akimov. 2010. A Typology of Shared Service Provision in Australian Local Government. *Australian Geographer* 41 (2): 217–231.

Dollery, B.E., B. Grant, and L. Crase. 2011. Love Thy Neighbour: A Social Capital Approach to Local Government Partnerships. *Australian Journal of Public Administration* 70 (2): 156–166.

Dollery, B.E., B. Grant, and M. Kortt. 2012. *Councils in Cooperation: Shared Services and Australian Local Government*. Sydney: Federation Press.

Dollery, B.E., M.A. Kortt, and J. Drew. 2016. Fostering Shared Services in Local Government: A Common Service Model. *Australasian Journal of Regional Science* 22: 225–242.

Domberger, S., and P. Jensen. 1997. Contracting Out by the Public Sector: Theory, Evidence, Prospects. *Oxford Review of Economic Policy* 13 (4): 67–78.

Domberger, S., and S. Rimmer. 1994. Competitive Tendering and Contracting in the Public Sector: A Survey. *International Journal of the Economics of Business* 1 (3): 439–453.

Drew, J., D. McQuestin, and B.E. Dollery. 2019. Good to Share? The Pecuniary Implications of Moving to Shared Service Production for Local Government Services. *Public Administration* 97 (1), 132–146.

Feiock, R.C., A. Steinacker, and H.J. Park. 2009. Institutional Collective Action and Economic Development Joint Ventures. *Public Administration Review* 69: 256–270.

Frey, B.S., and R. Eichenberger. 1999. *The New Democratic Federalism for Europe.* Cheltenham: Edward Elgar.

Fukuyama, F. 1995. *Trust: The Social Virtues and the Creation of Prosperity.* New York: Free Press.

Hawkins, C.V. 2009. Prospects for and Barriers to Local Government Joint Ventures. *State and Local Government Review* 41 (2): 108–119.

Hefetz, A., and M. Warner. 2007. Beyond the Market Versus Planning Dichotomy: Understanding Privatisation and its Reverse in US Cities. *Local Government Studies* 33 (4): 555–572.

Hefetz, A., and M.E. Warner. 2012. Contracting or Public Delivery? The Importance of Service, Market, and Management Characteristics. *Journal of Public Administration Research and Theory* 22: 289–317.

Henderson, A.C., ed. 2015. *Municipal Shared Services and Consolidation.* London: Routledge.

Hirschman, A.O. 1970. *Exit, Voice, and Loyalty.* Cambridge, MA: Harvard University Press.

Holzer, M., and J. Fry. 2011. *Shared Services and Municipal Consolidation: A Critical Analysis.* Alexandria: Public Technology Institute.

Homsy, G.C., and M.E. Warner. 2014. Intermunicipal Cooperation: The Growing Reform. In *Municipal Yearbook*, 55. Washington, DC: International CityCounty Management Association.

Hooghe, L., and G. Marks. 2001. *Multi-Level Governance and European Integration.* Oxford: Rowman & Littlefield.

———. 2003. Unravelling the Central State, But How? Types of Multi-Level Governance. *American Political Science Review* 97 (2): 233–243.

———. 2009. Efficiency and the Territorial Structure of Government. *Annual Review of Political Science* 12: 225–241.

Hoon, Y., and D. Hyun. 2014. Comparative Study on the Collaborative Governance Type for the Metropolitan Economic Regions in Case of Korea and Japan. *GRI* 16 (1): 141–168.

Hulst, R., and A. van Montfort, eds. 2007. *Inter-Municipal Cooperation in Europe.* Vol. 238. Dordrecht: Springer.

Hulst, J.R., and A. van Montfort. 2012. Institutional Features of Inter-Municipal Cooperation: Cooperative Arrangements and their National Contexts. *Public Policy and Administration* 27 (2): 121–144.

KPMG. 2015. *Shared Service Analysis: Final Report 27 May 2015*. Sydney: KPMG.

Kwon, S., and R. Feiock. 2010. Overcoming Barriers to Cooperation: Intergovernmental Service Agreements. *Public Administration Review* 70: 876–884.

Latsis, S. 1972. Situational Determinism in Economics. *British Journal for the Philosophy of Science* 23 (1): 207–245.

Lidstrom, A. 2017. Public Authorities and Intermunicipal Cooperation in a European Context. *Urban Affairs Review* 53 (2): 403–409.

McGinnis, M.D. 1999. *Polycentric Governance and Development: Readings from the Workshop in Political Theory and Policy Analysis*. Ann Arbor: University of Michigan Press.

Nahapiet, J., and G. Ghoshal. 1998. Social Capital, Intellectual Capital and the Organizational Advantage. *Academy of Management Review* 23 (2): 242–266.

Oakerson, R. J. 1999. *Governing Local Public Economies*. Oakland: ICS Press.

Oates, W.E. 1972. *Fiscal Federalism*. New York: Harcourt, Brace Janonovich.

Oates, W.E. 1999. An Essay on Fiscal Federalism. *Journal of Economic Literature* 37 (3): 1120–1149.

Ostrom, V., and E. Ostrom. 1999. Public Goods and Public Choices. In Polycentricity and Local Public Economies. In *Readings From the Workshop in Political Theory and Policy Analysis*, 75–105. Ann Arbor: University of Michigan Press.

Pérez-López, G., D. Prior, and J.L. Zafra-Gómez. 2015. Rethinking New Public Management Delivery Forms and Efficiency: Long-Term Effects in Spanish Local Government. *Journal of Public Administration Research and Theory* 25 (4): 1157–1183.

Putnam, R.D. 1995. Bowling Alone: America's Declining Social Capital. *Journal of Democracy* 6 (1): 65–78.

Rodrigues, M., A.F. Tavares, and J.F. Araújo. 2012. Municipal Service Delivery: The Role of Transaction Costs in the Choice between Alternative Governance Mechanisms. *Local Government Studies* 38: 615–638.

Rosenau, J.N. 2003. *Distant Proximities: Dynamics Beyond Globalization*. Princeton: Princeton University Press.

Savitch, H.V., and S. Adhikari. 2017. Fragmented Regionalism: Why Metropolitan America Continues to Splinter. *Urban Affairs Review* 53 (2): 381–402.

Silvestre, H.C., R.C. Marques, and R.C. Gomes. 2018. Joined-Up Government of Utilities: A Meta-Review on a Public–Public Partnership and Inter-Municipal Cooperation in the Water and Wastewater Industries. *Public Management Review* 20 (4): 607–631.

Silvestre, H., Correira, A. M., Marques, R. and Dollery, B. E. (2019). Shared Services in Brazilian Local Government: Urban Development in Small Counties. *Public Administration* 19 (3): 686–702.

Steinacker, A. 2004. Game Theoretic Models of Metropolitan Cooperation. In *Metropolitan Governance: Conflict, Competition, and Cooperation*, ed. R. Feiock, 46–66. Washington, DC: Georgetown University Press.

———. 2010. The Institutional Collective Action Perspective on Self-Organizing Mechanisms: Market Failures and Transaction Cost Problems. In *Self-Organizing Federalism: Collaborative Mechanisms to Mitigate Institutional Collective Action*, ed. R. Feiock and J. Scholz, 51–72. New York: Cambridge University Press.

Steiner, R. 2003. The Causes, Spread and Effects of Intermunicipal Cooperation and Municipal Mergers in Switzerland. *Public Management Review* 5 (4): 551–571.

Tavares, A.F., and P.J. Camões. 2010. New Forms of Local Governance: A Theoretical and Empirical Analysis of Municipal Corporations in Portugal. *Public Management Review* 12 (5): 587–608.

Tavares, A.F., and R.C. Feiock. 2014. *Intermunicipal Cooperation and Regional Governance in Europe: An Institutional Collective Action Framework*. Glasgow: European Consortium for Political Research.

Teles, F. 2016. *Local Governance and Intermunicipal Cooperation*. Amsterdam: Springer.

Tiebout, C.M. 1956. A Pure Theory of Local Government Expenditure. *Journal of Political Economy* 64 (5): 416–424.

Tomkinson, R. 2007. *Shared Services in Local Government*. Aldershot: Gower Publishing.

Voorn, B., M.L. van Genugten, and S. Van Thiel. 2017. The Efficiency and Effectiveness of Municipally Owned Corporations: A Systematic Review. *Local Government Studies* 43 (5): 820–841.

Warner, M.E. 2006. Inter-Municipal Cooperation in the US: ARegional Governance Solution? *Urban Public Economics Review* 6: 221–239.

———. 2011. Competition or Cooperation in Urban Service Delivery. *Annals of Public and Cooperative Economics* 82 (4): 421–435.

Weber, C., and B. Weber. 2010. Social Capital and Knowledge Relatedness as Promoters of Organizational Performance: An Explorative Study of Corporate Venture Capital Activity. *International Studies of Management and Organization* 40 (3): 23–49.

Wollmann, H. 2011. Reorganising Local Governments: Between Territorial Consolidation and Intermunicipal Cooperation. *The Croatian Public administration* 11: 681.

CHAPTER 10

Political Economy of Local Government Reform

10.1 Introduction

In common with public sector transformation at higher tiers of government, local government reform has been keenly contested. Indeed, even the term "reform" and the manner in which it has been applied to local public sector reform has been controversial (Wallis et al. 2007). For instance, Cooper et al. (1998, p. 10) have observed that the use of the term "reform" has been "so badly abused that it has lost much of its value", especially since "it keeps us focused on the past and on the negative instead of on the possibilities of the future".

In the literature on public sector transformation two meanings have been associated with reform (Wallis et al. 2007). In the positive use of the term, reform denotes irrevocable change and discontinuity. However, it also carries normative connotations. Thus it suggests the existence of an "initial undesirable state of affairs or even a 'crisis' of some proportion that can be improved by means of a specific reform process" (Wallis et al. 2007, p. 17). In addition, "the normative notion that reform has improved matters rather than simply changed an initial state of affairs is much more controversial and invokes value judgments on what constitutes positive change". In this chapter, we employ reform in its positive sense.

Public sector reform has a long tradition in the modern era (Millward 2011). In the literature, scholars have typically argued that it is possible to identify two major modern reform epochs: "Progressive-Era" Public Administration (PPA) and "New Public Management" (NPM) (Hood

B. Dollery et al., *Local Public, Fiscal and Financial Governance*,
https://doi.org/10.1007/978-3-030-36725-1_10

1994). The PPA wave of reform originating in the nineteenth century focused largely on the eradication of arbitrary decision-making and the application of due process in administration. In her analysis of the genesis of PPA, Yeatman (1997, p. 175) has argued that PPA is best conceived as a drive to "professionalize the public service in the sense of ensuring that selection and promotion were on merit rather than patronage, rule rather than discretion governed how public bureaucratic process and decisions operated, and public service was orientated by norms of impersonality, correct procedure and consistency". A number of commentators have maintained PPA should be seen in the context of its time insofar as it introduced mass production organizational techniques drawn from the private sector into public administration (Wallis et al. 2007). Put differently, PPA embodied the modernization processes already adopted in large-scale production in the market economy.

The NPM public sector reform movement—sometimes also referred to as "new managerialism" or "generic managerialism"—sought to liberate managers in public agencies from "rigid adherence to immutable civil service rules by giving them 'freedom to manage'" as well as "change the focus of the civil service away from its by now traditional PPA emphasis on procedural rectitude towards the achievement of outcomes or 'getting results'". Numerous scholars have argued that—in common with PPA—NPM constituted a modernization process by integrating post-Fordist managerial practices employed in the private sector into the operation of the public service.

While this long-run perspective on public sector reform has undoubted merit, it serves to obscure the uneven and discontinuous nature of reform processes. For instance, Hood (1994) has argued that real-world reform has been disjointed and far from incremental thereby presenting immense challenges to scholars attempting to explicate the genesis of public sector reform and its transformation through time. As a consequence, a voluminous literature has arisen around this question comprising a host of different and often conflicting perspectives on the problem (Wallis et al. 2007). For example, in his *The Future of Governing*, Guy Peters (1996) offered four alternative models of public sector reform. In a similar vein, in the *Art of the State*, Christopher Hood (2000) employed contemporary cultural theory in order to explain public sector reform processes. In their *Market Failure, Government Failure, Leadership and Public Policy*, Joe Wallis and Brian Dollery (1999) applied various recent developments in economic analysis, including new institutional economics and the theory of transformative leadership, to public sector reform. Catherine Casey (2002) brought organizational sociology to bear on the problem of reform in her *Critical Analysis of Organizations.*

Other scholars have examined whether the introduction of NPM constituted an enduring "revolution" in public administration and the various forces which have shaped its evolution. For example, contributors to *Transcending New Public Management* (Christensen and Laegreid 2008) provided comparative perspectives on the transformative processes in public administration wrought by external pressures, different national institutional structures and "cultural compatibility". Similarly, in their *Comparative Governance*, Peters and Pierre (2016) argue and advance a framework for considering how forms of governance may change through time.

While attempts to account for the genesis, nature and implementation of public sector reform in general have shed considerable light on local government reform processes, the more complex and variegated complexion of municipal structures in different national contexts, as well as the subordination of local government to higher tiers of government in most countries, have introduced additional complications. This has rendered it even more difficult to establish a common pattern of motives, processes and outcomes of municipal system reform policies and programs. Perhaps the most significant impact of these complexities on the scholarly literature on local government reform has been to concentrate attention on the use of alternative theoretical prisms through which to examine reform processes.

Local government reform can be comprehensive or it can simply address a single or narrow range of municipal operations. A useful taxonomic framework within which to consider this matter has been developed by Garcea and LeSage (2005), who distinguished between five categories of reform. Firstly, there are financial reform programs that consist of changes to the financial circumstances of local government, including any changes to revenue sources (i.e., both "own-source" revenue and intergovernmental transfers), expenditure (i.e., financial responsibilities and financial restrictions) and financial management. The second category is functional reforms that involve changes in the number or types of function performed by local authorities, including a reassignment of functions between local government and other tiers of government. Next are jurisdictional reforms which consist of changes to the authority and autonomy of local government, including general competency powers, specific bylaw-making powers, and the like. The category of organizational and managerial reforms involves changes to the administrative, executive, and management processes of local councils. The final category is structural reform programs which comprise changes to the boundaries, numbers and types of local authorities.

Given the myriad complexities of local government, both within and between different countries, scholars of local public sector reform have concentrated a good deal of their attention on empirically based comparisons of reform processes across different nations and across different local government systems within specific countries. In this chapter we will consider some of these studies in more detail.

This chapter is divided into three main parts. Section 10.2 focuses on the theory of local government reform by considering the problem of conceptualizing public sector reform, theoretical insights into the nature of local government failure, new institutional economics and policy leadership. Section 10.3 concentrates on comparative empirical studies of local government reform programs by discussing (a) comparative municipal reform in the Anglosphere countries and (b) comparative local government reform in European nations. The chapter ends with some brief concluding remarks in Sect. 10.4.

10.2 Theoretical Considerations

10.2.1 Conceptualizing Public Sector Reform

Given the complexities of local public sector reform, it is hardly surprising that intellectual discourse over the nature of reform has drawn on numerous disciplines and spawned a vast literature. A useful and concise way to understand how scholars have conceptualized public sector reform is to consider the analytical frameworks developed by some leading scholars in the field. To this end, we briefly consider the work of Peters (1996), Hood (2000) and Pollitt and Brouckaert (2004), who have all sought to conceptualize the various perspectives employed in public sector reform in advanced democracies in terms of policy paradigms.

In his *The Future of Governing*, Peters (1996, p. 16) argued that while reform *per se* had been a worldwide phenomenon, the pattern followed by reformers had been "extremely piecemeal and unsystematic", which required explanation. In order to shed light on this question, Peters (1996) advanced four models that had been employed to motivate and shape public sector reform programs: the market model, the participatory model, the flexible model and the deregulated model. According to Peters (1996, p. 18), "each of the four alternatives contains a clear idea about the source that is producing problems in the public sector" and prescribes the best ways of improving the operation of the public sector.

The market model rests on a "basic belief in the virtues of competition and an idealized pattern of exchange and incentives" (p. 22). Peters (1996, p. 28) contends that the market model has three central pillars; the superior efficiency of markets, the failings of public bureaucracies and an embrace of the generic qualities of management as "management is management, no matter where it takes place".

In contrast to the market model and its emphasis on the evils of public sector monopoly, the participatory model holds that public sector hierarchies lie at the root of the problem since a "hierarchical, top-down style of management restricts employee involvement, alienates workers, and reduces employee commitment" (Peters 1996, p. 47). In essence, the participatory model assumes that individuals are motivated by social incentives, such as participation, rather than by material incentives, like pay and perquisites. Nonetheless, in common with the market model, it prescribes "a decentralised bureaucracy with some transfer of power to the lower echelons of organizations as well as to the clients of the organizations" (p. 71).

The flexible model prescribes "flexible government" that can respond efficaciously in a stochastic environment by means of "appropriate policy responses to environmental changes rather than merely responding in habitual ways to inherently novel challenges" (Peters 1996, p. 72). The flexible model thus emphasizes organizational agility above other administrative attributes such as continuity and coherence.

Finally, the deregulation model sees the root of public sector problems as the hidebound rigidity of bureaucratic rules regardless of circumstances, thereby emphasizing the problematic nature of the rules and procedures guiding public sector operations rather than bureaucratic structure *per se*. From the perspective of policy remediation, the deregulation model stigmatizes "internal regulations within public organizations as the principal source of dysfunctions so often observed in the public sector" (Peters 1996, p. 109) and prescribes procedural change rather than structural change.

A different conceptualization of public sector reform is offered by Hood in his *The Art of the State*. Hood (2000, p. 6) argues that "the variation in ideas about how to organize public services is a central and recurring theme in public management, and that such variation is unlikely to disappear". Moreover, the elements subsumed under NPM are far from novel and indeed have a long history in public administration.

Invoking the concepts of "grid" and "group" from cultural theory, Hood (2000, p. 9) postulates four main approaches to public sector reform: the "fatalist", "hierarchist", "individualist" and "egalitarian" perspectives. Under this schema, grid signifies "the degree to which our lives are circumscribed by conventions or rules" thereby "reducing the area of life that is open to individual negotiation". By contrast, group denotes the extent to which "group choice is constrained by individual choice" (p. 8). While grid relates "rules versus discretion" debates in public administration, group deals with how to organize such activity. Table 10.1 summarizes the four perspectives:

From Table 10.1 it is evident that hierarchism rests on "orderly rules of behaviour and authority structures" with "little faith in impermanent self-organizing or self-steering processes" (Hood 2000, 73). In this view, agent-principal relationships are directed by fixed operating procedures along traditional PPA lines. The individualist approach is diametrically opposed to hierarchism presuming that "markets will ordinarily produce better results than bureaucratic hierarchies" because they automatically link individual achievement and public outcomes. By contrast, the egalitarian slant assumes that "communitarianism and participative

Table 10.1 Hood's four perspectives on public administration

Grid	*Group*	
	Low	*High*
High	"Fatalist way" Low co-operation, rule-bound approaches to organization Example: Atomized societies sunk in rigid routines	"Hierarchist way" Socially cohesive, rule-bound approaches to organization Example: Stereotypical military structures
Low	"Individualist way" Atomized approaches to organization stressing negotiation and bargaining Example: Chicago-school doctrines of "government by the market"	"Egalitarian way" High-participation structures in which every decision is debated Example: "Dark green" doctrines of alternatives to conventional bureaucracy

Source: Adapted from Hood (2000, Table 1.1, p. 9)

organization, in the form of radically decentralized self-governing units rather than conventional large-scale state structures" are superior to both the market and bureaucratic systems (Hood 2000, p. 120). Under this view, group solidarity and not rule-based constraints or market incentives can secure the cooperation of employees. Finally, in stark juxtaposition to the other perspectives, the fatalist model holds that "public organization and policy is inescapably unpredictable and chaotic, defying any clear-cut theory" (p. 146). Given its pervasive pessimism, the fatalistic perspective is cynical of the prospects of any reform program successfully modifying public administration for the better. Hood argues that fatalism plays a valuable role in conceptualizing administrative reform since it carries the implicit caveat that "widely shared assumptions turn out to be false, powerful empires spring up from nowhere while confidently backed plans produce outcomes quite different from, and even the very reverse of, what was expected" (p. 150), thereby underlining the "defects and shortcomings of the other three polar approaches to public management".

A third conceptual framework has been offered by Pollitt and Brouchaert (2004) in their *Public Management Reform*. Four perspectives on public sector reform are developed: "Maintain", "modernize", "marketize" and "minimize". Each is centered on postulated relationships between the "political system", the "market economy" and "public administration and law". Each approach emphasizes a different configuration between these three social systems and each represents an alternative public sector reform strategy available to politicians.

The maintain strategy hinges on tightening resource constraints. It thus advocates the implementation of measures designed to "tighten up traditional controls, restrict expenditures, freeze new hiring, run campaigns against waste and corruption and generally 'squeeze' the system of administration and law"(p. 186). In essence, the maintain strategy thus attempts to diminish the resources used by the public sector.

By contrast, the modernize strategy seeks to induce reform by improving administration processes. It relies on "bringing in faster, more flexible ways of budgeting, managing, accounting, and delivering services to their users", usually by importing techniques from private sector entities. Nonetheless, it vigorously asserts the importance of public sector service provision and thus attempts to "strengthen rather than dilute the state" (Pollitt and Brouchaert 2004, p. 187). Two main policy instruments are employed. On the one hand, "top-down" measures aimed at increasing bureaucratic capacity and reducing bureaucratic "red tape" are invoked, and on the other hand, "bottom-up" processes implemented to encourage active co-production participation by recipients of public services.

The marketization strategy involves exposing public administration to market forces. This is primarily done through employing market-type mechanisms in the operation of the public sector wherever possible. In addition, it seeks to stimulate competition between public entities and private firms to improve operational efficiency. The introduction of these measures runs counter to many longstanding public sector processes and thus can cause significant disruption.

Finally, the minimization strategy seeks to shift functions and public service provision previously undertaken in the public sector to the private sector. This is done using various policy instruments, such as competitive tendering, contracting out and privatization. A well-known danger associated with this approach is that it can deskill the public sector and thereby severely reduce administrative and technical capacity. This means *inter alia* that it is difficult in practice to reverse minimization.

Pollitt and Brouckaert (2004) argue that each of these four strategies has comparative advantages in respect of their differential impact on public expenditure discipline and process legitimacy. For example, whereas the modernize strategy can be more effective in terms of financial prudence, it may not have much influence on legitimacy. Similarly, while the maintain approach does least to alter the *status quo*, it is unlikely to have decisive effects on spending or legitimacy. In stark contrast, the marketize strategy will probably have a considerable effect on budgetary outlays and legitimacy, but in diametrically opposing ways, since the polity may assume that "fiscal priorities predominate over a service ethic" (p. 191). Finally, while the minimization approach can be expected to reduce the public sector in aggregate, it may not secure a balanced budget if tax reductions lower tax receipts.

Notwithstanding these incongruities, Pollitt and Brouckaert (2004, p. 193) argue that all four strategies present "a picture of a dynamic strategy which is being pursued by the top tiers of the public service hierarchy". Furthermore, they all constitute "metamanagement" and enable senior managers to "avoid the hurly-burly of 'operations'". While senior managers "set targets" and "redesign organizations", lower echelons must "actually achieve these targets and manage restructured entities". In sum, all of the strategies carry the advantage that they "can be carried out in response to the demands of politicians for lower costs and higher legitimacy" or they "can be launched independently by the new mandarinate, requiring nothing more from the political leadership than sympathetic acquiescence".

10.2.2 Analytical Systems for Diagnosing, Designing and Guiding Municipal Reform

Local government policymakers are fortunately able to draw on a voluminous literature for diagnosing any problems associated with the operation of their local government systems, determining whether any remedial policy intervention is warranted, and designing and implementing a reform program. In Sect. 10.2.2, we briefly consider the most important strands in this literature.

10.2.2.1 Theory of Local Government Failure

The phenomenon of government failure—defined as the inability of a government agency or agencies in a given tier of government or in a federal system of multi-tiered governments to operate optimally—is a common theme in policy analysis. Government failure occurs at all levels of government, including local government.

In the literature, scholars have developed numerous taxonomies of government failure. For instance, O'Dowd (1978, p. 360) proposed a tripartite classification comprising "inherent impossibilities" ("where a government attempts to do something which simply cannot be done"), "political failures" (where political constraints rule out effective implementation of a government policy) and "bureaucratic failures" (where the "administrative machinery" of government miscarries). Along similar lines, Dollery and Wallis (1997, p. 114) advanced a typology of government failure consisting of "legislative failure" (where allocative inefficiency derives from the excessive provision of public goods), "bureaucratic failure" (where public servants lack adequate incentives "to carry out policies efficiently"), and "rent-seeking" (where citizens pursue wealth transfers from public programs). A more comprehensive taxonomy was advanced by Weisbrod (1978, pp. 36–39) encompassing "legislative failure", "administrative failure", "judicial failure" (where the legal system generates sub-optimal outcomes) and "enforcement failure" (through poor enforcement or non-enforcement of regulations). However, the most refined classification system was created by Charles Wolf (1989). Wolf shaped a theoretical analogue of conventional market failure in welfare economics by ascribing "non-market failure" to the unusual characteristics of the "demand" and "supply" for public goods. He proposed four generic types of "nonmarket failure"; "internalities and private goals", "redundant and rising costs", "derived externalities" and adverse distributional outcomes typically manifest in "power and privilege" differences in the public sphere rather than "income and wealth" differences evident in market relationships.

In the local government realm, at least three analogous taxonomies of local government failure have been developed (Dollery and Wallis 2001; Dollery 2002). Firstly, in his *Public Choice Theory and Local Government*, Boyne (1998) constructed a typology of competitive classifications in local government that shape the degree of government failure. He distinguished between "three distinct forms of competition" in local government. In the first instance, competition exists between public organizations for "a share of tax revenues and service responsibilities" (p. 1). Secondly, political parties compete for authority to determine policy choices in given local authorities. Finally, Boyne (1998, p. 1) proposed "competition between governmental and private organisations for control over the production of public services". In order for vigorous Tiebout-type competition to prevail in local government, Boyne (1998, p. 22) argued that several conditions must be met. These conditions include "horizontal fragmentation" (there must be a large number of local councils in a given local government system), "vertical fragmentation" (there must be several tiers of government that compete), and "substantial local autonomy" (where "local communities should have the discretion to innovate, experiment and develop distinctive policies"). If these conditions are not met, then local government failure will manifest itself.

Secondly, Bailey (1999) extended the "exit" and "voice" framework developed by Hirschman (1970) to consider how local public service consumers can influence the provision of these services. Under the Hirschman (1970) structure, exit refers to the capacity of citizens to choose between different providers of a given service. In contrast, voice denotes the ability of citizens to express their preferences for public services through various mechanisms, including voting in elections, directing complaints to public service managers and completing customer surveys, without the need to move between municipal jurisdictions.

Bailey (1999) argued that both exit and voice have various limitations as methods of reducing government failure in local government. Bailey (1999, pp. 47/48) identified five chief characteristics of local services that inhibit the effectiveness of voice. Firstly, "legal and institutional barriers" in terms of diluted political representation, electoral and procedural irregularities, inadequate public hearings, and other factors can inhibit political attempts to improve municipal services. Secondly, "information asymmetries" between bureaucrats and local residents on the nature and costs of local service provision can limit the efficacy of voice. Thirdly, when local services are highly differentiated—such as educational standards in different public schools—voice may only affect a particular school rather than the whole school system. By contrast, for undifferentiated services, like water supply, voice will have more general effects. In the fourth place, the socioeconomic characteristics of the population of a given local government area can be decisive, with better-educated, affluent groups more likely to efficaciously express voice than their poorer, less educated counterparts. Finally, the greater the relative importance of some public service to the perceived welfare of a population, the more important voice will be as a means of addressing government failure.

In common with voice, Bailey (1999, p. 48) has argued that exit has various limitations. For instance, the non-excludability characteristic of local public services may preclude exit altogether due to the expense of relocation, such as inadequate environmental protection legislation across an entire local government system. Similarly, natural monopolies preclude exit where they cover large geographical areas. Legislative impediments to entry by alternative suppliers of a service may negate exit possibilities, as in the case of regional water authorities. In large countries with uneven concentrations of population, like Australia and Canada, spatially immense municipal jurisdictions with low populations typically create spatial barriers to exit. Finally, the availability of imperfect information may mean consumers are unaware of the relatively poor quality of the local services they receive, which can induce them to underestimate the benefits of exit.

Both Bailey (1999) and Boyne (1998) premised their taxonomies on the assumption that government failure is less acute at the municipal level than at higher tiers of government. In marked contrast, Dollery and Wallis (2001) argued that government failure is likely to be far more widespread at the local level and proposed a quadrilateral typology of local government failure. Byrnes and Dollery (2002) extended this typology to rest on five key pillars: "voter apathy", "asymmetric information and councillor capture", "iron triangles", "fiscal illusion" and "political entrepreneurship".

In the first place, Dollery and Wallis (2001) argued that voter apathy is typically greater at the local level for five main reasons. In many municipal systems voters regard local elections as less important than provincial and national elections because higher tiers of government usually exert control over local authorities. Secondly, in local government elections many candidates are not affiliated to political parties and information on candidates is harder to secure. Thirdly, municipal elections frequently get insufficient attention from news media. Fourthly, Dollery and Wallis (2001, p. 57) contend that in local government "governance and management roles are often confused in the eyes of many citizens, who cannot readily distinguish between elected representatives and professional public servants, making it difficult to assign responsibility for previous policy outcomes". Finally, it is comparatively difficult to establish accountability in local governance due to the ubiquitous influence of higher levels of government.

Dollery and Wallis (2001) contend that asymmetric information and councillor capture is a significant problem in local government which arises from principal-agent relationships between bureaucrats and politicians as well as between politicians and voters. Various factors make the agency problem more acute in local government. Dollery and Wallis (2001, p. 61) argue that municipal managers are much better informed than councillors and thus "by manipulating the asymmetry of information to their advantage, managers can capture councillors and thereby achieve the policy outcomes they desire". Moreover, unlike state and national politicians, municipal representatives usually do not have political advisers to assist in assessing information from local managers. In addition, selective behavior can affect municipal outcomes, where selective efficiency is employed by "bureaucrats to control their master's choices by being efficient at the things they want to do, and inefficient at those they do not" (Wintrobe 1997, p. 251).

Following the theory of rent seeking, "iron triangles" refers to the establishment of three-way colluding associations (or "triangles") between local interest groups, elected councillors and bureaucrats that seek to influence the share of a municipal budget dedicated to specific programs. Byrnes and Dollery (2002) argued three factors exist that make the problem of "iron triangles" more acute at the local level. Given information asymmetry between managers and largely part-time elected officers, as well as the extensive use of standing committees, interest groups can easily identify councillors with powers over certain municipal functions and form alliances with them. Secondly, because a comparatively high proportion of tax revenues are fixed and invariant with respect to local public service consumption, interest groups have incentives to endeavor to redistribute service provision. Thirdly, owing to the horizontally fragmented nature of local governments, iron triangles will have a greater impact on policymaking since local authorities typically attract less media scrutiny.

Fiscal illusion refers to the misperception of the costs and benefits of government by the citizenry of a given fiscal jurisdiction. Although five generic kinds of fiscal illusion have been identified by economists, two relate strongly to local government; the "fly-paper effect" and "renter illusion". The fly-paper effect describes the conjectured tendency for lump-sum grants from national to state and local governments to increase public expenditure by more than an equivalent increase in income from other sources. It is argued that voters misperceive intergovernmental grants as "gifts" to their jurisdictions and disregard the fact that tax liabilities rise correspondingly at a higher level of government. By contrast, renter illusion assumes that since property taxes constitute a major source of income for local government, only local residents who own property will accurately estimate the tax-price of municipal services. Local government will thus be more susceptible to this form of fiscal illusion.

Finally, in the present context political entrepreneurship refers to the phenomenon where persons elected to local government use their office to generate favorable publicity in order to pave the way to election in higher tiers of government. This can lead to local government failure because the inefficient use of resources by political entrepreneurs to capture the attention of voters may give rise to systematic allocative inefficiencies. Byrnes and Dollery (2002, p. 57) argue that "councils can be conceived of as breeding grounds for political entrepreneurs to not only capture the attention of political party officials at higher levels of government, but also of prospective voters in federal and state seats". They contend that three factors explain the greater magnitude of political entrepreneurship at the local government level. Firstly, given local government is typically the lowest level of government in multi-governmental national systems, usually with the greatest number of elected representatives, the absolute number of political entrepreneurs is likely to be higher at this level than at any other tier. Secondly, given the comparatively greater degree of voter apathy and relative lack of interest by the news media in local government, particularly in large cities, ambitious local representatives have incentives to engage in costly "eye-catching" local initiatives to raise their profiles amongst voters. Lastly, because state and national jurisdictions are normally bigger in terms of spatial area and population than local authorities, political entrepreneurs have incentives to offer local services to benefit regions much larger than their own municipal area to attract public attention.

10.2.2.2 New Institutional Economics

Conventional economics has traditionally rested on several central assumptions, including rational maximizing behavior, stable preferences, perfect information and costless market exchange, and it has largely treated both private firms and public organizations as institutional "black boxes" simply representing a technological relationship between inputs and outputs. However, the development of new institutional economics (NIE), with its emphasis on "institutional realism", has served to "open the black box" of public sector institutions (Wallis et al. 2007; Rutherford 1996). In this regard, Rutherford (1996, p. 186) has ascribed the development of NIE to an absence of "institutional content at the core of neoclassical theory" which hampered the ability of standard economic analysis to embrace new theoretical insights and limited its application to the public sector.

While NIE broadly adopted the neoclassical mode of analysis, it has nevertheless incorporated several additional insights, such as "bounded rationality" proposed by Simon (1975). NIE thus assumes that people possess only a limited ability to process information and consequently do not incorporate all information on any given transaction in their decision-making. Moreover, bounded rationality infers that the full complexities of economic exchanges cannot be fully incorporated in either formal contracts or market mechanisms. Furthermore, since bounded rationality precludes complete contracts between agents and principals, "opportunistic behaviour" can arise where economic agents can conceal preferences and actions in contracts. These characteristics of real-world economic processes attach central importance to institutions in economic analysis (Williamson 1979).

Frant (1991) has argued that NIE has three main conceptual foundations. Firstly, following Coase (1937), it emphasizes the centrality of transactions costs when an organization decides on whether it should produce an input itself or whether it should purchase the production factor through the market. Secondly, drawing on the Coase (1960) insights on the optimal assignment of property rights in the presence of externalities, key significance is assigned to property rights in economic analysis. Finally, NIE is anchored to the Alchian and Demsetz (1972) property rights approach to the analysis of "team production" within the organization.

Property Rights

NIE differentiates between three chief kinds of property rights. Firstly, user rights define the right to use a specified asset by prescribing the ways in which an asset can be deployed. User rights also impose restrictions on the use of an asset, which serve to constrain its economic value. Secondly, rights to derive income from an asset and determine its contractual use are important. Finally, rights exist to alienate an asset by sale or other means. However, in NIE property rights also embrace social norms. For instance, Alchian (1977, p. 131) has noted that "the rights of individuals to the use of resources (i.e. property rights) in any society are to be construed as supported by the force of etiquette, social custom, ostracism, and formally enacted laws supported by the state's power of violence of punishment".

In the real world, property rights must be measured, demarcated, maintained and enforced. This process imposes costs that can be reduced where social norms on property coincide with legally defined rights. In this way social institutions that reinforce property rights recognition are welfare enhancing since they serve to minimize these costs (Eggertsson 1990). This NIE framework departs from conventional neoclassical economics that holds *inter alia* that all property rights are privately held and costless to maintain, protect or transfer. Once it is recognized that real-world property rights differ sharply from the idealized neoclassical conception, then the importance of institutions designed to accommodate imperfect property rights becomes apparent (Milgrom and Roberts 1992).

All complex productive activity involves the combination of various productive inputs to generate output. This typically means employing assets owned by different people under different conditions. In a market system, the permanent or temporary transfer of property rights over productive assets is handled by means of contracts that stipulate the conditions attached to the specific transfer in question. Contracts occupy a central role in NIE generally and the economics of property rights in particular. Given the importance of contractual relations in determining the nature of economic organization, NIE places considerable emphasis on the economic logic of contractual arrangements (Cheung 1983), including in the public sector. As we have seen, this emphasis is reflected in NPM-style contractualism.

Transaction Costs

Transaction costs are closely related to property rights economics in NIE (Wallis et al. 2007). Whereas a transaction is defined as an agreed exchange or transfer of goods and services across technologically discrete boundaries, transaction costs represent the aggregation of all costs surrounding an agreement of this kind (Williamson 1985). Transaction costs play a key role in a market system, variously described as the "costs of using the price system" (Coase 1937, p. 390) and the costs of "running the economic system" (Arrow 1969, p. 48). Transaction costs are thus completely different from production or transformation costs comprising the costs associated with transforming input factors into outputs.

Two perspectives exist on the nature of transaction costs. Firstly, transaction costs have been intimately entwined with property rights. For instance, Eggertsson (1990, p. 14) has observed that transaction costs "arise when individuals exchange property rights to economic assets and enforce their exclusive rights". In this sense, transaction costs cover the costs of negotiating, enforcing and maintaining property rights (Barzel 1982). Secondly, more recently, scholars have construed transaction costs as comprising the resources deployed in the establishment and maintenance of exchange-facilitating institutions in market economies. For example, it has been argued that transaction costs encompass all costs included in the "creation or change of an institution or organization" as well as the "use of the institution or organization" (Furubotn and Richter 1992, p. 8).

The origins of transaction costs derive from Ronald Coase's (1937) paper in which he explored the question of why firms and markets coexist when they perform the same functions. Coase (1937) argued that firms and markets—as two alternative institutional methods of organizing economic activity—operate simultaneously because using the price mechanism has transaction costs. To minimize the costs of economic activity, economic agents will attempt to minimize transaction costs by employing either markets or organizations, depending on which represents the least cost approach. Transaction cost theory generalizes these insights by stressing the key role of institutions in enhancing economic relationships.

The application of transaction costs hinges on the nature of the transactions in question in order to determine which institution is optimal. Following this logic, the most important attributes of transactions are transactional uncertainty, transactional frequency, and the centrality of transaction-specific assets. For instance, in the case of a specialized transaction involving significant investments in specific assets—or high "asset specificity"—then we can anticipate ongoing bilateral bargaining between the parties involved in the transaction. Along similar lines, a lack of perfect information will induce pervasive uncertainty and thereby limit the usage of long-term contracts. Analogous arguments apply to transactional frequency. For example, where there is little or no asset specificity, infrequent transactions will normally require contracts. Infrequent transactions can thus simply occur through standard market mechanisms. These transaction cost arguments apply equally in a public sector context.

Agency Theory

The third pillar of NIE is agency theory which centers on principal-agent relationships (Wallis et al. 2007). A principal-agent relationship exists where a principal delegates responsibilities to a contracted agent whose conduct significantly affects the welfare of the principal. Principal-agent relationships are an integral part of all complex economic, political and social activities. For instance, with respect to the public sector, Moe (1984, p. 765) has argued that "the whole of politics can be seen as a chain of principal-agent relationships, from citizen to politician to bureaucratic superior to bureaucratic subordinate and on down the hierarchy of government to the lowest level bureaucrats who actually deliver services directly to citizens".

Trade-offs by principals represent a key feature of all principal-agent relationships. For example, should a principal delegate a specialized function to a contracted agent, then the principal can minimize costs if the specialized agent can adequately perform these tasks. However, given that the interests of the principal and agent are not identical, "agency failure" will occur if the agent does not increase the well-being of the principal. Since the interests of principals and agents typically diverge in most real-world relationships, agency theory examines the costs associated with agency relationships and the efforts aimed at minimizing these costs.

Three main categories of agency costs have been identified (Jensen and Meckling 1976). Firstly, "monitoring costs" arise since agents' behavior must be monitored and incentives developed to encourage the desired behavior. Secondly, resources must be invested by agents in order for them to be able to guarantee successful outcomes to principals. These outlays constitute "bonding costs". Finally, "residual loss costs" will accrue to principals contingent on any divergence between their interests and those of their agents. In sum, total agency costs comprise monitoring costs, bonding costs and residual loss costs.

Aggregate total agency costs vary in accordance with the characteristics of agency relationships. For instance, in an agency relationship, specialist agents typically have more information than principals about both the function in question and the comparative advantage of their own performance. The resultant information asymmetry enables agents to exploit principals through "shirking behaviour" or "opportunistic behaviour" which runs contrary to the interests of principals. Total agency costs are proportionate to the extent of this behavior.

Although agency theory was initially developed to examine modern corporations, which are almost always characterized by a separation between ownership (principal) and control (agent), it was later extended to all forms of economic organization, including public sector entities and voluntary organizations (Wallis et al. 2007). This literature shed further light on the problem of agency failure by invoking the concepts of "adverse selection" and "moral hazard". Adverse selection refers to the informational asymmetries in principal-agent relationships flowing from pre-contractual opportunism. For instance, in contemporary franchise arrangements, large franchise corporations frequently have more information on the market potential of prospective franchises they wish to sell. As a result, they can negotiate contractual arrangements with franchisees on the basis of this information asymmetry to their benefit. Secondly, moral hazard arises from post-contractual opportunism, where agents pursue their own interests rather than those of principals. In these circumstances, action sought under a contract, which is not directly observable, may be shirked by agents.

Recent developments in agency theory have broadened its focus further to include sources of employee motivation beyond simply material remuneration, such as organizational identity. In real-world organizations, including local authorities, a great deal of effort is frequently devoted to instilling non-economic motives into workers in the hope of transforming the identities of employees to align with organizational objectives. This can *inter alia* limit the extent of moral hazard under conditions where it is difficult to monitor behavior effectively (Akerlof and Kranton 2005). Various methods of modifying employee identity have been devised, including inspirational organizational leadership, which have *inter alia* been applied to the implementation of local government reform.

10.2.2.3 Policy Leadership and Local Government Reform

A voluminous body of scholarship in the social sciences has been devoted to the phenomenon of leadership (Northouse 2018), which encompasses economic theories of leadership (Wallis et al. 2007). While the conceptual prisms offered by the government failure paradigm and NIE have had a significant impact on the design of public sector reform, they have largely been silent on the policy leadership necessary to implement reform.

In the realm of public policy, most theories of leadership view it as encompassing the marshalling of a target group toward some specified objective, where the "group" can consist of teams, communities, organizations, local governments and nations. Furthermore, the networks through which leadership is exercised may span across numerous communities, organizations and public bodies even if the ultimate target group consists of the nation (Wallis et al. 2007).

NIE illuminates how leadership can be exercised through networks since it distinguishes between markets, hierarchies and networks as alternative conduits of social coordination. Whereas all three mechanisms seek to coordinate actors by assembling and sharing dispersed resources, networks rely more on trust than contract or authority as their primary instrument of coordination. In essence, leadership networks comprise individuals willing to let principal actors take the lead in given circumstances to generate an effective group response.

The "policy cycle" framework on public policy processes can illuminate how leadership operates in the arena of public policymaking. If we conceive of policymaking as a process that characteristically passes through five stages of "agenda-setting", "policy formulation", "decision-making", "implementation" and "evaluation", then policy actors exercise policy leadership through policy networks by exercising influence at each stage in order to steer public policy in a given direction (Wallis et al. 2007).

Policy networks can thus be seen as providing the mechanism through which policy leadership can provide coherence to a policy process by steering it toward particular goals. Burns (1978) has made a critical distinction in this regard between "transactional" and "transformational" forms of leadership. In essence, "transactional" policy leadership works through existing policy networks to effect incremental policy changes. By contrast, "transformational" policy leadership creates its own leadership network outside the prevailing structure of policy networks and then transforms these policy networks in order to implement comprehensive reform.

Three modes of transformational leadership have been identified in the literature. Firstly, Wallis et al. (2007, p. 94) observe that the "defining characteristic of an 'exploratory' style of transformational policy leadership" consists largely of "an openness to ideas and actors outside those of the prevailing 'establishment'". In contrast, they note that there is the "cohesive" style of leadership "exhibited by a 'strong' team characterized by a shared commitment to advance one another into positions from which they can reconstruct policy according to shared principles and penetrate, break up and reconfigure policy networks that are viewed as potential sources of resistance". Finally, there is a "supportive style of transformational policy leadership that seeks to broaden the scope of policy change and deepen its transforming impact through a style that is both challenging and facilitative".

The type or style of policy leadership employed relates to the nature of the policy change that is sought (Wallis et al. 2007). A key distinction in this regard must be drawn between "normal" and "paradigmatic" policy change. Thus, for paradigmatic policy change, in its early agenda-setting stage exploratory leadership is efficacious, whereas in its implementation stage cohesive leadership is more appropriate and in its evaluation stage supportive leadership is effective.

10.3 Empirical Studies

As we have noted earlier, the institutional complexities of local government systems, the complications of different multi-governmental relationships and a myriad of other real-world differences between different national structures have rendered theorizing on local government reform exceedingly difficult. For these reasons, much can be learned about the nature of reform motives, processes and outcomes from comparative studies of local government reform in practice. A vast literature has arisen around comparative local government reform (Kuhlmann and Brouckaert 2016). Most work in this area has focused on the comparative analysis of local government reform in countries that exhibit similarities to a greater or lesser extent. Moreover, the great bulk of comparative empirical work has considered specific types of policy reform, notably structural reform through municipal mergers, rather than the full range of reform programs, such as Dollery and Robotti (2008). However, a few comparative studies exist that have considered the full gamut of policy reforms. In Sect. 10.3, we examine two of the more comprehensive of these studies in more detail in order to shed light on commonalities in municipal reform between different countries.

10.3.1 Comparative Analysis of Anglo-American Countries

In their *Local Government Reform: A Comparative Analysis of Advanced Anglo-American Countries*, Dollery et al. (2008) gathered contributions from leading scholars in Australia, Britain, Canada, Ireland, New Zealand and the United States on the motivations, processes and outcomes of local government reform in these countries. Dollery et al. (2008, p. 190) then attempted to provide "a comparative thematic overview of the determinants, goals and objectives, nature and scope, and effects of those reforms; to provide observations regarding the prospects for, and the nature and scope of, additional reforms". In this section, we consider their findings.

Dollery et al. (2008) distinguished between "primary" and "secondary" determinants of local government reform programs in the six Anglosphere countries. Primary factors comprised "perceived problems within the municipal systems", "intergovernmental politics" and "political rationality", whereas secondary determinants encompassed "demographic trends", "political legacies and cultures", "judicial decisions", "extra-national (regional/international) initiatives", "ideational frameworks" and "imitation". With respect to primary determinants, Dollery et al. (2008, p. 190) found that while "there was a widespread perception among elected and appointed officials of all levels of government in the six countries under review that municipal systems could and should be reformed", differences existed "regarding the nature, causes, effects and significance of municipal system problems". In terms of intergovernmental politics "municipalities were not always losers in intergovernmental contests nor did higher-tier governments seeking to force reform always accomplish their objectives" (p. 192).

Amongst secondary factors, demographic trends proved influential and "diminished the size of some municipalities, increased the size of others, and brought the populations of other councils geographically much closer together" (p. 193). Similarly, ideational considerations "informed reform, sometimes powerfully", especially NPM doctrines. Finally, policy imitation proved important provoking a tendency "to copy or adopt, in whole or in part, proposed or actual reforms of other jurisdictions". However, "the fact that the reforms were often not identical, either across countries or between the various sub-units in federal countries, suggests that there are limits to imitation" (p. 195).

Secondly, Dollery et al. (2008) considered similarities in terms of the "goals and objectives" of local government reform programs. Two strong similarities were identified; (a) to improve "the governance, management and service provision capacity of municipal governments" and (b) to improve "the governance, management, and service provision capacity of the higher tiers of government through municipal reforms", with the exception of the United States.

Thirdly, Dollery et al. (2008) examined the "nature and scope of reforms" across the six countries in question in terms of structural, functional, financial, jurisdictional as well as organizational and managerial reforms. Commonalities in structural reform included reducing the number of local authorities, boosting "larger one-tier municipal governments over smaller one-tier entities and over two-tier structures", the establishment of "expansive regional authorities" in place of small regional entities, a preference for general purpose government instead of special purpose bodies, and the formation of "sub-municipal entities and venues that facilitated general citizen participation" (p. 197).

For functional reform, policymakers had limited aims, focusing on the "expansion and contraction of existing functions", the realignment of functions and the realignment of roles and responsibilities between tiers of government. Under financial reform, Dollery et al. (2008, p. 202) concluded that, in general, it "entailed only relatively minor adjustments to the existing financial frameworks", even though sometimes "major reforms to various facets of the financial frameworks were proposed … most were not implemented", with the net result of "substantial continuity in the traditional fiscal frameworks".

In terms of jurisdictional reform, the main emphasis fell on the transfer of general competence powers to municipal governments. In this regard, "some general competence powers were conferred upon some, or all, municipal governments in Australia, New Zealand, Ireland and Canada", but not Britain and the United States. With respect to organizational and managerial reform emphasis fell on "electoral systems, the composition of councils and their committees, and the composition and powers of executive and administrative bodies" (p. 206), especially in Australia, Britain, Canada and New Zealand.

Finally, managerial reform efforts were directed at three main areas: corporatization, commercialization and democratization. Corporatization aimed at determining "what local governments should do and how they should do it to maximize effectiveness and efficiency in performing their functions" (p. 208). In particular, reforms in all six countries seek to minimize political interference by elected officers in the management of municipalities through the more rigid separation of policy and administrative functions. Commercialization largely focuses on the greater use of markets to acquire inputs and allocate public services. Common trends across all six nations included compulsory competitive tendering for the provision of services by private firms, the privatization of some local services and greater use of intergovernmental agreements for the provision of some services. Democratization seeks to align management practice more closely with democratic governance. In all Anglosphere countries this took the form of efforts to improve transparency and accountability, enhance public consultation, increase public participation, and strengthen the rights of local residents relative to local authorities.

Dollery et al. (2008) also considered commonalities in the impact of these reforms on the local government systems in the six Anglosphere countries. In terms of the effects of reforms on the main dimensions of local government, they concluded that in none of the six countries had municipal reform programs radically transformed the operation of local government systems, even though they had "some significant effects on municipal governance and multi-level governance". In sum, while all countries underwent substantial reforms and significant changes occurred, the operation of local government was not fundamentally transformed.

10.3.2 Comparative Analysis of European Countries

In their co-edited volume *Local Public Sector Reforms in Time of Crisis*, Kuhlmann and Brouckaert (2016) assembled contributions on local government reform from leading scholars across 28 European countries. Contributors examined three broad categories of local government reform: (a) "External administrative reforms" comprising (1) "territorial re-scaling" that dealt with both "territorial upscaling" through municipal mergers and "territorial trans-scaling" through "inter-local cooperation" and (2) "reorganizing local service delivery" through NPM policy at the horizontal level, like corporatization and outsourcing, and vertical reorganization by transferring functions from higher tiers of government to local government; (b) "internal administrative reforms" comprising (3) "managerial reforms" focused on "reform projects of internal reorganisation, process re-engineering, new budgeting and accounting systems, performance management tools and human-resource-related modernization"; and (c) "democratic reforms" encompassing (4) "participatory reforms, direct democracy and citizen involvement" (Kuhlmann and Brouckaert 2016, pp. 4/6).

Kuhlmann and Brouckaert (2016, pp. 8/10) argued that five "institutional key features" have decisive effects on the nature of local government reform programs in particular countries. Firstly, "state structure and type of government" are important. In this regard, unitary states with "centralised administration central governments" have a comparative advantage in securing local public reform. Much the same is true with "majoritarian systems of government" compared with "consensus-orientated governments where negotiations, bargaining and overall orientation towards compromise are predominant".

Secondly, "administrative structure and tradition" is critical. Countries with "legalistic administrative cultures" and a "predominance of rule orientation" typically proceed more slowly with local reforms. By contrast, countries with a "public interest/common law tradition" are less hesitant and more readily borrow techniques from the private sector. "Post-communist" countries with experience of "at-best rudimentary relevance of legal norms in day-to-day administrative work" form a special case, with little in common with each other in terms of local government reform.

Thirdly, the "functional responsibilities and autonomy of local governments" is deemed important. Kuhlmann and Brouckaert (2016, p. 9) argue that "local authorities with a broad range of functions are more inclined to reform their administrations than functionally weak local governments" since they face more intense pressures from local residents. The strength of local autonomy hinges on the existence or otherwise of a "general competence clause" characteristic of continental European and Scandinavian countries. By contrast, the British *ultra vires* tradition allows local authorities to undertake responsibilities specifically assigned to them and can be revoked at any time. Accordingly, it is easier in the latter case to reform local government.

Fourthly, "territorial structures" are important insofar as geographic size is critical for the "operational viability", "democratic quality" and "capacity for reform". In this regard, Kuhlmann and Brouckaert (2016, p. 9) contend that "large-scale systems can be expected to be more capable of coping with the reform-related transaction and opportunity costs than are small municipalities", especially given their larger resource bases.

Finally, "local democracy" has significant ramifications for local government reform. Kuhlmann and Brouckaert (2016, p. 10) argue that "the nature and impacts of local public sector reforms can be expected to depend on the type of local democracy" in general and the "distribution of decision-making powers within local authorities" in particular. In general, they contend that reform will proceed more readily in local government systems with strong "committee systems" rather than with strong "mayor systems".

Contributors to *Local Public Sector Reforms in Time of Crisis* examined a total of 28 European countries that Kuhlmann and Brouckaert (2016, pp. 10/14) grouped into six clusters: The "continental European Napoleonic type" consisting of Belgium, France, Greece, Italy, Portugal, Spain and Turkey; the "continental European federal type" comprising Austria, Germany and Switzerland; the "Nordic type" made up of Denmark, Finland, Iceland, the Netherlands, Norway and Sweden; the "Anglo-Saxon type" containing Ireland and the United Kingdom; the "Central European type" covering the Czech Republic, Estonia, Hungary, Latvia, Lithuania, Poland and Slovakia; and the "South Eastern European type" involving Bulgaria, Croatia, Romania and Slovenia. Kuhlmann and Brouckaert (2016) contend that each of these clusters of local government types possesses different combinations of the five "institutional key features" outlined above. This renders them more or less amenable to effective local government reform programs.

In a final chapter summarising the findings of the various contributors to *Local Public Sector Reforms in Time of Crisis*, Kuhlmann and Brouckaert (2016, p. 351) observe that "there are commonalities within and between clusters". Thus, "between clusters, organised pressure seems to be brought by central/state government on local government through hiving off more competencies than resources, while simultaneously centralizing financial controls and fiscal frames, and imposing functional recentralisation". As a consequence, this "pressure on local government organizations produces a pattern of reactions in the shape of internal management reforms (performance-related measures), external reforms (mergers, cooperation and so on), and/or marketised measures".

10.4 Conclusion

As we have seen, a vast research effort has been directed at the question of public sector reform, including local government reform. Scholars have labored to produce a range of conceptual frameworks for characterizing the nature of reform, developing alternative models of public sector reform, creating the theoretical tools required to diagnose public sector problems, design remedial policies and successfully implement policy reform initiatives. This chapter has sought to distil the major strands of this voluminous body of work into a single digestible summary as well as outline two major comparative studies of local government reform in order to assess cross-country commonalities.

It is evident that while considerable progress has been made, the highly country-specific idiosyncratic nature of local government has rendered it extremely difficult to generate common features of the nature, causes and kinds of local government failure, effective forms of policy implementation and policy remediation. While it is clear that for countries with broadly similar institutional characteristics, commonalities exist, it would seem that few general policy measures are universally applicable.

References

Akerlof, G.A., and R.E. Kranton. 2005. Identity and the Economics of Organizations. *Journal of Economic Perspectives* 19 (1): 9–32.

Alchian, A. 1977. *Economic Forces at Work*. Indianapolis: Liberty Press.

Alchian, A., and H. Demsetz. 1972. Production, Information Costs, and Economic Organization. *American Economic Review* 62 (4): 777–795.

Arrow, K. 1969. The Organization of Economic Activity: Issues Pertinent to the Choice of Markets Versus Non-market Allocation. In *Public Expenditure and Policy Analysis*, ed. R.H. Haverman and J. Margolis, 43–51. Chicago: Markham.

Bailey, S.J. 1999. *Local Government Economics*. Basingstoke: Macmillan.

Barzel, Y. 1982. Measurement Costs and the Organization of Markets. *Journal of Law and Economics* 25 (1): 27–48.

Boyne, G.A. 1998. *Public Choice Theory and Local Government*. Basingstoke: Macmillan.

Burns, J.M. 1978. *Leadership*. New York: Harper and Row.

Byrnes, J., and B.E. Dollery. 2002. Local Government Failure in Australia: An Empirical Analysis of New South Wales. *Australian Journal of Public Administration* 61 (3): 54–64.

Casey, C. 2002. *Critical Analysis of Organizations: Theory, Practice, Revitalization*. New York: Sage.

Cheung, S. 1983. The Contractual Nature of the Firm. *Journal of Law and Economics* 26 (1): 1–21.

Christensen, T., and P. Laegreid, eds. 2008. *Transcending New Public Management: The Transformation of Public Sector Reforms*. Aldershot: Ashgate Publishing.

Coase, R.H. 1937. The Nature of the Firm. *Economica* 4 (3): 405.

———. 1960. The Problem of Social Cost. *Journal of Law and Economics* 3 (1): 1–44.

Cooper, P., B. Brady, L. Hidalgo-Hardeman, O. Hyde, A. Naff, K. Ott, and H. White. 1998. *Public Administration in the Twenty First Century.* Fort Worth: Harcourt Brace.

Dollery, B.E. 2002. Public Choice Theory and Municipal Efficiency: A Taxonomy of Local Government Failure. *Economia* 53 (2): 1–14.

Dollery, B.E., and L. Robotti, eds. 2008. *The Theory and Practice of Local Government Reform.* Cheltenham: Edward Elgar.

Dollery, B.E., and J.L. Wallis. 1997. Market Failure, Government Failure, Leadership and Public Policy. *Journal of Interdisciplinary Economics* 8 (2): 113–126.

———. 2001. *The Political Economy of Local Government: Market Failure, Reform and Leadership.* Cheltenham: Edward Elgar.

Dollery, B.E., J. Garcea, and E. LeSage, eds. 2008. *Local Government Reform: A Comparative Analysis of Advanced Anglo-American Countries.* Cheltenham: Edward Elgar.

Eggertsson, T. 1990. *Economic Behavior and Institutions.* Cambridge, MA: Cambridge University Press.

Frant, H. 1991. The New Institutional Economics: Implications for Policy Analysis. In *Policy Analysis and Economics*, ed. D.L. Weimer, 111–125. London: Kluwer.

Furubotn, E.G., and R. Richter. 1992. The New Institutional Economics: An Assessment. In *New Institutional Economics*, ed. E.G. Furubotn, 1–32. London: Edward Elgar.

Garcea, J., and E. LeSage. 2005. *Municipal Reforms in Canada.* Toronto: Oxford University Press.

Hirschman, A.O. 1970. *Exit, Voice and Loyalty.* Cambridge, MA: Cambridge University Press.

Hood, C. 1994. *Explaining Public Policy Reversals.* Buckingham: Open University Press.

———. 2000. *The Art of the State: Culture, Rhetoric and Public Management.* Oxford: Oxford University Press.

Jensen, M.C., and W.H. Meckling. 1976. Theory of the Firm: Managerial Behavior, Agency Costs, and Ownership Structure. *Journal of Financial Economics* 3 (3): 305–360.

Kuhlmann, S., and G. Brouckaert, eds. 2016. *Local Government Reform in Times of Crisis.* London: Macmillan.

Milgrom, P.R., and J. Roberts. 1992. *Economic, Organization and Management.* Englewood Cliffs: Prentice Hall.

Millward, R. 2011. Public Enterprise in the Modern Western World: An Historical Analysis. *Annals of Public and Cooperative Economics* 82 (4): 375–398.

Moe, T.M. 1984. The New Economics of Organization. *American Journal of Political Science* 28 (4): 739–777.

Northouse, P.G. 2018. *Leadership: Theory and Practice*. London: Sage.
O'Dowd, M.C. 1978. The Problem of Government Failure in Mixed Economies. *South African Journal of Economics* 46 (3): 360–370.
Peters, B.G. 1996. *The Future of Governing: Four Emerging Models*. Lawrence: University Press of Kansas.
Peters, B.G., and J. Pierre. 2016. *Comparative Governance: Rediscovering the Functional Dimension of Governing*. Cambridge, MA: Cambridge University Press.
Pollitt, C., and G. Brouckaert. 2004. *Public Management Reform: A Comparative Approach*. Oxford: Oxford University Press.
Rutherford, M. 1996. *Institutions in Economics: The Old and the New Institutionalism*. Cambridge, MA: Cambridge University Press.
Simon, H.A. 1975. *Reason in Human Affairs*. Oxford: Basil Blackwell.
Wallis, J.L., and B.E. Dollery. 1999. *Market Failure, Government Failure, Leadership and Public Policy*. London: Macmillan.
Wallis, J.L., B.E. Dollery, and L. McLoughlin. 2007. *Reform and Leadership in the Public Sector: A Political Economy Approach*. Cheltenham: Edward Elgar.
Weisbrod, B. 1978. Problems of Enhancing in the Public Interest: Towards a Model of Government Failures. In *Public Interest Law*, ed. B.A. Weisbrod, J.F. Handler, and N.K. Komesar, 30–41. London: University of California Press.
Williamson, O.E. 1979. Transactions Cost Economics: The Governance of Contractual Relations. *Journal of Law and Economics* 22 (1): 233–261.
———. 1985. *The Economic Institutions of Capitalism*. New York: Free Press.
Wintrobe, R. 1997. Modern Bureaucratic Theory. In *Perspectives on Public Choice*, ed. D.C. Mueller, 429–454. Cambridge, MA: Cambridge University Press.
Wolf, C. 1989. *Markets or Governments*. New York: MIT Press.
Yeatman, A. 1997. The Reform of Public Management: An Overview. In *Managerialism: The Great Debate*, ed. M. Considine and M. Painter, 173–187. Melbourne: Melbourne University Press.

Name Index[1]

[1] Note: Page numbers followed by 'n' refer to notes.

B. Dollery et al., *Local Public, Fiscal and Financial Governance*,
https://doi.org/10.1007/978-3-030-36725-1

Subject Index[1]

[1] Note: Page numbers followed by 'n' refer to notes.

B. Dollery et al., *Local Public, Fiscal and Financial Governance*,
https://doi.org/10.1007/978-3-030-36725-1

The manufacturer's authorised representative in the EU is Springer Nature Customer Service Centre GmbH, Europaplatz 3, 69115 Heidelberg, Germany. If you have any concerns regarding our products, please contact ProductSafety@springernature.com

Printed and bound by CPI Group (UK) Ltd, Croydon, CR0 4YY
30/09/2026
02225459-0015